BERA Dialogues

Series Editor: Donald McIntyre

Other Books in the Series

Please contact us for the latest book information:
Multilingual Matters Ltd, Frankfurt Lodge, Clevedon Hall,
Victoria Road, Clevedon, Avon BS21 7SJ, England

BERA Dialogues 12
Series Editor: Donald McIntyre

Researching the Early Years Continuum

Edited by
Pat Broadhead

MULTILINGUAL MATTERS LTD
Clevedon • Philadelphia • Adelaide

Library of Congress Cataloging in Publication Data

Researching the Early Years Continuum/Edited by Pat Broadhead
BERA Dialogues: 12
Includes bibliographical references
1. Early childhood education–Great Britain. 2. Articulation (Education)–Great
Britain. I. Broadhead, Pat, 1951- . II. Series.
LB1139.3.G7R47   1995
372.21–dc20   95-31910

British Library Cataloguing in Publication Data

A CIP catalogue record for this book is available from the British Library.

ISBN 1-85359-312-5 (hbk)
ISBN 1-85359-311-7 (pbk)

Multilingual Matters Ltd

UK: Frankfurt Lodge, Clevedon Hall, Victoria Road, Clevedon, Avon BS21 7SJ.
USA: 1900 Frost Road, Suite 101, Bristol, PA 19007, USA.
Australia: P.O. Box 6025, 83 Gilles Street, Adelaide, SA 5000, Australia.

Typeset by Formatvisual, Weston-super-Mare.
Printed and bound in Great Britain by WBC Book Manufacturers Ltd.

Contents

Notes on Contributors

Angela Anning was a headteacher of a nursery-infant school before moving into higher education. She has also taught in the secondary and further education sectors. In her current post as Senior Lecturer in Early Years and Arts Education at the University of Leeds, she is involved in initial training, in-service and higher degree work. Her research interests include teachers' craft knowledge and art and design at Key Stages 1 and 2.

Judy Arrowsmith has taught in Sarawak, Malaysia (VSO) and in Scottish schools. She works in the Social Science and Social Work department of Moray House Institute, Heriot-Watt University, Edinburgh. Her current research interests are parent–staff partnership and the use of ethos indicators in school self-evaluation and improving school effectiveness.

Carol Aubrey is a Senior Lecturer at the University of Durham and until recently Director of PGCE (Primary). She trained and worked as a primary teacher before becoming an Educational Psychologist. She has written widely on special education and school psychology. Her current research interests are pedagogical subject knowledge in early years mathematics.

Keith Bardon combines primary science advisory work for Kirklees Local Education Authority with work as a curriculum consultant working with experienced teachers and initial training students. Prior to this, he was head of science in a middle school. His research was carried out towards an MA in Applied Educational Studies, now successfully completed.

Sally Beveridge is a Lecturer in Special Needs and Primary Education at the University of Leeds. She has considerable teaching and research experience in the area of special needs education. She is currently involved in initial training, Advanced Diploma and higher degree work and research into special educational needs.

Sue Billett is Head of Professional Studies at the University College, Scarborough. She directs primary, initial teacher training and PGCE courses as well as managing other professional courses. Her research interests lie mainly in the area of early years education.

Pat Broadhead has taught predominantly across the early years of education. In her current post as Lecturer in Education at the University of Leeds she is involved in initial training, in-service and higher degrees. As well as long-standing research interests in the early years she is currently involved in researching school and teacher development.

Sheridan Earnshaw combines primary science advisory work for Kirklees Local Education Authority with work as a curriculum consultant working with experienced teachers and initial training students. She has worked with teachers for nine years and prior to this, taught in the early years. Her research was undertaken for an MA in Applied Educational Studies, now successfully completed.

Dianne Lamont is the head of an integrated nursery school in Fife. The research was carried out in her previous post where, also as head, she was involved in a Scottish Office Education Department (SOED) funded project into parent–teacher collaboration.

Ann MacNamara is a Lecturer in Mathematics Education at the University of Leeds in the areas of initial training, inservice and higher degrees. Prior to this, she taught in nursery and across the primary range.

Val Monaghan is a teacher in charge of a 52-place nursery in Leeds. After a number of years in secondary and further education, she retrained for nursery and has worked in a variety of inner city settings. Her research formed part of a now successfully completed MEd thesis.

Sheila Rye is a nursery school headteacher in Bradford. She has previously worked in the advisory service, in first schools, in a combined centre, in adult education and with the playgroup movement.

Diane Shorrocks is a Senior Lecturer in Education at the University of Leeds. She has taught in primary schools and is involved in initial training. She is currently Director of the MAK2 Project which is developing national assessments for Key Stage 2 Mathematics. Prior to this, she directed the ENCA 1 Project – the Evaluation of National Curriculum Assessment at Key Stage 1. She has ongoing and wide interests in child development studies.

1 Researching the Early Years – Issues and Foci

PAT BROADHEAD

The title of this volume, *Researching the Early Years Continuum*, might seem to pre-suppose an established consensus regarding the nature of such a continuum. In fact, no consensus as yet exists – partly because of the inevitable complexity of such a continuum, and also perhaps because some fundamental questions remain only partially explored. This opening chapter endeavours to render explicit some of the complexities in order to contribute to the important and current debate about these fundamental, early years questions. It also aims to indicate how the book as a whole aspires to inform considerations about continuity, consistency and appropriateness in provision and practice across the early years and more generally to offer research-based perspectives in support of the ongoing debate.

Clearly one book cannot address all such questions, so it seems appropriate to identify those questions that will be addressed. First we need to consider what is meant by 'the early years'. Linked to this, what is the current legacy both of the principles and of the types of provision evolved from the past, and what are the associated issues to be identified and considered in a search for cohesion and coherence? These are each addressed in this chapter as a first step in considering whether what is now needed is a coherent early years framework within which a continuum of learning and development might be possible. Having identified some aspects of this domain, the next question is concerned with the identification of issues of importance at particular points on the learning-development continuum. Lastly, what might underpin and influence educators' and caregivers' decisions about where to invest their efforts and energies in terms of enhancing their professional knowledge base and thus their practice? A fuller consideration of the latter two questions is founded in the research reported.

This collection of research papers is drawn from authors working in higher education, in local education authorities (LEAs) and in nursery and primary schools. The findings offer insights into:

- provision for special needs children
- the nature and extent of parental involvement and its impact upon parents, children and practitioners
- the very young child in a school setting
- the development of subject knowledge for practitioners and for children
- the impact of the National Curriculum and assessment on early years practice
- the identification of practitioner rationales to underpin decisions about appropriateness in a learning, caregiving environment.

The research findings offer some general theoretical insights into the above. These insights support a view that within a proposed continuum, there is a need to locate and integrate practice-related ideas. The collected research thus includes the experiences of practitioners who, with varying kinds of support from outside collaborators, have explored and confronted their own distinctive research issues and problems. From these specific, context-related studies set alongside outsider-determined research, emerges evidence of the links between the growth of knowledge and understanding and enriched practice and provision. If the early years of care and education are characterised by discontinuities and lack of consensus, then well-focused initial training and support for ongoing professional growth are potential catalysts for emerging consensus at practitioner level. If a conceptual framework for underpinning and promoting continuity and cohesion is to be established, the complexities of a learning-development continuum need to be asserted and understood. This volume hopes to make a contribution by reporting related research and by adding a voice to the call for an urgently needed research agenda.

The Early Years: Historical and Current Context

This research focuses, in the main, on children between the ages of three and seven years, in a range of educational contexts and on their teachers and their parents. It is important to acknowledge, however, that provision for young children is made in a wide range of types of settings. It is necessary, therefore, to explore aspects of the wider contexts of provision, both current and historical, prior to any intention to inform considerations of a continuum of learning and development with research findings.

It is proposed that the 'early years' begin at birth. Some children under school age, and usually from about six months of age, are provided for in settings underpinned primarily by a caring philosophy rather than an educational philosophy. Herein lies one challenge to consensus. Provision for the pre-statutory school-age child is diverse with a substantial tradition founded on self-help. While diversity has brought choice and should be celebrated, it has also brought fragmentation. In the statutory sector, provision has long been funded separately by social services and education departments, these being increasingly supplemented by the self-help growth in the voluntary sector and more recently by growth in the private sector. Indeed the latter two providers have grown considerably in number; and playgroups, for example, now cater for more children than do any other form of provision, with private provision rapidly expanding (HMSO, 1990).

Recent years have seen a striving towards consensus with the establishing of integrated services funded jointly by social services and education. This has centred, as David (1990) recounts, around an 'educare' principle. This draws on the best of each philosophy, combining education's emphasis on all aspects of human development with social work's emphasis on the family, health, protection and nurturing. However, as Gilkes (1987), Hevey (1986) and others have pointed out, in reality partnerships, consensus and consistency of practice and provision are difficult to attain when pay and working conditions are so dissimilar across the sectors, when joint training is minimal and when such well-established philosophies lead their proponents to see partnership as a potential diminution of their own traditions.

The belief in the need for an understanding of continuity and progression across the early years is, historically speaking, relatively recent. The Hadow Report of 1931 (Board of Education, 1931) recommended that 3–7 year olds be taught separately from 7–11 year olds, and while it recommended close liaison between the sectors it had little to say on a continuum of provision. Indeed Hadow postulates a deficit model of young children: 'The scope of attention in young children appears to be very limited, as they are lacking in the powers of mental organisation' (ch. 3, para. 37). This view has been extensively challenged elsewhere (Donaldson, 1978), and several chapters in this volume also reveal a somewhat different perspective. Hadow's most oft quoted statement has been seen by many as embodying an underlying tenet in early years provision: 'The curriculum is to be thought of in terms of activity and experience rather than of knowledge to be acquired and facts to be stored' (ch. 7, para. 35). It is perhaps also worth noting that the 'rather than' replaced 'as well as'. The forthcoming chapters looking particularly at the child's acquisition of subject knowledge lead one to appreciate that young children are as much concerned with knowledge and facts as they are with activity and experience – perhaps the 'as well as' should have remained in place.

However, these chapters, and others, also inform our thinking about the influences of adult structuring, via the provision of activity and experience, on the acquisition of knowledge, facts and, perhaps most importantly, understanding.

Moving on from Hadow, Plowden (CACE, 1967) did much to establish a principle of 'child centredness'. Once again, the emphasis was interpreted as being on activity and experience, of active rather than of passive learning, of the child being self-directed and self-motivated and of the adult supporting the quest for knowledge through appropriate provision.

The philosophies which had come to underpin provision for the nursery child had drawn on the works of innovators such as Froebel, Isaacs, Montessori and MacMillan (see Anning, 1991). These philosophies then began manifesting themselves in provision for 5–8 year olds with the enhanced status ascribed to these approaches moving them chronologically upwards. While Plowden was perceived as giving these philosophies and practices a stamp of official approval, any 'ground gaining' overall was as much the result of political commitment as of shared ideologies, with a then-prevailing political will and resultant financial commitment significantly enhancing the amount of pre-five provision to become available, particularly in the educational and some social service sectors. In effect, there was to be more of this type of provision around, enabling it to be significantly influential beyond its own sector.

The 1970s thus saw a proposed expansion of nursery provision, notably in the form of nursery classes attached to infant and primary schools – a far cheaper, more flexible form of provision than nursery schools. The extent of the growth in provision varied considerably from one part of the country to another. Further, as Osborn (1981) reported, the growth in the number of under-fives in infant classes was simultaneously beginning to increase proving even cheaper than nursery classes because of diminished staffing ratios. By 1989, there were more under-fives in reception classes of primary schools than there were in the nursery classes attached to primary schools (HMSO, 1990). While the authors of the chapters in this volume would advocate the span of early years continuing to eight, particular considerations need to be given to provision for four and five year olds. *A Framework for the Primary Curriculum* (NCC, 1989a) notes: 'To establish artificial boundaries between the education of children under five and that received by five year olds would be both counter productive and an opportunity lost' (para. 4.5).

Cleave & Brown (1991b) viewed this statement with some suspicion, believing it to herald the intention to infiltrate established early years work with a National Curriculum philosophy; the National Curriculum emphasis being, they claim, on preparation for the next phase rather than entitlement at a given phase as early years ideology would advocate.

The need to avoid boundaries within an early years framework is to be endorsed, but it must also then be asked, what of the post-five child, required under the terms of the 1988 Act to be taught the National Curriculum? What kinds of impact will this legislation have in a search for continuity and cohesion? The official line is as follows: 'The first key stage begins with a pupil becoming of compulsory school age and ends at the end of the school year in which the majority of pupils in his/her class attain the age of seven (ERA, 1988: Sub-section III, Section 10). Exploring the concept of 'compulsory school age' is, of itself, complex. The 1944 Education Act, Section 35, identifies it as the beginning of the term after which the child reaches five years. Under the 1948, Education (Miscellaneous Provisions) Act, entitlement can be claimed, by parents, from the fifth birthday. This places 'compulsory school age' in a somewhat grey area in terms of entitlement to receive a National Curriculum. And, of course, it does not address questions of how the learning experience is structured both for compulsory recipients and for younger children in the classroom. Thus far, legislation is not in place relating to teaching methods.

So, what of the reception child, the five year old mentioned above, together with many who are still four? Once a year admission is being undertaken in September on a rapidly increasing basis, because children bring with them a guaranteed and much needed income source in these days of diminishing staff and budgets. Some providers might want to offer a form of schooling more strongly teacher-determined than traditional nursery provision, where the emphasis is on children pursuing their interests in an appropriately structured environment, supported by informed adults. In many cases, these young children are undoubtedly capable of operating at level one and perhaps level two of the National Curriculum (Sylva, 1991). Yet Sylva also draws attention to the fierce outcry in the United States of 'too formal too soon'. This leads then to questions about the kind of teaching–learning environment from which children do benefit as they move through these early years. What kind of structure is valuable? Does teaching to the National Curriculum provide the appropriate kind of structure, or does it serve only to accommodate legislative requirements? Reconciling content with mode of delivery is as much a key issue for early years as it is across the whole of the primary sector and would surely be a fundamental issue within a conceptually founded framework.

Research is consistent in its findings concerning the inappropriateness of much of the current provision for four year olds in school in relation to their emotional, social, physical and intellectual needs in terms of both content and provision (Bennett & Kell, 1989; Cleave & Brown, 1991b). This also has implications for five year olds, being so close in developmental terms. Thus, despite the consensus which supposedly followed on from Plowden endorsing a transfer of tradition and practice from the nursery school into the infant school, research has consistently revealed a pattern of inappropriate provision for four year olds in school. However, it has also to be borne in mind that while we might be pressing our four year olds in school (and perhaps our five and six year olds) into premature academia (at the cost perhaps of the caring part of the educare principle), our three and four year olds in nursery may also have been exposed to an imbalanced curriculum with considerable emphasis being given to activity and experience and much less emphasis being given to the acquisition of knowledge and understanding.

It might seem at this point that the development of an early years framework within which a continuum of development and learning is located is unlikely to emerge. History, politics and economics might seem to militate against it. We have seen how, from a period of political and economic commitment in the 1970s and early 1980s, a new and still evident concern has emerged – the plight of the four year old in a primary school setting. What hope then for a period when political commitment is spasmodic and economic commitment is weak? An examination of the research agenda which paralleled this earlier growth of provision will be helpful in so far as it was commissioned to inform policy and expansion and still has much to offer in a search for ways forward in the formulation of a cohesive, conceptually founded framework. Developing consensus would seem to be as much about knowing which questions to ask as it is about sharing informed perspectives. Research is concerned with both dimensions and could potentially have much to offer as a catalyst for cohesion in the search for a framework to underpin provision and a continuum of development and learning to inform practice.

What Can Research Offer?

The 1980s and the early nineties have seen a relative lack of large-scale funding of educational research into early years provision. Comparatively speaking, the seventies and early eighties were characterised by the then perceived importance of and expansion of provision for young children and research into that provision. This section draws on the seminal work of Margaret Clark (1988) so as to explore the development of these comparative differences from the seventies and the nineties and consider a possible agenda for the next century.

Margaret Clark's (1988) report, *Children Under Five: Educational Research and Evidence*, was commissioned in the early eighties by the then Secretary of State, Sir Keith Joseph, 'to carry out a critical evaluation of research into the education of under fives undertaken over recent years'. Her review of the links between expanding provision and associated research in the seventies is worth recalling. In 1974, a Nursery Education Management Committee was established, by the DES (Department of Education and Science now DfEE, Department for Education and Employment). Short-term studies were initiated, leading to the identification of 19 topics requiring further research or development projects. These topics included: 'Continuity and progress – a descriptive study of children's experiences in schools between the ages of 3 and 7 or 8 years, to show the extent and nature of continuity and progression, in the curriculum.' The recognition of the need to understand children's learning and influences upon it across the breadth of the continuum was thus acknowledged.

At about this time, the Social Science Research Council (SSRC; now Economic and Social Research Council, ESRC) decided to increase expenditure on the preschool area and commissioned research into key topics. Barbara Tizard was appointed to undertake a review of then current research. The DES Management Committee considered the recommendations made to them along with Barbara Tizard's report to the SSRC and determined the following five areas of priority for further research:

(1) What parents want and why in the realm of preschool provision.
(2) Co-ordination of services for under-fives.
(3) Parental involvement in nursery education.
(4) Continuity and progression in the educational experience of children between three and eight years.
(5) Problems associated with the integration of handicapped children into normal nursery classes.

Following on from further short-term projects undertaken by the Management Committee, 19 research projects were recommended. Four were given priority (drawing also on further recommendations by Tizard to the SSRC). These concerned:

(1) Rural areas.
(2) Continuity of experience and curriculum across the 3–8 age range.
(3) Teacher training.
(4) Ethnic minorities.

The emphasis on the need to know more about how continuity of experience is maintained remained a high priority.

In April 1975, SSRC awarded a large part of its money to Jerome Bruner for research into the preschool field. The Oxford Preschool Research Unit was established and a number of influential publications ensued, with a remit to ensure that the research was accessible to practitioners. The DES awarded grants to research the experiences of young children at home (Hutt & Davie, published Hutt *et al.*, 1989), the development of materials for assessment and evaluation, and the investigation of the aims, roles and development of nursery staff (National Foundation for Education Research in England and Wales NFER). Further research was undertaken in various quarters following on from the 'boom' promoted by DES/SSRC interest. Such research was generally perceived as high priority and (significantly) fundable, but only for a relatively brief period. Margaret Clark comments on the possible limitations of the ensuing priority-linked studies leading, in her view, to a diminution in subsequent funding. She maintained that these subsequent, more extensive research studies failed to set their topics (as listed by the DES) in the wider range of educational contexts identified and described in the previous, short-term studies. While these later studies resulted, in her view, in the identification of further, related priorities, the findings did not lead on to the establishment of a cohesive context for research planning. Such a context might have emerged, however, had the political will and commitment continued beyond the mid seventies, and it might yet be revived.

Margaret Clark concludes her report by identifying six research priorities, proposed as a framework within which to consider issues rather than exploring these early years issues in isolation. These are, in brief (for fuller discussion see Clark, 1988: 279–280):

(1) Studies of continuity of children's experience between three and eight.

(2) The development of literacy and numeracy in young children.

(3) Quality and appropriateness of experience for children for whom English is a second language.

(4) Children in rural areas.

(5) Pre-service and in-service courses for teachers and other staff.

(6) An evaluation of the extent and quality of educational and other provision, including children under mandatory school age in reception classes.

Some revision and expansion might now be timely. For example, continuity of experience might now need to incorporate birth to eight. To literacy and numeracy might be added the exploration of the child's world, including scientific, geographical and historical perspectives. Artistic, musical and dramatic expression are clearly also part of this world. While recognising the special needs of second language learners it might now be argued that quality for them is similar to that offered for any child within the age phase but that, yes, particular account must be taken of their special needs. Early priorities had also included parental involvement and teacher training, the latter perhaps now in need of re-focusing as professional development to take account of ongoing impact from initial training onwards. Both parental involvement and professional development are clearly integral, conceptual framework issues. If a framework for understanding and action is to emerge, it clearly needs to be underpinned by reference to related research. Starting points and directions must be considered.

The Research Reported in this Book

A brief outline of the issues addressed by this volume was given at an earlier point in the chapter. It now seems appropriate to provide further detail on the forthcoming chapters and to comment on the contribution they might make to a research-based framework with some potential to conceptualise the early years and to a continuum of development and learning that might inform practice.

The chapters have been organised chronologically in relation to the age of the children with whom each is concerned. The first four chapters thus focus on nursery settings. These are followed by two chapters which introduce a focus on two aspects of transition, one relating to parental involvement in the nursery and in the primary school, and one relating to provision for four year olds in school in rural and town settings. Two chapters then look at aspects of mathematics in reception classrooms. These are followed by a focus on the summative assessment of Year 2 children. This chapter links to the next which looks at assessment and science in Year 2 children and on to a final chapter which looks at factors influencing the delivery of science in infant and junior classrooms. Thus is the age-range three to eight considered.

Three of these chapters look at aspects of significant parental involvement – parents as partners in their children's learning and development. There are clear implications from these studies in relation to the educare principle of linking development and learning at home and at school as an integral issue within an early years framework. Across the age-phase related chapters, there are reports of children's learning and teacher action in three subject areas: English, particularly language development and literacy skills; mathematics, particularly aspects of numeracy; and science. This is not intended to reflect their location at the core of the National Curriculum; nor is this intended to suggest that other subject areas are in any way marginal to development and learning. Rather, the studies reveal the foundations that these areas can lay for subsequent learning when the subject areas are interpreted and provided for appropriately and assiduously. Threaded through the chapters, with a range of emphases, is the strand of professional development.

In Chapter 2 Sally Beveridge addresses special needs in a context of different types of provision, from fully separate to fully integrated. She explores dimensions of home–school links and the associated importance of early intervention. Earlier we remarkd on the need to celebrate diversity in forms of early years provision while avoiding fragmentation. Sally Beveridge describes a continuum of integrated settings for special needs children. She reports on the perspectives of parents and teachers, going on to identify significant dimensions of integrated preschool provision for further investigation. Reflecting back on priorities and recommendations outlined earlier reveals a recommendation to 'research problems associated with the integration of handicapped children into normal nursery classes'. Sally Beveridge's findings and agenda setting broaden out this rather narrow proposal by addressing the issue of special needs in the early years from a more positive and timely perspective.

Val Monaghan reports in Chapter 3 on research into the development of language through story in the nursery where she is teacher in charge. Two groups of children were tested and compared. The experimental group were exposed to an intensive intervention programme of stories and story-related experiences. While the methodology will be of particular interest to practitioners in similar circumstances the findings, concerned with the extent to which activities, in this case carefully structured shared experiences, increased opportunities for language development, are particularly pertinent. Val Monaghan's research, rather than being undertaken within a context of 'combatting disadvantage', is founded on a professional development perspective in that the more the educator knows and understands, the better all children's needs will be served. Val Monaghan has clearly allowed this principle to inform her own practice. Working from an action research perspective her findings contribute both to theoretical and contextual perspectives.

Dianne Lamont's (Chapter 4) research is the first of three studies to draw attention to parental involvement in the early years, each of the studies moving well beyond a view of parents as helpers. It has long been recognised that parental involvement issues are central to the early years debate. Margaret Clark advocated its inclusion within a research agenda and as noted earlier, parental involvement is fundamental to the application of the educare principle with the need to acknowledge the experience of the whole child and to link home and school in these early years. The family and parenting are key issues in relation to the care and education of young children. Dianne Lamont's research examines how a school staff endeavoured to effect improvements in learning through revisions in practice leading on to policy development. Simultaneous with the focus on their own practice, staff liaised with parents via questionnaire, interview and joint viewing of filmed interactions between adult and children. Subsequent changes in the interactive styles of both staff and parents with children are documented. As head of the nursery, initiator of the research and collaborative researcher with staff, Dianne Lamont also explores the tensions of being a manager with a commitment to professional development via research alongside a desire for staff to take ownership of that research; and this in a community where the nursery and its existing practices were already seen as having high status with no perceived need for change. Ethical dimensions are considered. This research draws attention to the extent (or limit) to which any kind of initial training can prepare educators for the significant and important responsibilities of assessment – a theme developed further by Diane Shorrocks (in Chapter 10) and Sheridan Earnshaw (in Chapter 11). The development of professional expertise and the implications in relation to initial and in-service training are dimensions also explored by Carol Aubrey (in Chapter 9) and Diane Shorrocks (in Chapter 10).

Continuing the focus on links between home and school, Sheila Rye (Chapter 5) reports on her research into the setting up of consultations with parents in a large, inner-city multi-racial nursery. Semi-structured interviews with parents, the majority of whom had a first language other than English, revealed a desire on the parents' part to know more about what their children did at nursery and about what they were learning. The chapter reports findings which underpinned subsequent procedures for consultation established by staff and the impact of these procedures upon the levels of communication between staff and parents in relation to the children's learning. Sheila Rye's research offers considerable insights into the involvement of parents from ethnic minority groups – another of the priorities identified by the Nursery Management Committee in the mid seventies. Further to this, it considers an issue raised both in the Dianne Lamont's (Chapter 4) and Angela Anning & Sue Billet's (Chapter 7) research – the role of professionals other than the teacher in relation to early years provision. One of the fundamental issues within the complexity of provision concerns the range of types of practitioners working in early years settings. Their disparate initial training and means of further professional development have long been recognised as potentially undermining cohesion and consistency in provision. Sheila Rye's research gives important insights into the potential that practitioner research has for addressing consistency and cohesion in relation to this particular issue.

Following on in a similar vein of parents and practitioners, Judy Arrowsmith in Chapter 6 draws interesting parallels with both Dianne Lamont's and Sheila Rye's research, from a broader yet complementary perspective. While the previous two authors were, respectively, head and teacher in charge in a nursery setting, Judy Arrowsmith was an outside researcher intent on building working relationships with insiders founded on confidence and trust. Initial interviews with staff and parents were followed by dissemination of the findings as a basis for decisions, by staff, about how partnerships with parents would be developed. The chapter charts developments in two nursery settings and draws also on related research undertaken in four primary schools. Both studies take account of the idiosyncratic and cultural climates of specific settings, revealing parental–professional relationships as dynamic, not static. This study is also a timely and pertinent reminder that well-considered forms of parental involvement should not cease with the child's transition to primary school.

Continuing this theme of transition, Angela Anning & Sue Billet (Chapter 7) have studied, from a perspective somewhat different from previous studies, that unfortunate legacy of previous expansion now, it seems, entrenched by financial need in schools – the four year old in a primary school setting. This research also embraces a priority identified by both the Nursery Education Management Committee in the mid seventies and by Margaret Clark in her final recommendations, but somewhat neglected in the interim – namely that of provision for young children in rural areas. Their LEA-funded research contrasts provision in two small village schools with provision in two large town schools. It provides qualitative data extracts which illuminate the nature of children's experiences in the respective settings. It identifies and explores some interesting implications in relation to how such research might, in the past, have affected LEA policy in relation to concerns about localised needs – in this case, a very high proportion of rural schools. Given the substantial movement of money to individual schools, such influence is rapidly diminishing. This has implications for the future of locally funded research initiatives, for local policy development and for the related training dimension in early years provision. As well as looking at the continuing plight of four year olds in school, this study draws attention to the wider significance of these issues.

Ann MacNamara's report of her research (Chapter 8) is the first of the chapters to look at children as learners and the contribution professionals make to learning and development. Ann MacNamara's research focuses on the development of mathematical skills in the early years. The research offers an informed challenge to notions of deficiency that may yet prevail concerning young children and their powers of mental organisation. It investigates a particular mathematical skill – subitising – in children in nursery and then in reception settings, also following a small group as they move from one setting to the next. The research has implications for the baseline of expectation of four and five year olds in reception classes as well as for mathematical, classroom practice. Along with the remaining chapters, Ann MacNamara's work contributes to a view of 'activity and experience' as only a part of the young child's entitlement (albeit important). This particular mathematical ability is clearly evident. Yet it may be potentially constrained and even diminished because of particular teaching methods adopted, and perhaps because the teacher's knowledge of developmental potential within a particular age-phase may be only partially informed.

Carol Aubrey's research (Chapter 9) into the growth of pedagogical subject knowledge in the learning of mathematics was undertaken in reception classrooms. This chapter is concerned with mathematical data handling. It informs understanding of the need for subject knowledge alongside the development of practitioner understanding of the learning process and associated pedagogical knowledge. Carol Aubrey offers case studies of the background, beliefs, attitudes and practice of two reception teachers, one novice and one experienced. The high level of expository detail gives clear insights into the current condition of these two teachers' mathematical thinking and to links with classroom organisation and planning at these points in their careers. It illuminates issues relating to support for beginning teachers who may, like the one in this study, find themselves initially overwhelmed by the mathematics curriculum and by the responsibility for its implementation. It also shows the extent to which an experienced teacher, both in terms of mathematical knowledge and pedagogical subject knowledge, may still struggle, to some extent, when trying to deal effectively with the diversity of individual need in the classroom.

Within a context of children's learning, Diane Shorrocks (Chapter 10) reports on the statutory requirements of assessment in the early years. Diagnosis and assessment are fundamental to a concern with quality provision; summative assessment at the end of Key Stage 1 is a statutory requirement, set in a context of public accountability. Are these conflicting dimensions for early years educators? By drawing on data from a national project Diane Shorrocks offers a comprehensive consideration of the relationship between Teacher Assessment and SAT assessment at Key Stage 1. She comments, in the light of the data, on the relative appropriateness and usefulness of each approach to assessment. She also draws attention to the correlation between developments in teaching and learning resulting from these assessment procedures and goes on to consider the corresponding training and support required by early years teachers in the development of assessment related skills.

The final investigations of children's learning and the role of the adult, focus on science, with two complementary chapters. The first of these was undertaken by Sheridan Earnshaw (Chapter 11) in the capacity of advisory teacher. Continuing the assessment theme, it draws on research with Year 2 teachers, exploring links between personal subject knowledge and assessment and planning. Sheridan Earnshaw's research endorses conclusions drawn by Diane Shorrocks: that teachers are now required to consider what should be taught and in what ways, as well as asking what children have learned and their evidence for it. Sheridan Earnshaw's observations of science sessions – content, organisation, management and teacher assessment – along with pre and follow-on interviews with teachers, illustrates the extent to which the knowledge and competence of teachers (both as planners and assessors) has influence on the potential outcomes for learners. The second of Diane Shorrocks' concluding comments concerns the links between competence in these areas and training and support. Sheridan Earnshaw's research draws on data concerned with the levels and types of science-related training received by her sample teachers, her conclusions adding substantive weight to Diane Shorrocks' discussion. Post-Dearing, teacher assessment should re-acquire higher status. It clearly has a role to play in establishing and maintaining quality provision right across the early years continuum. Sheridan Earnshaw's research is a timely reminder that 'one-off' intensive training of the type offered to teachers when the science National Curriculum was introduced is insufficient for maintaining the required levels of professional development. She looks to a future that might avoid making further mistakes by offering appropriate levels of support to practitioners.

The second of the two science-focused chapters (Chapter 12), by Keith Bardon, also looks at factors influencing the delivery of science. Keith Bardon's research centres on infant and lower junior classrooms. It seemed appropriate to conclude the volume by reiterating an important point made earlier – that movement towards a continuum of learning and development across the early years should not be made at the expense of continuity between Key Stages 1 and 2. Such lack of continuity could signal a real danger for seven year olds if they find themselves in settings as inappropriate to their needs as many four and five year olds have found themselves – this may be a legacy already forming. Keith Bardon's research leaves us with a timely pointer to the need to look for similarities, rather than differences, in the experiences of both teachers and learners in their respective domains.

On conclusion of the following chapters, a postscript (Chapter 13) examines the possibilities of moving forward with a research agenda in the search for a cohesive and conceptually founded early years framework and for an integrated continuum of development and learning.

2 Dimensions of Preschool Provision for Children with Special Educational Needs

SALLY BEVERIDGE

Background

The Warnock Committee (DES, 1978) regarded early educational intervention as crucial for children with special educational needs. Accordingly pre-five provision, which it described as the 'key' for promoting children's learning, was identified in the Warnock report as one of the three most important priorities for service development.

When considering what shape this early provision should take, the Committee acknowledged the role of parents as their children's primary educators, and endorsed the development of home-based services such as those based on the Portage model (White & Cameron, 1987). At the same time, though, it emphasised the immense importance of nursery provision. Indeed, it recommended very strongly that nursery provision should be expanded for all children, and not just those with special educational needs. It regarded mainstream nurseries as potentially the most appropriate form of provision for the majority of children with special educational needs, but recognised that if their needs were to be successfully met, then this required:

- positive attitudes on the part of both parents and staff
- appropriate accommodation and equipment
- generous staffing levels
- thorough planning of the integration, taking into account all the children's needs

- regular advice and support for staff from local authority support services (para. 5.52).

In addition to mainstream placements, where children's needs were more specialised, smaller and more intensively resourced and supported, nursery units might be attached either to primary schools or, in the case of the most severe and complex needs, to special schools. Irrespective of whether children attended mainstream or special nurseries, though, the Committee stressed that parental involvement and interdisciplinary collaboration were essential to the success of the intervention.

Although the 1981 Education Act was based to a large extent upon the Warnock report, it did not adopt all of the Committee's recommendations. The same remains substantially true of its re-working within the 1993 Education Act. LEAs (Local Education Authorities) have a responsibility to make provision for children from the age of two years if they have identified special educational needs, but any provision which is made before the statutory school age of five years can be deemed special. Nationally, there has been no general expansion of nursery provision, and there is a great deal of variation between LEAs with respect to their preschool policies and practices. Some have followed the principles and framework put forward in the Warnock report, whereas others provide little choice for parents outside the special school sector. Nevertheless, in a number of authorities a continuum of more or less integrated placements can be described, ranging from special schools (which may take children from as young as two years old), through specially resourced community nurseries, to mainstream nurseries and classes.

Mitchell & Brown (1991) have described a general consensus among those working in early intervention that their aims are: to provide early stimulation as a basis for subsequent learning; to minimise existing difficulties; and to try to prevent later difficulties from arising. Bailey & Wolery (1992), on the basis of their study of different intervention schemes, have similarly been able to identify some common goals. Importantly, they include among these a consideration of family priorities:

(1)   to support families in achieving their own goals;
(2)   to promote child engagement, independence and mastery;
(3)   to promote development in key domains;
(4)   to build and support children's social competence;
(5)   to promote the generalised use of skills;
(6)   to provide and prepare for normalised life experiences;
(7)   to prevent the emergence of future problems or disabilities.
(Bailey & Wolery, 1992: 35)

Despite these shared aims and purposes, though, there are distinct forms that early provision for children with special educational needs can take, each of which is underpinned by a rather different set of beliefs and priorities. So, for example, very early help of a highly specialised nature may be provided with the aim of paving the way for later mainstream placement; or longer-term special assistance may be given, in either separate or integrated contexts. By contrast, high-quality mainstream early years provision may be developed which aims, through responsiveness to the full range of children's needs, to minimise the need for more specialist intervention.

There is no firm empirical evidence to support the greater effectiveness of one or another approach for particular children, and therefore the preferred approach, for both their parents and teachers, must be at least in part based on their 'accumulated wisdom' (Bailey & Wolery, 1992), beliefs and priorities. Their perceptions of the nature of the children's needs, their views on the extent to which specialist intervention is required to meet these, and the weighting they give to the relative advantages and disadvantages of integrated and separate provision will all be significant. It was with the aim of exploring a range of teacher and parent perspectives on early intervention, and the hope of identifying dimensions which merited further study, that I undertook a preliminary investigation into these questions.

The Investigation

The investigation was based upon detailed interviews with a small sample of parents of preschool children with special educational needs and their nursery teachers. The sample was not randomly chosen. I wanted to include parents and teachers with experience of quite different nursery provision. Accordingly I directly approached staff involved in three diverse specialised nurseries and asked them to participate in the study. I also asked each of them to select two parents who were willing to be interviewed. Mainstream nursery contacts were made through a Child Development Centre whose pre-five teacher approached two parents and their children's teachers on my behalf.

The nursery settings

The nursery settings were as follows:

Nursery A – a child and family service for those with learning disabilities, run by a voluntary agency.
Nursery B – the nursery class of a special school for primary children with moderate learning difficulties.

Nursery C – a large resourced community nursery attached to a special
school for pupils with moderate learning difficulties.

Nursery D – a small resourced mainstream nursery attached to a special
school for pupils with moderate and severe learning
difficulties.

Nursery E – a mainstream nursery attached to a primary school.

The teacher with responsibility for each nursery was interviewed. In the
case of nursery B, the head teacher of the school also participated in the
interview. Table 2.1 summarises some factual detail about the staffing of
the nurseries, the children who attended, and their likely future school
placement.

Table 2.1 The nurseries

	Nursery A	*Nursery B*	*Nursery C*	*Nursery D*	*Nursery E*
Children's ages	0–4 years	3–5 years	2–5 years	3–5 years	3–5 years
Range of needs	All special needs	All special needs	Mainstream: special (30:25)	Mainstream: special (14:4)	Mainly mainstream
Class size	Various small groups	11	55 (in 3 rooms)	18	26
Full-time (FT) or part-time (PT)	PT	FT	PT & FT	PT	PT & FT
Staff experience	Mainly special educ.	Mainly special educ.	Special educ. and main-stream	Special educ. and main-stream	Mainstream
Staffing ratio (approx.)	1:3	1:4	1:5	1:6 and 1:9	1:13
Where the children with special needs go next	80% to their local nursery	Most stay in special school*	Approx. 30% to mainstream school	50+% to mainstream school	Individually decided

Note:
* Special school B as a whole integrates approximately 10% of its pupils each year
into their local mainstream schools

The parents and their children

Eight mothers, one of whom was a foster mother, agreed to be interviewed. Their children ranged in age from 2 years 9 months to 5 years 6 months. Four already had statements of special educational needs, and four were at various stages in the formal assessment process. One child had Down's syndrome and one cerebral palsy; the others were described as showing general developmental delay and/or language difficulties. Almost all had additional areas of difficulty, commonly in their behaviour (generally ascribed by their mothers to frustration), and in individual cases, autistic symptoms, diabetes and impairments of vision, hearing, articulation and motor co-ordination had been diagnosed. Each one of the mothers said that she had been aware of her child's difficulties before these were confirmed by professionals, and two felt that it was only after considerable persistence on their part that professionals took their concerns seriously. For most, professional confirmation occurred when the child was between 12 and 24 months old.

Prior to attending nursery, nearly all had some involvement with their local Child Development Centre and, through that, speech or physiotherapy where appropriate.

The children's nursery experience

Most of the children began to attend nursery at between two and three years of age. Four attended on a full-time basis and for the others, their part-time attendance was supplemented by additional provision, for example at playgroup, day nursery or Child Development Centre. All but two mothers said that the choice of nursery for their child had been informed or led by professional advice, and without exception they expressed confidence that it had been the right choice.

The reliable assessment of preschool age children is notoriously difficult, but nevertheless the mothers and teachers showed a remarkable degree of agreement on the specific needs of the children. The mothers were aware of the nurseries' aims for their children and in several cases used the phrase 'what we're aiming for at the moment' when describing them. This conveys an impression that these mothers felt involved in decisions about appropriate aims. Their relationships with professionals were a dominant theme in all of their interviews, and this impression of close and positive links with nursery staff was confirmed in numerous ways. One mother explained that 'I wouldn't say we live in one another's pockets – I'm not that sort of person', but went on to describe a number of joint home–school initiatives which she characterised as forming a 'partnership' between herself and the nursery. The following comments represent the views expressed by most mothers:

'It's really nice to be able to get to know them ... you need to have a good relationship with the teachers.'

'They make you feel comfortable. They make you feel you're not the only person with a problem. You do think it's something you're doing wrong ... but they make you at ease, that it's not your fault, and you're not the only parent to go through it.'

'I don't think you should under-estimate the value of help and support for the parents... [and] the family.'

'We do feel a part – we don't feel as if our role has been taken off us... it's not one-way, they ask us for our advice, what we would like them to do ... so you are part of the nursery, you don't feel like an outsider.'

'I don't think they've alienated me in any way because from the very beginning... they included me, they listened to me, they respected what I said. That to me means a lot.'

Given the apparent quality of their home–school relationships it is perhaps not surprising, but nevertheless notable, that when the mothers and teachers were asked to say what they saw as the main strengths of the particular nurseries, there was a great deal of agreement. Table 2.2 summarises their views. From part (a) of Table 2.2, it can be seen that staff attributes and parent–teacher relationships are a key factor for both parents and teachers across all the settings. What teachers describe as being 'welcoming of parents' appears to be experienced by the mothers as a 'relaxed and helpful approach', and both agree that a strength of the nurseries is that staff listen to what parents have to say. Nevertheless, there is a slightly different emphasis in their perspectives: while the teachers tend to give primary emphasis to their relationships with parents, for the mothers in this sample weight is generally given first to staff relations with their children, and second to relationships with themselves. This difference in emphasis is similar to that found among a larger sample of parents by Sandow, Stafford & Stafford (1987). The importance ascribed to the relationships which are developed between staff, pupils and parents is a finding which is not unique to provision for children with special educational needs. According to one recent study, it is the indicator of 'what makes a good school' that is most frequently referred to by parents during the early years (Hughes, Wikeley & Nash, 1990). One further difference in perspective, which recurs in a subsequent section of the interviews, concerns the nature of staff expertise. Whereas the teachers tend to emphasise the importance of staff skill and experience, among the mothers a key factor is their determination and commitment to meeting the children's needs.

Part (b) of Table 2.2 shows perspectives which are specific to individual nurseries. Again, there is considerable agreement between teachers and parents. For example, both see the support they receive, respectively from other professionals and from other parents, as strengths of particular nurseries. In addition, relationships with other children are significant to both parents and teachers when judging the quality of a preschool setting. The approach to the curriculum, however, reveals certain differences in expectations and assumptions, such that whereas some teachers and parents view specialised approaches as particularly relevant to the effectiveness of their intervention, others are sure that more 'normal' methods should apply.

Views on Early Intervention

From the mothers' perspective it was evident that they saw early nursery provision as important both for themselves and for their children.

Table 2.2 Teacher and parent perspectives on the main strengths of the nurseries

Teachers	Parents
(a) All nurseries	

Staff who are/do:
  Welcoming of parents
  Understanding and supportive
  Experienced and skilled
 	
  Listen to/develop positive
  relationships with parents
	Staff who are/do:
	  Relaxed, helpful
	  Develop good relationships with children
	  Determined/committed and put
	  children's needs first
	  Listen

(b) Specific nurseries	
Staff have good support Early admissions/full-time placement Small numbers Mainstream peers/mix of children Curriculum - specific skills work, behaviour management Curriculum - free flow/work at own pace Therapists on site Integration and expertise	Other parents give support Early admissions/full-time placement Small classes/good staffing ratio Mainstream peers/mix of children One-to-one attention, skills work, special equipment/ toys, work on behaviour Independence, imagination, variety of activities Equal treatment for all/acceptance, valuing and respect for children

Many were open in discussing the value of respite – of time away from each other's company – both for themselves and for their child's independence. Several also referred to the social, emotional and practical support they had derived from their own attendance at the nursery. A flavour of their views on the role of early intervention in helping their children is given by the following comments:

'The earlier the better... they need pushing.'

'Parents do give in, you're bound to... [teachers] think of teaching points in everything they do, in a way that you don't do or even think of doing at home.'

'It can prevent early problems getting worse.'

'It will give [skills] that will help him withstand the pressures of life that are to come.'

Among six of the mothers, there was some optimism that nursery was providing their children with skills that would help them succeed in a mainstream school.

Although the mothers were very positive about early intervention, one was also quite explicit that 'a lot of what [son]'s done, he's done for himself'. Interestingly, she was the only mother to refer to turning down earlier offers of specific help, because her son was already 'naturally starting to do things'. Two of the teachers were also circumspect about how far it is possible to say that their interventions have definitely led to children's progress. Nevertheless, all of the teachers considered early intervention to be of great importance for children with special educational needs: 'vital', 'essential' and 'fundamental' being some of the adjectives they used. Like the mothers, they saw intervention as bringing advantages for parents as well as for their children. All referred to their relationships with the children's parents and to ways in which they attempt to provide parental support. Indeed, for nursery A, the service to families represents a fundamental aim, and the teacher from nursery D also described support for parents as a primary purpose.

When talking about the benefits to the children, three common themes emerged: the acceleration of early learning; the provision of a sound basis for subsequent learning; and the prevention of later difficulties, 'frustrations, angers and anxieties'. For these benefits to arise though, as one teacher pointed out, there is a need for early accurate assessment. The difficulty in establishing a reliable assessment picture in the early years has already been referred to. The need to involve parents and all relevant professionals together in the assessment process, is a topic which recurred in a number of parent as well as teacher interviews. While some understanding was expressed about professional reluctance to 'label' a child as having special needs too quickly, the risks of not providing help when it was needed were viewed as far more significant. Serious concerns were raised about a perceived tendency to say of preschool age children whose development seems slow, 'all children develop at different rates, don't worry'. As one mother put it, 'a line has to be drawn somewhere – if a child needs help, it should be given', and this seems to be the general consensus among both parents and teachers.

Nevertheless, teachers from all except nursery B did point to potential disadvantages as well as advantages which can arise from early intervention. These are generally associated with the inadvertent fostering of dependence among both children and their parents. For children, this might result from an over-emphasis on one-to-one attention, adult direction and praise, which was seen by one teacher as a risk particularly associated with special schools and classes. For parents, examples were described where an unnecessary level of dependence on the 'special' label and on professional guidance and advice had developed. One teacher also pointed out that professionals can make parents feel they should be stimulating their children all the time: 'we can create a situation which is full of anxiety', and where the intervention adds to rather than alleviates stress.

The explicit aims of the five nurseries in this study are very similar, and there was a certain degree of consensus between the teachers about the ideal form that early intervention should take. That is: it should be offered as early as possible; it should be sufficiently flexible to meet the individual needs of children and families, for example through providing both home-based and nursery-based involvement; there should be sensitive, skilled and sufficient staff; and the intervention should be seen as a partnership between children, parents, teachers and other professionals.

However, there was rather less agreement on how specialist the nursery setting for intervention should ideally be. The teachers' views were understandably influenced by the forms of provision they have experienced and, in the case of nursery B, by their knowledge of those children referred later to the school who had not received appropriate help from mainstream services during their early years. The teacher from nursery A felt that intervention should take place initially in a specialist setting, and only later in a mainstream setting when 'the parents were more sure themselves about their child's ability, more sure about what they [parents] were doing and felt able to face the outside world'.

The headteacher from school B felt strongly that expertise should be concentrated where it is needed and that the ideal form therefore might be resourced units in mainstream schools. The teachers from nurseries C, D and E also referred to the importance of skilled and motivated staff, but they all expressed a strong commitment to the ideal of intervention in fully integrated settings.

Perspectives on Integration

Six of the eight mothers interviewed were hoping for mainstream education for their children, and the majority of the teachers too had very positive attitudes to integration. When discussing what they saw as the advantages of integrated provision, individual mothers and teachers referred to benefits for both mainstream and special staff, and for the parents of all the children concerned. However, the majority of their comments related to the children themselves.

For the children with special educational needs, potential benefits that were mentioned included curriculum breadth and challenge, higher expectations and a greater degree of independence. Most discussion, though, focused on their interactions with mainstream peers. One teacher aired some concern that parents might expect too much from peer interactions, and another pointed out that often children with learning difficulties can have difficulty with their social skills and relationships. Nevertheless, both mothers and teachers viewed mainstream peers as important models who could help the children's learning. A typical comment from a mother on the incentive peers can provide was: 'It stimulates him to be around children who are doing what three and four year olds should be doing – it encourages him to do the same.' Interactions with peers are not restricted to the classroom or school context, and for many parents it was very important that their children should have local friends, feel they belong to their local community and generally 'feel a part of the whole'. Furthermore, several emphasised their view that:

'Special school might be nice and relaxed, but life isn't like that, life is having to compete.'

'He's got to learn to live in the real world.'

'It's not going to help him protecting him from the real world.'

When thinking about potential benefits of integration for mainstream children, most teachers were a little tentative in their replies, but hoped that it would result in their developing increased tolerance, empathy and understanding, and that this would continue with them into adult life. The teachers from nurseries C and D pointed out that such a response was not inevitable, and that staff had to be prepared to plan for and work on this.

Most parents also expressed the hope that integrated provision would act to promote more positive attitudes towards special needs. They hoped mainstream children would learn:

'To take children with special needs for granted and not look on them as different.'

'To see them just as children.'

Several parents were open in describing their own previous prejudices before their 'eyes were opened' by having a child with special needs, and most described difficult encounters they had had with public reactions to their children's behaviour. Not surprisingly, therefore, they had strong views on the need to 'educate society'. One mother spoke for many when she summed up her feelings about integration as follows: 'The children would feel part of the real world, their parents would feel that they weren't being shut away and treated as different and it would do the mainstream children good.'

Three of the teachers used the explicit language of rights and equal opportunities when referring to integration as representing an 'inherent right' and an 'entitlement'. This does not mean though that they were not aware of the practical difficulties involved in ensuring that integration is a positive and productive experience for all concerned. There was a great deal of realism among both staff and parents about the extent to which different children might benefit and, in many of their interviews, there was an implicit endorsement of the argument put forward by the headteacher of school B that: 'it's just not good enough to say integration is a good thing... there are things which have to be in place' to make it work.

Their views on what specifically does need to be in place are summarised and grouped by theme in Table 2.3. The table also indicates the numbers of teachers and parents who referred to each theme, and it is interesting to note the degree of agreement in their perspectives. Comparison with Table 2.2 reveals a number of areas of overlap with what they regard as the main strengths of their current position. Just as in the earlier part of their interviews, the responses of mothers and teachers show a different emphasis in relation to staff attributes, with the mothers making most frequent reference to attitudes, understanding and

Table 2.3 Integration: What needs to be in place?

Teachers	Parents
Staff who:	
• are skilled and experienced/have expertise	
• have positive attitudes	• are positive, aware understanding, committed, determined
• have appropriate knowledge, support, training	• are informed, trained
• have realistic but high expectations	• have appropriate expectations
• are flexible enough to respond to very different needs	• are able to meet different needs
(4)	(5)
Support:	
• of children; flexibly organised and fostering independence, not dependence	• at an appropriate level
• of children, parents and staff; properly organised	
• financial	• financial
(5)	(4)
Planning:	
• to ensure integration is a positive experience for all	• to ensure the learning of other children is not disrupted
(2)	(3)
An ethos which:	
• neither denies nor overemphasises difference, but responds to the needs all children have	• does not label/isolate/make the child feel different, but does respond to his/her special needs
(2)	(2)
A headteacher who:	
is positive and welcoming, and does not make integration decisions purely on the basis of financial implications*	
(2)	(2)
Home–school links which:	
• allow two-way communication	• give both parents and professionals support
(1)	(1)

Note
* Individual mothers had experienced interviews with headteachers in local primary schools in which their perception was that the whole focus had been on the amount of money their child would cost the school, and whether the finance provided with their statement would cover this.

commitment and the teachers stressing the importance of skill, expertise and experience.

If the aspects of good practice which they identified were not in place, then the mothers were alert to a number of problems which could arise for their children. If they were not given specific help when they needed it, for example, then they might lose confidence and become frustrated, withdrawn and unhappy. Without an appropriate level of support in the class, other children might become resentful of any additional attention they received, and they might be made to feel very different from the rest of their peers. A number of parents were quite explicit that they did not want their child to cause disruption to the learning of others which, as one of them put it, 'would not help anybody'.

The head of school B felt very strongly that too often the mainstream system does not work well for children with special educational needs, who may arrive at a special school after unhappy mainstream experiences which lead them to view themselves as failures. By contrast with mainstream schools, he argued, parents can be sure that if their child is in a special school then the staff have the experience, expertise and positive determination to help them. The staff, together with the special facilities and good interdisciplinary liaison which their children might need, can represent a real strength of the special school setting. The teacher from nursery A was equally concerned to emphasise that special schools are not 'second best' but provide 'a real alternative'. For some parents, they offer: 'comfort and assurance that their child will not be seen as different... will be well and truly looked after and won't come to any harm'. For two of the mothers who were interviewed, these arguments were clearly persuasive.

Dimensions of Educational Provision

Several of the mothers in the study referred to how difficult they had found it to decide upon what would be the most appropriate provision for their children. This was true at the preschool stage, but not surprisingly they tended to see the process of decision-making about school placement as even more difficult. Government circulars are explicit that this process should be informed by an 'agreed understanding' between parents and professionals, concerning both the nature of the child's needs and also the provision needed to meet those needs. In practice, most of the mothers felt that their choices were at least informed if not determined by professional guidance. The issue of parental choice is an important one, because as a result of the 1993 Education Act parents of children with statements will for the first time have the right, with certain provisos, to choose the school their child attends. If they are to exercise this right actively and positively, then they need appropriate information to guide their choice. Both mothers and teachers in the study were quite clear that any decision must be based upon a balancing of priorities between: (a) the child's needs for specialist help and resources; and (b) her/his need for access to as 'normal' a range of learning experiences as possible, including the opportunity to interact with mainstream peers.

Three dimensions of educational provision emerge from the interviews as particularly significant. These are first, the ethos of the school or nursery; second, the intensity of the intervention it provides; and third, the level of integration it promotes.

Ethos

Both the mothers and the teachers said that the quality of relationships between children, parents and staff were of prime importance. Several mothers commented that the extent to which they felt they and their children were welcomed by teaching staff was a significant criterion in their decision about school placement. There was general agreement that if the placement is to be successful then this requires staff who are committed, motivated and determined to help children with special needs. While both mothers and teachers saw such positive attitudes as fundamental, their emphasis was slightly different. Among the mothers, a commonly expressed view was that, given the necessary level of commitment, teachers would develop appropriate skills and expertise, much as they had done as parents: 'After all, we [parents] don't have any choice, we just have to get on with it.'

Notably, it was one of the two mothers not seeking mainstream placement who expressed reservations about staff expertise in ordinary schools. These reservations were shared by the special school head and nursery teacher. Among the teachers generally, greater weight was given to the need for staff to be supported in acquiring knowledge, skills and expertise in working with children with special needs. Nevertheless, both mothers and teachers expressed views similar to those of the Warnock Committee, that it is not sufficient for teachers to 'merely accept' a child with special needs into their classes: rather, they must actively plan to meet their needs.

Intensity of intervention

Traditionally, special and mainstream settings have tended to adopt very different approaches to early intervention. Typically, many special schools have been characterised as highly structured and directive. Their interventions usually incorporate intensive one-to-one work on individualised skill-based programmes. By contrast, mainstream nursery provision has usually been characterised as involving a child-directed, 'free flow' approach, in which the emphasis is on encouraging children to develop their concepts and skills through active exploration of their environment. In this context, interventions rarely entail formalised one-to-one work.

Increasingly, however, it has been acknowledged that each of these traditions has strengths to offer. There is no doubt that some children need more explicit structure and support than others to help them make best use of the learning opportunities which are generally available in mainstream settings. Among these children will be many who have learning difficulties. Equally though, it has been demonstrated that successful intervention for children with special needs cannot be wholly teacher-directed, but must build on the children's own initiatives (Bailey & Wolery, 1992). Those mothers who had experience of both types of approach were convinced that both were important for their children. They felt that a 'more disciplined and formal' style provided the 'groundwork' for their children's learning, but that it was in the less tightly structured contexts that the child 'comes out', is 'more herself' and uses 'his own imagination'.

There were, as previously discussed, diverse views about the degree to which specialist forms of intervention were required, but the general view among the mothers appeared to be that they wished for the 'least different' approach that would effectively meet their child's needs. In one mother's words: 'What I like is they don't treat your child any differently because they have special needs... but they are responsive to the special needs your child has.'

Level of integration

The nurseries in the study can be viewed as representing points along a continuum of fully separate to fully integrated provision. Few of the staff thought of it in this way though, for they were aware that it is a misleading over-simplification to equate placement with the level of integration actually experienced by a child. So, for example, most of the children at specialist nursery A also had part-time involvement in mainstream settings; the children at nursery C spent varying proportions of their day in more separate or more integrated contexts depending on staff assessment of their needs; the children at nursery D were seen to become more fully integrated over time; and so on. It has often been pointed out that simply placing children with special needs in mainstream classes does not guarantee their successful integration. Indeed, in practice they may remain as separate as if they were in a special setting, unless steps are taken to promote positive interactions with their peers.

For many of the mothers and teachers I interviewed, integration represents an equal opportunities issue. From this perspective, as Hegarty and his colleagues (Hegerty, Pocklington & Lucas, 1981) have argued, it cannot be seen as only having implications for the children with special needs. If integration is thought of as 'their problem' then the task is to 'fit into' a framework that was not designed with their needs in mind. By contrast, if integration is conceptualised as having relevance for all children, then provision can be planned which anticipates and attempts to meet the full range of needs. One mother summed up the views of several others when she described her son's involvement in such a setting: 'He's mixing with ordinary children, he has the opportunity to talk with them, play with them. He gets individual attention when he needs it, he is encouraged when he needs to be encouraged and sheltered when he needs to be sheltered... It's doing him good.'

In introducing this investigation, I drew attention to the view of the Warnock Committee that, given certain conditions, mainstream nursery is the most appropriate form of provision for the majority of children with special educational needs. In the absence of a large-scale experimental programme it is not really possible to explore this proposition empirically, because the majority of children with special educational needs do not have statements and therefore many will not have any formal preschool education at all. Certainly their parents are unlikely to have alternative forms to choose between. For that minority who have statements, however, the interviews lend strong if qualified support to the principle of integrated nursery provision. If this is to be as successful as possible, the perspectives of the mothers and teachers in this study do provide several pointers for schools.

The 1993 Education Act requires that all schools not only make explicit but also regularly review their policies in relation to special educational needs. As indicated in Table 2.3 there are a number of crucial dimensions involved for schools: these include positive staff attitudes and commitment, good home–school communication, appropriate levels of support and active planning which aims to promote positive interactions and learning experiences for all.

3 The Development of Language Through Story in the Early Years of School

VAL MONAGHAN

The Context

Within a nursery setting, it is widely accepted that children will be given lots of first-hand experience and plenty of opportunities to talk. With this in mind, during the late 1970s I had attended a course concerned with communication skills in the early years. This course was based on the work of Joan Tough (1976). It had examined the different uses of language evident in children's conversation and teacher promotion of those uses. Subsequently, I had begun to suspect that although my skills as teacher might be enhanced, I was not necessarily more proficient at developing the children's communication skills; something still seemed to be missing.

About the same time, and influenced by the work of Beryl MacDougal and teachers in Cleveland, I had changed the organisation of my nursery classroom, developing a resource-based workshop approach. The intention had been to give children more scope for directing their own learning with independent access to resources in a supportive and stimulating environment.

As well as developing the classroom as a resource-based workshop, I had worked with the nursery staff in starting to use the local environment as a resource, taking the children out, giving them experiences and providing common ground between adults and children.

In this setting and with these experiences some silent children had started to talk, but others still seemed unable to capitalise on these experiences. Two recollections remain memorable and were, I think, influential on my own developing ideas about the whole area of language. Two children went to the local bakery and were enthralled; they saw bread dough being mixed and they saw the scones go into the oven in layers. On returning to school one could only respond to questions about the trip with a blank silence; the other could only comment: 'One up and down.' The whole experience had initially appeared to make very little sense to these children until they had gone to the mark making area. They had then each given a very well observed visual account of the visit even though they had been unable to express themselves verbally.

Another child, unable to recount the simplest of activities could draw complex maps of his trips to the seaside in dad's van. In the course of a small piece of classroom research into concept development in young children, Gareth, whose expressive language in school had appeared limited, revealed a vast stock of knowledge about the world largely communicated to me through hand signs.

About the same time, I was witnessing my own children's language development in the home. Hearing them engrossed, together in 'storying' for long periods, I began to see the potential for children extending their experiences into other possible worlds and drawing on the resources of storybook and TV characters. This was the sort of sustained activity I had rarely witnessed in the nursery setting and fuelled my desire to look more closely at the area. I was now beginning to suspect that, despite our best efforts and contrary to the claims of nursery teachers, one of the prime aims of the nursery curriculum – to develop the children's language – was not being fulfilled. The challenge presented by Tizard & Hughes (1984) in the study of children's learning at home and at school rang uncomfortably true: 'This study suggests that children's intellectual and language needs are much more likely to be satisfied at home than at school' (p. 256).

It seemed that the nursery school or class might be offering better opportunities for developing social skills than for developing language skills. Classrooms are often noisy and crowded, resources limited and experience was leading me to believe that there was perhaps a lack of understanding of the real antecedents of language development on the part of the staff. Consequently, verbal exchanges suffered from the constraints of time, numbers of demands from other children and lack of any shared experience between adult and child.

A certain level of language competence is required for children to be perceived as potentially successful students in school. For here we are faced with the issue of teacher expectation whereby a child might be dismissed early in their school career because they appear not to have the linguistic tools with which to function adequately. However, as the Tizard & Hughes (1984) study revealed, children can be more verbally proficient in the home than they seem to be in the nursery setting. The Bristol study directed by Gordon Wells (1986) also looked at children's language in the home and went on to link the findings to future progress in school. After investigating a range of possibilities, one of his most substantial findings was that the only common factor correlating with success later in school was the child's experience of having stories read, discussing and recalling the story on a parent-to-child basis as a normal and natural part of family experience. This led me to a consideration of the nature of story and its role as a cultural amplifier as identified by Bruner (1986). This is the conceptual movement, by children into other possible worlds, locating characters and cultural myths and icons, building a conceptual map of events, contact with the symbolic, access to the shared cultural heritage. If stories are a key to success in school and if there is a link between story experience and language development, then it seemed useful to consider the role of story in the early years curriculum.

The Research Project

I thus investigated how exposure to stories affected children's language development. An intervention programme was designed in which a control group and an experimental group of similar ages were selected randomly (apart from age) from the class register. The control group was selected from the morning register and the experimental group from the afternoon register. Provision and overall age ranges are identical for each session. Less than 10% of parents make particular morning or afternoon requests thus the majority of children are randomly assigned. Separating the groups in this manner cut out the possibility of contamination across groups and simplified practical application of the intervention programme in a busy classroom where, as teacher in charge, I had other responsibilities and minimal time available for engaging in this research but which I nevertheless perceived as important.

Each group began with six children but one child whose inherited language is Punjabi was dropped from the control group because translating facilities were not available. It was felt that she would not have been able to show her true language ability and the findings would not have been comparing like with like. One child was withdrawn from the experimental group due to extremely sporadic attendance, which meant she was not available for the pre or post intervention story test, thus the research continued with five children in each group. The programme lasted for a six-week period. All the children were tested before and after the intervention programme was completed to see whether there was any change (a) in their level of language needed to function in school and (b) in their ability to tell and retell a story.

Working from the view that language acquisition is an interactive process, the intervention programme was designed to promote interaction between parent and child, teacher and child, other adults and child and between the children themselves. The main vehicle for this interaction was the story material itself, but the experiences offered to the experimental group by the intervention programme as well as being the means of delivering the story material also provided a commonly shared context for all participants. This set of experiences gave another dimension along which language development might take place. I wanted to increase their exposure to story telling and story-telling techniques. This could have been achieved by increased exposure to whole class story times. However, bearing in mind Wells' (1986) and Tizard & Hughes' (1984) findings and linking this to Bruner's (1986) consideration of cultural amplifiers, it seemed more appropriate to replicate home-based experiences, as far as possible with one-to-one and small group experience (two to three children) for the experimental group and with parental involvement.

The Library at Home and School

At the beginning of the six-week period members of the experimental group were taken individually by the class teacher to the local library with their mothers. The intentions were partly to ensure familiarity with the library and to give an opportunity for joining – all the children but one joined the library at this time. It was also intended to emphasise that the focus of the intervention programme was books and stories adding a practical dimension to the brief outline of the project given in an introductory talk to parents. The final purpose of the library visit was to start to build up a common context of experience between all parties involved in the programme. This visit did unexpectedly offer another appropriate opportunity for the group because the local library had planned a story-telling session during the third week of the project to which all the children in the experimental group were taken with the help of two of the mothers. This consolidated the experience of the initial visit in an entirely appropriate way and was greatly enjoyed by the children. The subject was 'On the Farm' and the children were involved in making a large group picture, singing, story telling and seeing and handling some live farm animals.

In addition to the public library the experimental group was given access to a special box of books in class from which they were encouraged to select a book to take home every day. The normal class library system allows the children one book a week; the experimental group took advantage of this extra availability so their access to books was considerably increased. This opportunity was much more eagerly taken up than anticipated and once established, was responsibly used with no further intervention from the teacher. The aim of this feature of the intervention programme was to encourage and support interaction between parents and children in the area of stories and books. In addition to extra library facilities parents were asked to keep a diary during the six-week period, the aims being to help focus the parents on the story-reading activity and to provide empirical data for the study. A sheet of suggestions as to how the diary might be used was given to each parent. The parents were also given a leaflet reproduced from Barrie Wade's (1984) *Story at Home and School* with a few simple hints and suggestions about appropriate interaction on the part of the adult. The leaflet encourages parents to further the story-reading experience by talking about the stories and by encouraging the child to participate in telling and retelling. The leaflet was part of the attempt to heighten the parents' awareness of their children's involvement in story telling and retelling.

The In-class Intervention Programme

There were several elements to the in-class intervention programme. A group of parents were recruited to provide an extra adult in the classroom every afternoon. The parent would read to individual or pairs of children, targeting the experimental group. Parallel with this I, as the class teacher, temporarily released from normal duties by the presence of a student teacher in the classroom, withdrew experimental group children in small sub-groups to give them extra experience of story making on a more structured basis than that offered by the visiting parent.

I worked with a pre-selected group of stories all chosen for particular reasons. The first story to be used was John Burningham's *The Shopping Basket*. This was chosen partly for the familiar mundane subject matter, partly for the simple element of fantasy and partly because it lends itself to work with 'props'. The work with this story was gradually extended from an initial reading, to reading and talking about the story, to use of magnetised enlarged illustrations, and finally to small world props in conjunction with illustrations. The children were encouraged to develop an awareness of the structure of the plot which is in fact circular and which can easily be demonstrated with the use of the props. They were also encouraged to work as a group using the props to act out the story adopting the role of one of the characters or as 'director' and actually move the characters and illustrations around appropriately. It was hoped that this experience might feed into their own independent 'storying' activities at home and at school by opening them up to the possibilities of the use of props and giving them some skills to bring to this activity.

The other main focus of attention was the traditional story *Goldilocks and the Three Bears.* This was chosen partly because it was assumed it was likely to be familiar to most of the children and their parents, thus giving a mutuality of context between home and school, partly because it is an easy story to tell and retell because of this very familiarity and because of its repetitive nature, and partly because it lends itself to the use of props readily available at home and at school. The children were encouraged to participate in the retelling of this story at an increasingly sophisticated level. At first they were merely listening to the story; they were then encouraged to join in. This proved a popular activity and the children soon took individual character parts with one child able to take the part of the story teller. The intention was to heighten the children's awareness of the conventions of story telling in terms of simple story structure and the fact that although different people might tell the story at different times, whether the story is written down or spoken, its essential elements remain the same. It was hoped that this might increase their own ability to organise events into a story and to adopt a format appropriate for retelling.

The other two stories which were used for this more structured focus were *The Three Billy Goats Gruff* and *Wake up Bear* by Lyndley Dodd. *The Three Billy Goats Gruff* was chosen for its familiarity to both children and parents, for its very clear structure, and for its repetitive nature which lends itself to being told as well as read out loud. The Lyndley Dodd story, although not familiar to children and parents, is a simple, repetitive story with a deep structure that has the quality of a traditional folk tale which gives a sense of changing seasons and its effects on the animal kingdom. This story was read aloud with the aid of magnetised cut out illustrations from the book.

Testing the Children

Each of the children was tested at the beginning and end of the six weeks of the intervention programme using two different types of test now described.

The Marion Blank Test

This test was the Pre-School Language Assessment Instrument: (PLAI). It is designed to assess young children's skills in coping with the language demands of the teaching situation and thus identify children for whom any intervention or an adaptation of a teaching method would be beneficial (but not used in this way, in this research, rather as a measure of gains). 'The test is based on a model of classroom discourse wherein the teacher is seen as placing demands on the child that require varying levels of abstraction' (Blank, Rose & Berlin, 1978: 1).

The test comprises discrete pictures with 45 accompanying questions for the adult to ask the child. The questions require differing levels of

Table 3.1 PLAI Test – scores achieved on levels on abstraction

(a) Control group – (age range 3.7–4.7)*

Levels of abstraction	Christina %ile	Debbie %ile	Damien %ile	Rebecca %ile	Gareth %ile
Pre-test period					
Group 1	1–25	50	1–25	99	25–50
Group 2	50	50–75	25	99	75–99
Group 3	75–99	50	75–99	75–99	75–99
Group 4	50–75	25–50	75	99	99
Post-test period					
Group 1	1–25	25	1–25	99	–
Group 2	75	50–75	50	99	–
Group 3	75	99	75–99	99	–
Group 4	50	75–99	99	99	–

(b) Experimental group – (age range 38–48)

Levels of abstraction	Danielle %ile	Matthew %ile	Claire %ile	Ralph %ile	Mark %ile
Pre-intervention					
Group 1	25–50	50	1–25	75	1
Group 2	25	75–99	1–25	75	25
Group 3	25–50	75	50–75	50	1–25
Group 4	25	75	25–50	25–50	1
Post-test period post-intervention					
Group 1	25	99	1–25	75	50
Group 2	99	75	50–75	75	75–99
Group 3	75–99	75–99	25	50	50
Group 4	99	75–99	50	25–50	99

*Children listed in order of age in each group.

abstraction from the child, for example, at a simple level: 'What is the woman holding?'; answer 'a cup' would elicit full marks, whereas the answer: 'She's drinking a cup of tea', would score lower. Greater accuracy denoted a more adequate answer. At a higher level of abstraction, the child may, for example be being asked to predict the next action based on the picture and on information given by the adult and scored accordingly giving maximum value to the child's response. There are some benefits here from looking briefly at those forms of thought which Donaldson (1978) refers to in terms of 'disembeddedness', that is 'thought which has been prised out of the old primitive matrix within which originally all our thinking is contained'. Donaldson argues that if children cannot engage in disembedded thought then they have only limited access to the educational process. Thus there is an issue of entitlement here; children may be disadvantaged if they remain at low levels of abstraction. This research was concerned with identifying ways of helping children to develop maximum, possible levels of abstraction in a facilitative environment.

Table 3.1 presents individual children's scores in four groups of language skills which differ in the level of abstraction involved. Thus Group 1 represents the first level of abstraction – Matching Perception which is naming objects; Group 2 represents the second level – Selective

Table 3.2 PLAI test – scores achieved on a continuum of adequacy

(a) Control group

	Christina	Debbie	Damien	Rebecca	Gareth
Pre-test period					
Adequate responses	25	30	26	36	32
Inadequate responses	20	15	19	8	13
Post-test period					
Adequate responses	29	33	28	39	Did not
Inadequate responses	16	12	17	6	participate

(b) Experimental group

	Danielle	Matthew	Claire	Ralph	Mark
Pre-intervention					
Adequate responses	23	34	26	35	18
Inadequate responses	22	11	19	10	26
Post-intervention					
Adequate responses	32	29	24	36	30
Inadequate responses	13	16	21	9	15

Analysis of Perception, for example, the purpose of objects; Group 3 the third level – Re-ordering of Perception, for example, how the pictured events came about. At the fourth level of abstraction, Reasoning about Perception, the child is asked to theorise, plan and rationalise, for example, prediction skills or how to achieve a particular outcome. The table shows the percentile ranking of each child in the control and experimental groups respectively. The percentile ranking makes it possible to compare the child's performance to that of others from a similar age and background. If a child's score is above the 75th percentile, for example it indicates that he or she possesses skills in that area of discourse which are greater than three-quarters of his or her peers.

Table 3.2 shows the scores that each child achieved on the PLAI subsequently re-interpreted on a continuum of adequacy. The seven categories of interpretation are collated under two headings, Adequate responses and Inadequate responses, showing scores out of 45 for each heading. Blank (Blank, Rose & Berlin, 1978) remarks that 'In assessing the child's answer, the yardstick that we have selected is the degree to which the response reflects the child's grasp of the demand that has been posed'. Thus, even when the answer is deemed inadequate the child is given credit for attempting to deal with the material rather than giving a totally irrelevant answer with, for example categories of 'acceptable' and 'ambiguous', within the heading of 'Adequate response'. These particular aspects of the assessment (Tables 3.1 and 3.2) proved significant in terms of perceptible development during the six-week period – dramatically so for one or two subjects.

Test two – Barrie Wade: Telling and retelling a story

The second form of testing focusing on the child's ability to tell and retell a story, drew on Barrie Wade's (1984) book *Story at Home and School*. The children in both groups were individually read a previously unknown story. After two readings they were asked to retell the story. They were then asked to tell any story of their own choosing. These told and retold versions of the stories were scored out of ten for showing evidence of a beginning, middle and end and for character and setting. Children who offered a nursery rhyme for their own story were given a nil score as this was deemed to be a learned response not relevant to the question. Response to both aspects of the story-telling assessment gave an indication of general concentration, listening and sequencing skills as well as the child's ability to organise their own material. More importantly, this test indicated the child's grasp of the conventions of story structure at a very basic level.

Wade does not provide a systematic means of scoring, thus this research drew on models used by Poulson (1991) and Applebee (1983) and simplified these to a meaningful level for the sometimes elemental snatches of story offered by the very young children in the project. The children were thus scored within a range of two points per item on:

Beginning – e.g. 'Once upon a time there was...'
Middle – some kind of event/adventure.
End – some indication of finality.
Characters – i.e., not just 'he' or 'she'.
Setting – any extra information in terms of location, weather, feelings etc.

Pre and post-intervention

In terms of both levels of abstraction (Table 3.1(a)) and adequacy (Table 3.2 (a)) the control group shows some improvement in performance. Christina and Rebecca remain fairly constant (Table 3.1) whilst Damien shows small improvements (Gareth refused to participate in the post-test). Only one child, Debbie, in the control group achieved a dramatic

Table 3.3 Ability to tell and re-tell a story

(a) Control group

Retell	Christina	Debbie	Damien	Rebecca	Gareth	Combined gains
Interview (before test period)	2	6	2	4.5	0	4.5 points
Interview (after test period)	3	4.5	4	7	0	

Own story						
Interview (before test period)	2	2	0	8	0	6.5 points
Interview (after test period)	2	3.5	4	9	0	

(b) Experimental group

Retell	Danielle	Matthew	Claire	Ralph	Mark	Combined gains
Interview (before test period)	0	0	3	3	3	16 points
Interview (after test period)	0	9	4	5	7	

Own story						
Interview (before test period)	0	7	3	4	3	20 points
Interview (after test period)	9	8	7	6	7	

shift in any of the groups of discourse skills (see Table 3.1). She moved from between the 25th and 50th percentiles in Group 4 skills at the beginning of the period to between the 75th and 99th percentiles at the end of the period. This suggests that some measure of improvement may be accounted for by maturation and access to the more visually available activities, thus we clearly cannot discount their impact.

In relation to Table 3.1(b), in the experimental group, Danielle has improved considerably on Groups 2, 3 and 4 percentiles. Matthew (high scoring at pre-intervention) has made less impressive gains. Claire has improved considerably on 2 and by one percentile on Group 4. Ralph remains constant (also among the high scorers pre-test) with Mark as the most impressive of all in his progress, moving substantially across all groups. In Table 3.2(b), Danielle and Mark, the lowest scorers pre-intervention, have made the most substantial gains six weeks later. Matthew and Claire have diminished somewhat in terms of adequate responses. A consideration of Table 3.3 seems relevant at this point.

From Table 3.3 we can see Danielle had similarly notable results in the story tests (Table 3.3(b)). Although unable to retell the story on either occasion at the second interview her score for the telling of her own story moved from a nil score (she had responded earlier with a nursery rhyme) to a score of 9 with an extremely well-organised version of the *Three Billy Goats Gruff*. Mark remains remarkably constant pre and post-intervention. Matthew comes into his own with significant gains on the retelling of the story he has listened to and both Claire and Ralph show some progress. There is markedly less progress for any child in the control group. When the two groups combined gains are considered (final column) the disparities between control and experimental groups are marked.

Danielle and Mark – some further detail on the youngest and oldest children

It appeared that the experience of the intervention programme had considerably enhanced the self-esteem of both Danielle and of her mother. Perhaps being included in the project helped them feel special. This view is supported by the diary evidence which was meticulously and imaginatively kept by Danielle's mother throughout the period. It is detailed and lengthy, written as though Danielle is speaking in the first person and her mother took a great deal of time and trouble with it. I would suggest that the re-tell test (Table 3.3) was very difficult for a child of only just over three years and six months, but her own version of the *Three Billy Goats Gruff* demonstrates that possibly stories: 'can stimulate and develop our ability to organise affectively a range of material into coherent and meaningful wholes' (Egan, 1988: 105).

Interestingly the two youngest children in the experimental group, Danielle and Matthew, were the most frequent users of the library opportunity and the diaries reveal that they became sophisticated storytellers at home. These two children were also the ones who responded most enthusiastically to the focused work carried out in class and were keen to take the part of the story teller with groups of children. Both children made post-intervention gains in terms of levels of abstraction (Table 3.1(b)) suggesting a possible connection between the ability to organise material in a narrative form and ability in abstract forms of language.

The child whose overall progress was the most remarkable was Mark; his first PLAI test (Tables 3.1(b) and 3.2(b)) revealed a very inadequate language ability. This was not entirely surprising as I was aware that his use of language at school indicated some fairly muddled and hazy thinking. For example, during a trip to the local shop to buy baking ingredients, when asked to find a bag of sugar he pointed to a jar of pickled onions and on his return to school was unable to say anything sensible about the shopping trip. He found it very difficult to give coherent answers to the simplest questions and indeed his low score on the PLAI seemed to confirm what we already suspected. Most of his answers were inadequate, of those 66% were irrelevant and he did not score over the 25th percentile in any group. According to the test he presented as a child with special needs.

It has to be said that Mark was a reluctant victim of the intervention programme, sometimes even resorting to hiding under tables to avoid his daily dose of stories! On closer contact as a result of the intervention it became clear that his general knowledge was limited and he had great difficulty giving sensible expression to his everyday experiences. Life seemed to be a fairly baffling business for him. For example, after looking at the book *Going Shopping* by Sarah Garland, Mark was unable to relate his own experience of supermarket shopping or suggest any commodity he might buy there. He was also unable to identify common farm or wild animals with any certainty. Although from a caring and conscientious home, the diary evidence suggests that the input Mark received at home would not have enhanced his general knowledge or drawn upon the resources of children's literature to develop his language skills.

During the course of the intervention programme he became more and more excitable; hiding under tables became a joke. He developed quite a taste for stories as he gradually seemed to be making more sense of them. He was particularly keen on the story of Goldilocks and asked for it on many occasions although was never able to accept the symbolism of the doll prop representing Goldilocks in the story and always referred to 'the doll'. At the end of the programme his PLAI score reached the 99th percentile in two language groups and he offered 30 adequate responses, 73% of which were fully adequate (not shown on Table 3.2(b)), as against only 18 adequate responses 39% of which were fully adequate at the beginning. In addition, of his inadequate responses he progressed from 29% in the invalid category and 66% irrelevant to 80% invalid and only 20% irrelevant (not shown on the table). This shows that even though a proportion of responses remained inadequate, they *were* becoming more relevant. Mark's experience seems to be an extreme example of a child suddenly being able to make sense, to organise his thoughts. When asked to tell a story at the beginning of the period all he could produce was a little snatch about Fireman Sam, scoring 3. After the six-week period he produced a flood of words about Goldilocks, some of which were quite well organised within the conventions of story structure.

Evidence from the Project Diaries

There are examples in the project diaries, kept by the parents of the children in the experimental group, of children using the story material in an attempt to make sense of their personal experience. Claire gets a measure of 'naughtiness' from 'Dreadful David' and concludes that he is a baby which is a possible explanation for his unacceptable behaviour. There are several examples in the diary kept by Claire's mother of her using story material as a measure for her own or her sister's behaviour, or for the notion of 'naughtiness'. Incidentally, Claire is by no means a naughty girl (at school anyway) but she is clearly very aware of 'naughtiness' as a possible mode of behaviour. After listening to 'Wilberforce Goes Shopping' she comments: 'Naughty bear, running the trolley into the lady's bottom.' And then brings her sister Helen in for purposes of comparison: 'Helen slides down the bannister, I don't do that I just walk down.'

The diary again reveals Claire's preoccupation with acceptable and unacceptable behaviour in a comment on the story 'I'm going for a walk': 'You should go through the gate not through the fence.' Claire's mother's comment in the diary also shows that she uses story material to make sense of the experience of growing; it is a two-way process. The story makes sense of her own experience and her experience makes sense of the story. She has listened to the Pat Hutchins story 'Happy Birthday Sam' and comments: 'I stand on the chair to switch the light on. I can't reach my clothes.' She then started singing 'Happy Birthday'.

Claire's comments on 'I'm going for a walk' again reveal her matching up her own experience: 'I like walking on walls.' She has a clear concept of family – Mummy, Daddy, Claire and Helen – but the story of Goldilocks indicates that some families do not follow this pattern; Claire notices this and is puzzled: 'Where is Helen Bear?'

From his pre-test scores (Table 3.1(b)) we can see that Matthew is a child with a high level of literacy awareness at the beginning of the project, was particularly interested in a very simple book *Tom and Pippo Read a Story*. He asked for this book several times and in addition he had heard it at school several times. He is a child capable of appreciating more complex stories than this but possibly the attraction of this simple book for him is on a metacognitive level as he begins to see himself as a story reader and story teller himself. He is the child (Table 3.3(b)) who makes the most substantial gains in being able to retell a story he has just listened to. The diary reveals that he read the Tom and Pippo story to his little sister, thus adopting the role of dad who reads to Tom and Pippo in the story. In Matthew's version the last line of the story is: 'Pippo likes to read his own books.'

The next day he asked for this story again. His mother wrote: 'Then I read the book with Matthew pointing to the words and repeating the words after me and sometimes he would finish off sentences by himself.'

Three weeks later the diary reveals that Matthew's story-telling skills are becoming more sophisticated. Matthew has had a great deal of variety of stories read at home and at school and now sees himself as an accomplished story teller: 'Matthew sometimes makes up his own words. Matthew pretends to read stories to Faye, all different stories rolled into one from pictures, cards etc.'

The diary kept by Danielle's mother provides examples of Danielle using the story material as a measure for her own experience. She listened to the very simple story 'I'm going for a walk' and it served as a model for her own road safety training: 'Then I read it to my mammy and told her you should only cross the road when the green man comes on she said yes and that I'm a clever girl.' The diary shows that Danielle then went on to behave in a similar way to Matthew, beginning to now see herself as an accomplished reader and story teller: 'Then I read the story to my dolls and teddy bears.'

The story books that elicited the most interesting comments in the diaries are the simple books with a deep structure in terms of the everyday experience of small children. The Sarah Garland story *Going Shopping* enabled Danielle to reveal her full potential as a story teller as this quotation from Mum's diary shows: 'My mammy read this to me and I really enjoyed it. I read it to her then read it to myself. I didn't put it down for about 15 minutes. Later on I read it to my dolls and they enjoyed it too. I've started to read it like my teachers do, holding the book so the children can see the pictures. I also tell my dolls to stop it and listen to the story.'

This book also proved of interest to Mark, whose progress during the course of the project has been discussed. He was a child who had great difficulty finding the words with which to start to make sense of his life. *Going Shopping* provided a stimulus. In this story the mother is staggering under the burden of the weekly battle through the supermarket, a scene familiar to Mark, although at school he had been quite unable to talk coherently about it. He responded to this book at home with the following: 'Mark was asking about the fruit and veg. Mark said mummy was going to drop the baby because she had too many bags.' Here perhaps we can see Mark grappling with the beginnings of disembedded thought, conceptualising and predicting in the very personal context of his culture.

Some Conclusions and Considerations

Donaldson (1978) says that in order to achieve success in school the child's conceptual system must expand in the direction of increasing ability to represent itself in the world at large. Clearly the child is helped to achieve this through language and thus the school must assist home in providing the tools with which the child can make this step. The Wells' (1986) study clearly demonstrated the need to: 'Provide [the children with] a firm foundation on which to acquire those skills of literacy and symbol manipulation that are so important for later success in all areas of the curriculum' (p. 159). It was this work that was the impulse for the present study and for the precise nature of the intervention programme. The solution seems deceptively simple – children need stories; not initially as part of a class group but on a one-to-one or small group basis with an adult: 'Such an experience provides not only an introduction to literacy but also an entry into a shared world that can be explored through the sort of collaborative talk that is the most effective way of facilitating the children's learning and language development' (Wells, 1986: 160).

The gains revealed by this small-scale study for the children discussed above were such that I became convinced of the validity of both Wells' and Donaldson's treatise. The approaches to intervention utilised within this study sought to identify complementary roles for parents and teachers – both key adults in these young children's lives. These approaches seemed to have particular potential for developing abstract processes and disembedded forms of thought for children scoring low in these areas prior to intervention. Story telling is common practice in a nursery setting. In reiterating the value of story, this study is saying nothing new. Where I hope this study can make a contribution is to the status enhancement of a mode of interaction that may be seen by some as fairly low-level time filling. In sustaining and exploiting the potential of such interaction, I have learned also that accessing children's thinking and encouraging them to access it is not only about asking them questions or about modes of adult–child interaction (and this perhaps is one of the limitations of the Tough (1976) work). The context is crucial, as Tizard & Hughes (1984) revealed; shared experience, a sense of history and future together provide a richer and more meaningful context for children whose experience of the world and their culture are as yet limited. There is useful content adults can bring to the interaction and relevant contexts they can create in relation, in particular, to story telling. The research convinced me that story activities should be a high priority, deserving of quality time and careful planning in the early years curriculum with home and school working together on behalf of the child.

4 Curriculum Development and Staff Development through Research – Children, Staff and Parents Growing Together

DIANNE LAMONT

This chapter considers how, through practitioner research, an area of the nursery curriculum was developed. I shall outline how I became involved in the research, highlight the issues to emerge, and discuss the role of the staff in accepting and supporting the research and subsequent developments. I will show how the status afforded to the curriculum area increased child, staff and parental interest in the educational value of the activity. I will comment also on the interrelationship of curriculum development and staff development as it occurred during and as a result of the research.

I was appointed in 1989 to my first nursery headship and in 1991 elected to undertake a distance learning module on 'Monitoring Effectiveness'. The research was undertaken both for the course award and for its intrinsic value.

The nursery (comprising four nursery assistants, a caretaker and a cook) has high status in the community. The 60 part-time children and their parents were well known to staff. Likewise staff were well known because of their length of service. I was aware that expectations of what the curriculum would be, and the role of the staff in delivering the curriculum were well established in the eyes of both staff and community. I was also aware that changing these expectations would challenge long-held assumptions. None of this could be ignored if the education of all involved was to be affected. There seemed to be little value in demanding change and creating a new way of working without extensive discussion, explanation and a lot of 'taking-on-board' time. The period covered by the course work and the research period would be long enough to set ideas in motion and focus attention on a clearly defined area as long as we all felt secure with the focus.

My confidence that we would find success came from the staff experience of good nursery practice, my experience of working closely with parents as partners in their children's education during my educational home visitor days, from being involved in the training of early years teachers, and on the research front, from two recently completed research modules from the MEd programme at Stirling University. Colleagues undertaking the same module offered one support network, and, Local Education Authority (LEA) advisers and college staff yet another.

Planning the Research

The Monitoring Effectiveness module demanded that a curriculum area was monitored, evaluated and reviewed. In my view, baking seemed appropriate because of its potential to promote the following:

(a) children's vocabulary
(b) children's level of concentration
(c) children's ability to follow instructions
(d) children's independence.

Children also like this activity for obvious end-product reasons, for close adult contact and the small-group situation. It seemed to me that parents would find baking an area of interest but it would be necessary to establish the truth of this hypothesis. Three staff meetings were arranged for outlining course requirements for the award and for planning the research.

The agenda for these meetings was:

(a) Choosing a curriculum area and focusing on it for a term.
(b) Producing evidence of the educational nature of this nursery experience which would withstand scrutiny by parents and other assessors.
(c) Planning and observing learning and teaching in this curriculum area.
(d) Helping parents to value learning and teaching opportunities in this curriculum area.
(e) Understanding the research process.

For me, as stated above, baking had potential, but staff needed to consider other possibilities. However, staff rejected other areas of nursery experience on grounds of resources available, parental interest and personal preference and confidence. As a result of extensive discussion, baking was defined as an acceptable area for research, and it was decided to survey parents to see if they expressed interest in this area of our curriculum. My influence over the final choice was minimal, being restricted to emphasising personal strengths and preferences and the balance of resources available to carry out the research. Staff acceptance of the rigour of the research was more difficult. Some were happy to see it as my work, one was interested in the observation schedules, and all were daunted by all aspects of recording the work, whether recording was written, audio or video.

Staff involvement was crucial, and through discussion and sharing, commitment was given by all, including cook and caretaker; their support in particular ultimately proved crucial in protecting staff at times of stress. One member of staff volunteered to work with me, her student and one *small* group of children. The other nursery assistants agreed to support us by increasing their child/adult ratio on research days, conducting the parent survey and reviewing the video material and the observation schedules. Staff felt inadequate in dealing with the research ideas, the language, in gathering information and the presentation of data. I agreed to be responsible for putting the research plan together, for constructing, with their help, the questionnaires and interviews, and for video recordings. I would also write up our research findings. And so interest and excitement was generated out of fear of the unknown. Baking as a nursery experience had new status. It was all systems go!

Selecting the Research Methods

The methods had to be ones which staff could accept, feel comfortable with, and implement. They had to generate data which could easily be interpreted by all staff and equally easily be disseminated to parents and colleagues. Examples of questionnaires, interview schedules and checklists were discussed, and it was agreed that we would use:

(a) a questionnaire to parents (Appendix 1)
(b) interview schedules (Appendix 2, Appendix 3)
(c) observation schedules (Appendix 4, Appendix 5).

The questionnaire was given to a group of 30 parents. From this sample, 20 parents recorded that their children enjoyed baking and that they thought their children were learning by baking.

This reflected our perceptions and so these 20 respondents (same sample group) were interviewed using a 'never, sometimes, often' (LIKERT) schedule (see Appendix 2). From this emerged a group of 12 who wanted: (a) to participate in nursery baking sessions, and (b) more information/help with baking so that they could bake at home with children.

A second interview (see Appendix 3) of these 12 parents established that they viewed baking as an activity which kept children busy and happy. Some parents set out to teach their children about counting, weighing and taking turns when they were baking. These interviews were conducted as informally as possible with a member of staff asking the question and recording the responses on a duplicate of the sheet the parent had in front of her/him. Experience told us that forms presented difficulties to some parents and that they were comfortable to have their answers recorded for them. At a further meeting we discussed staff behaviour during a baking activity and a checklist was devised for observation of the staff/adult at work. Later it became evident that this could also be used when reviewing the video-tapes. A second checklist, to be used similarly, was constructed for observation of child behaviour. Finally, to collect data about language, a further schedule was devised to analyse the types of words used by the children during a session. Future staff meetings were scheduled for review and reporting progress to all involved.

The Group Selected

Of the parents who had expressed an interest in participating in sessions and having more information, six were able to give commitment for the research period; these parents and their children became the research group.

The parents were given the following information about the sessions available to them:

(a) Time in nursery to see the baking area and its equipment, and to learn about the layout and the organisation.
(b) Explanation of the recipes and the teaching input and learning outcomes.
(c) Observation of children and staff during a baking session.
(d) Review of video of this session with staff.
(e) Parent/staff joint session with children in nursery.
(f) Parent/child joint session in the nursery.
(g) Parent/child session baking at home.

We were fortunate that all involved stayed the course. There were no staff absences. Interest was sustained and energy flowed which the research group found a great support. The planned sessions were completed.

Issues

At this stage the research path was clear – the mechanisms were all in place, and the rest of this chapter could simply be a report of findings. However, many issues were raised by this research process and these, like the challenge to assumptions mentioned earlier, are worthy of consideration.

There was the issue of staff confidence in the learning/teaching opportunities in baking for the children. Staff were confident that children experienced growth in vocabulary, in concentration and independence as a result of baking, but had doubts that they could 'prove' this, or gather evidence. It was acknowledged that the research period would be a snap-shot of the process and that evidence gathered would contribute to the overall observations that staff had been compiling on the children, since term one. The video recordings could be continued beyond the research period to give further evidence of progress which staff could monitor, evaluate and review.

There was the issue of staff confidence about learning and teaching for parents. This raised questions about stages of teaching and what learning would be achieved by the children when the parents were involved.

The school climate was such that staff responded readily to parent enquiries and requests for advice, but there was limited experience of parents as learners or partners in the educational process of the nursery. Questions arose from the staff:

'But what if the parents don't do it like us?'

'Will the parents use the same language as us?'

'Will the children want to bake with the parents?' (from the student)

'How much will we need to teach the parents first?'

At this point I introduced some of Tizard & Hughes' (1984) findings on young children learning at home and raised the issue of accepting the child and parent language as our starting point. This was to encourage staff to value the parents' contribution to language development and to stimulate the growing partnerships.

The Video

At this point the use of the video came under discussion. Not only would staff see themselves, they would be seen with and by other adults! A decision was taken to review the recordings as a group including the parents and children. The use of the observation schedules (Appendices 4 and 5) with the video meant that two viewings were seen as necessary. The first viewing just to look, exclaim, note impressions, compliment and positively criticise. The second viewing allowed a closer focus on behaviour and the use of language. For me there was the idea that reviewing the video may highlight some curriculum and staff development issues, but this was not acknowledged at this point because I believed that the staff would come to see that they could instigate change and that I would permit them to initiate change. I could not share this idea at this point because, as previously stated, I was aware of the perils of leading from the front and was at pains to maintain staff ownership of their focus for change.

Body of Knowledge

Just as the first session was about to go ahead, one member of staff asked: 'Once we've done all the sessions, made the recordings and observations, and you've written it all up, what use will it be to us then?' This was a point which had to be dealt with, but there were short-term and long-term implications, and so, over our coffee breaks for a day or so the short-term issues were dealt with. We concluded that we would all have learned but at that point we were not sure what that learning would be. As Rowland (1988) puts it, learning is not only the result of what we do, but also of how we give meaning to what we have done.

I was trying to find a framework for what seemed to be around for us at that time. I was aware of staff observations and research literature I had briefly encountered on the module and I began to place these observations in slots in my learning file. For example, the 'what will we do with it?' question above I filed under Body of Knowledge, Rowland (1988) and noted:

(1) How does my 'body of knowledge' relate to the knowledge of 'others'?
(2) How does this relate to the external knowledge as presented in the research literature?
(3) How can such learning effect change in the classroom if we never get outside our own body of knowledge and view things from a different perspective?

(4) Is this learning of one's own body of knowledge part of a continuous process, or is it a result of a brief period of reflection and introspection, a kind of therapeutic interlude?

These references were anchor points for my own learning and formed another level of questions about the interface of literature and data gathered in practice. I was aware of a balance being struck between advancing my own learning through further reading of the literature and the need to work within the staff framework to maintain the aims of the research. This tension between the personal learning dimension and the professional strand remained throughout, but recognition of it seemed to allow me to keep both aspects in check and to allocate each their time.

Worthwhileness became an issue around week five of the research period, when more sessions than the original seven and more nursery space and time were required to give all parents the same experience of the baking sessions and video viewing. We concluded that another three baking sessions would need to be planned. At any one session two members of staff were dedicated to the small group while other staff fulfilled all the other roles and functions.

At this point, the commitment of the cook and caretaker were greatly valued as they stepped in and protected research time and normal nursery routines. The caretaker volunteered to be in school during all baking sessions as an extra pair of hands in the normal routine and the cook answered all phone calls to avoid interruptions to me. Time was also found to restate our research aims, including our need to have evidence of learning and teaching. Staff and the parents, with an awareness of curriculum areas we had emphasised the previous year, reflected on developments in that curriculum area and concluded that there would be positive outcomes which we had not considered. So after further sharing of fears and concerns, the worthwhileness of the research was re-established and our original aims seen in the context of other possibilities.

Staff made remarks at this time about the children not in the research group and I had to address this with them in terms of spin-offs and benefits to these children in the future. This reminded me of the spiral or cycles of enquiry referred to by Kemmis (1985) and I was able to translate this to staff to reassure them that time invested in the research would accrue benefits to all in the future.

The Headteacher's Agenda

Emerging for me at this time was a growing certainty that my parallel strand of staff development was weaving itself in, and that my aims would very likely be achieved as a result of the research process. Uppermost in my mind was the need for curriculum guidelines. Staff had been voicing a need for this for three terms, and I felt we would now achieve this at the end of the research period for baking and by the end of the school session in other curriculum areas. I was also of the opinion that the time was right to work with staff on producing the guidelines. Collaborating in the process of putting our thoughts on paper would offer many opportunities to develop a range of ideas about learning, resources and individual children. I also felt it was important that all staff had ownership of school policy documents.

I was not consciously working through the research to establish a critical community but I began to see a collaborative community emerge. We had agreed at the outset that I would record all data and write up the research. Would staff think this should also apply to the guidelines and policy? I knew that this had not been part of their experience to date and yet, in the climate being fostered through our regional INSET, open exchange and reciprocal criticism were being encouraged. I decided a waiting game was in order and set my sights on the beginning of the next session to achieve documentation.

I was nurturing a lot of commitments at this point – staff to research, my commitment as manager to staff development, my commitment as an employee to LEA policy requirements and that to the Monitoring Effectiveness course award – an intricate and delicate web. Throughout I was aware of my own professional perspective being challenged and reshaped, especially with regard to supporting staff and the importance of feedback to all concerned. I had expected to feel conflict between the demands of the research and the day-to-day running of the school. However, a sense of shared purpose and growth towards a new and vital school ethos sustained me. I felt we were on course to achieving aims in all areas of commitment.

I began to detect a new strand of personal development which was about emancipation. For me it was freedom from the expectation of staff that I would tell them how I wanted things done giving me a sense of freedom to work alongside them as a partner, something I also wanted them to value in their growing partnership with parents.

I hoped that staff equally felt free to negotiate and challenge our practices. I had yet to discover if this would be the case. Was I experiencing what Cicourel (1981:52) observes as the interaction of the tension of the micro and macro structures we operate within 'because all daily life settings reflect several levels of cultural complexity'? Webb

(1990a) seemed to state the dilemmas with clarity: 'When reflecting on everyday classroom practice, practitioners immediately come up against the context of power and authority in which that practice is located' (p.28).

Taking it Seriously

Time was limited, and so it was important that everyone met their commitments to the sessions. On the agreed research days there was an air of anxiety until all were assembled and the session underway. Nursery life went on as normal, adding authenticity to our video recordings – unexpected visitors, telephone calls, the odd mini-crisis! The stress at times was tangible, but never unbearable, humour prevailed, enjoyment was evident. Parents took it seriously. They signed up eagerly for their baking sessions, discussed them with staff, anticipated them with their children and encouraged each other consistently. This was an encouraging aspect of the parent involvement because previously parents had not always kept their rota appointments. We were aware of parents talking to one another about their involvement in the school day and that the idea of the research taking place with their children was intriguing. The experience of working with staff on this research was invaluable when we again embarked on Scottish Education Department funded research, 'Working together – Parents and Staff in Nursery Settings' (SOED, 1992).

Children's Issues

Children eagerly prepared for each session. Hygiene routines were faithfully observed without adult prompting, and six eager faces awaited the researchers each time. Another group of equally eager recruits had to be re-directed, and other staff reported that they had to offer baking more frequently during the research period. The new equipment was attractive to the children, they enthusiastically shared their experiences with the other children, staff and parents and set up their own display of the recipe card and end product for all to see.

Evidence

As the programme of baking sessions progressed, we were aware that our intuitive expectations were being confirmed through the use of the observation schedules in conjunction with the video recordings. Our expectations of growth in language, levels of concentration and independence were being revealed and some of our questions and issues about parents as partners were being highlighted. Parents initially pointed and gestured during sessions. Gradually, with growing confidence and the good staff model, the verbal input of the parents increased. In the early tapes there was a high level of questioning of children by adults. This decreased and was replaced by more demonstrating, explaining, encouraging and commenting on the process. The interaction between the children increased as the research progressed and the adult verbals became less dominant.

Adult input was high at the beginning and end of each session. This we concluded was about setting the scene, and re-directing. For children we thought it was about establishing trust and confidence. At the end of a session adults and children seemed to need to recap and share the experience without staff present. We learned that there was a great deal of conversation later, at home, concerning the sessions in school, so much so that extended family became aware of the research as children wanted them to share the cakes and biscuits and sometimes asked family to repeat the recipe at home.

Effects of Parents' and Children's Knowledge of their Involvement in the Research

Parents began asking staff more about their child's interest in baking. Parents reported that, at home their knowledge of baking was questioned by the children and that they felt more able to respond positively. They, in turn, found themselves asking their children about the baking sessions in school. Staff would then check out what the parent did know about the process used by the child and in some cases the mum became the learner as the child talked and demonstrated her/his way through a session. The child as teacher was a new idea for some staff and for many parents. Staff took account of the knowledge the parents and children had gained and this enabled further, informal discussion of teaching and learning to take place.

Staff reported an awareness of spending more time explaining aspects of their work to parents. The initial feeling of insufficient time for children and parents had dissipated and staff now found they had quality time with both.

Sharing Observations

At project meetings the research staff (headteacher, parent, nursery assistant) made the findings available to all. The video-tape then became to some extent a check on what was recorded on the observation schedules. The opportunity also existed for future observation, with more time available to use the video-tape.

Staff were most comfortable to view the video-tape and then to use the observation schedule, especially if working in tandem, confirming each other's observations initially, and as a more open and analytic approach developed giving criticism and suggestions as to further action. For the parents the learning process was different. They expressed surprise at their child's ability to concentrate for so long (usually half an hour), to follow lots of instructions, and to use new words correctly. Towards the end of the research period, they were also noting how well organised was the children's approach to the activity and how much less they depended on the adults. This increased independence was reported by other members of staff who were aware that the research group children were taking a lead in other baking sessions. The benefits were in growths which were real and positive aspects of change – change which was observable by all concerned.

Curriculum development had been the focus, but in researching the curriculum, there had been enormous gains in staff development. The research outcomes had inspired staff so much that they began to approach their work with children with new confidence. The important changes for staff were evident in:

(1) Their systematic use of observation.
(2) Their analysis of children's behaviour and language.
(3) Their systematic planning, teaching and learning.
(4) The developing capacity for matching targets to children's developmental stage.

The approach to nursery organisation gradually changed to take account of:

(1) The planned use of space.
(2) Structured layout within a learning area with labelling and easily accessible equipment.
(3) The creation of an environment in which the potential learning and achievements for children were obvious to children and parents.

The research outcomes enabled us to support children in:

(1) Making choices.
(2) Taking the initiative for their own learning.
(3) Acting independently of adults.

We were also able to observe leadership skills in the children and this gave feedback to staff that change was taking place.

As a staff, we had come to value the research process. Engaging in research had emphasised for us the importance of:

(1) Discussion.
(2) Consultation.
(3) Parent involvement in planned teaching and learning.
(4) The value of monitoring progress.
(5) Job satisfaction.

That these benefits accrued to us was due to:

(1) A growth in trust of each other.
(2) A better understanding of our professional selves.
(3) A growth in our knowledge of learning and teaching.

The Final Phase

Moving into the final weeks of the research period required some discipline. I knew that we were going to have the material required for the course award and I had to move towards compiling it for module accreditation. I had to prevent myself at this point from following the staff development needs that were now presenting themselves.

I knew we had gone through the action research cycle and that we had clarified our ideas, examined our practice, had collaborated and reflected together and now were able to evaluate what we had done and the point at which we had arrived. But the move from the research process to the curriculum development and the staff development issues had to wait. The importance of the time being right had been proved before and with this knowledge I disciplined myself to write up the research and wait.

The finished report met the deadline post by half an hour and was well received by the course tutor who requested permission to copy the video for use on her early years courses. Staff morale at this point soared – recognition. I responded by offering to make the nursery assistant and parents available to talk to students about their experience. On this note the term ended and the research process was complete.

Staff Development and Curriculum Development

And so as a whole staff we re-entered the cycle at the beginning of the new term. Development had occurred for all of us. I had learned to wait. I had created a school climate where staff and parents having worked together, were preparing to consider changes. Children were going to find that their learning environment was changed to present more challenging opportunities. Children would be given more control, more choice over their learning in the baking area, staff would acknowledge that these choices were possible, workable and effective. We had all the evidence that these things were possible, and our discussions and observations enabled us to plan further change together, to commit our thinking to a curriculum guideline, and to re-shape a policy on children learning. At this point the curriculum guideline was forming in my mind as was the policy statement, but the practical issues of nursery layout and equipment had priority for the beginning of the new session and that was our starting point.

Day one of the term was spent setting up the play rooms, selecting and rejecting resources and negotiating space priorities to accommodate to the ways of learning we wanted to suggest and develop. Decisions were based on knowledge gained by staff during home visits to new children prior to the summer break and on the development stages and interests of the returning children. Staff were aware that they were planning with children's learning and choices in mind. Previously starting points would have been activities, product and the adult intention. The research had shown us that the children could work independently of staff and we had to allow those who had achieved independence to continue with their newly acquired freedom. The ability of our new children to work independently was the burning question in staff. Only time would tell. New children and parents absorbed our new practices – they did not know the old! Parents who were bringing second or subsequent children to our care remarked on our changed layout and approach and commented with amazement on their children's easy adjustment to nursery. Staff held their breath but also marvelled at how well it was working – some of us didn't want to believe that children could be so independent – but it was happening in front of our eyes, and we had planned for it to be this way. Staff had moved from a position where they held that because of the children's experiences before nursery they had to be directed and controlled, with the adult dominant in the baking area. The feedback from children and parents reinforced their newly held opinions on choice and independent activity in the nursery. This in turn reflected on my role to guide them towards a greater understanding of why this way of working with children is educationally sound. This was achieved through further staff meetings and directed reading from up-to-date literature. I hoped that the literature would clarify understanding of our experience in the way that Rowland (1988:60) describes 'where the text echoed experience – sense could be made of it. To put this another way, understanding has to be grounded in experience and not texts, even though the latter may help to illuminate that experience.' At this point I had a request for a new book for staff use – a modern dictionary so that terminology and jargon was understood.

We also read and discussed our LEA guidelines on curriculum for nursery children. The time seemed right to pursue the staff development dimension. I thought at the outset that the college module would provide a framework for raising staff and curriculum development issues, and it had. Only briefly in the early stages was there a suggestion that staff co-operation would mean I would gain the award. I had addressed this at the time and resolved not to exploit staff or parents in pursuit of the award, mainly because I hold that my professional development should be geared to improved service delivery to children, staff and parents. With this triangulation clearly upfront, exploitation was not an issue. Rewards had accrued to everyone when the tutor had asked permission to use our video with college students. On reflection, the fact that the research was linked to an award-bearing course only served to give us positive features such as time scales, targets and the momentum to keep going. There may also have been the element of learner-readiness and a sense of needing to make changes within a familiar environment with trusted colleagues. The experience gained through the research period and the subsequent teaching year resulted in a massive shift in staff attitude and expectation. During that year staff agreed to monitor the changes in block play of a group of children and to make their plans and records available to the local adviser. The feeling was that they had the support of one another in facilitating the change and an expectation that I would respect their rate of progress towards change. The resulting policy document includes reference to children, staff and parents and highlights their influence on the curriculum, resources, organisation and record-keeping. Adhering to the original plan that I would be responsible for all aspects of writing up, I produced a draft document and gave it to staff for their comment. Staff were keen that the document would be useful for students as well as themselves and so requested that it should include references to books and articles held in our staff library and that the importance of personal reading should be emphasised. The document was formally discussed at two staff meetings, after which it was produced in its final form. A three-fold leaflet explaining to parents the learning opportunities in baking was also discussed and agreed, thereby translating our policy statement for parent information. I found this triangulation of policy, guideline and parent leaflet consolidated much of my thinking about theory of learning, theory into practice and communicating with parents.

Our document is unique to our nursery but its birth process is one which is replicable. It is essential that such documents reflect staff intention, parent and child needs and LEA policy on the curriculum and its delivery. There is no sure-fire recipe except that which states 'go slowly, establish trust, minimise threat and build confidence'. The early stages are the most important – feelings, fear and doubts must be addressed. This is invaluable and seems crucial to the acceptance and implementation of the policy.

This collaborative way of working is acknowledged in McNiff (1988:19) in the 'shifting centres model', an approach to developing understanding of personal learning and professional life in which 'teachers, teacher-supporters and clients are awarded equal status and responsibility for helping the other person's process of understanding to evolve'. The research group had established cohesion and a commitment to change which has benefited the whole school community. I found the experience very stimulating, a definite growth point in my own professional development, leaving me with total commitment to ensuring that policy reflects the thinking and educational needs of those who devise the policy and who have to implement it on a day-to-day basis.

Appendix 1: Questionnaire to parents

(1)   Some things that your child can do at nursery are:

        Painting   Growing

        Water   Sand

        Cooking   House

        Animals   Puzzles

        Gluing   Music

        Bricks   Books

Which does your child enjoy?

(a)   (b)   (c)

(d)   (e)   (f)

(2)   Some things your child can learn at nursery are:

        to trust others [   ]   to bake [   ]   to ask questions [   ]

        to enjoy books [   ]   to draw [   ]   to sing rhymes/songs [   ]

        to listen [   ]   to share [   ]   to play with others [   ]

Which of the above do you think your child has learned?

(3)   Has your child learned anything else? (Please state)

....

Appendix 2: Interview schedule 1

		Often	Sometimes	Never
(1)	I bake with my child at home	[ ]	[ ]	[ ]
(2)	My child asks me to bake	[ ]	[ ]	[ ]
(3)	My child has/had dough at home	[ ]	[ ]	[ ]
(4)	My child helps me with cooking	[ ]	[ ]	[ ]
(5)	My child tells me about nursery cooking	[ ]	[ ]	[ ]
(6)	I see my child playing at pretend cooking	[ ]	[ ]	[ ]
(7)	I would like to join a nursery cooking session	[ ]	[ ]	[ ]

(8) Is there anything else about cooking at home or nursery you would like to tell me about?

....

....

....

....

Appendix 3: Interview schedule 2

You replied to the first interview.

(1) Can you tell me why you let your child/children help you so much with cooking?

....

....

(2) What does/do your child/children get out of the cooking sessions?

....

....

(3) What do you enjoy most about these times?

....

....

(4) Do you set out to teach your child/children particular things during these cooking sessions?

....

....

Appendix 4: Observation schedule

Activity: _____ Date: _____

Adult/Parent	1	2	3	4	5	6

Organising _____

Naming _____

Demonstrating _____

Helping _____

Encouraging _____

Talking _____

Questioning _____

Listening _____

Other _____

Appendix 5: Observation schedule

Activity: _____ Date: _____

Child	A	B	C	D	E	F
Looking						
Listening						
Speaking (v.n.adj.)						
Helping						
Asking						
Counting						
Recalling						
Sharing						
Thinking						
Other						

5 Time to Talk

SHEILA RYE

Background

The impetus for this research came partly from my experience in adult education, playgroups and family centres, which convinced me of parents' deep interest in their children's education, and partly from recent research accounts of partnerships between parents and school, focusing on various aspects of children's education and development (e.g. Wolfendale, 1983; Edwards & Redfern, 1988; Athey, 1990).

Recently appointed as nursery team leader, I was interested in developing a partnership approach where staff and parents respected and shared each other's knowledge and expertise as educators of young children. As a first step I talked to staff and parents about how they perceived the existing partnership and how they thought it might be improved. What emerged from these initial discussions with parents was a consensus over the friendly and welcoming atmosphere, but a lack of knowledge about what their children did all day and what they were learning.

> 'I don't have a clue what he does at nursery – that's the only thing ... I ask him and "Oh, I played all day" – "What did you play?" – but you can't get it out of him [laughs]. I know nothing really – I don't know what he does.'

> 'Also I don't really know what the children learn during the day – I don't know – I know most of it is through play and social interaction – but in terms of actual learning I don't know what curriculum they have, and I'd like to know.'

Reflecting on these comments I was strongly reminded of what Tizard, Mortimore & Burchell (1981) have to say about establishing a working partnership with parents. Their research – a practical and balanced critique of the efforts of seven nursery and infant schools to develop parental involvement – showed that the daily beginning and end of session chats between parents and staff seldom moved much beyond milk, dinner money and the child's health. They identify individual consultations with parents as:

> in our opinion, the single most important opportunity for parental involvement. If a school can manage nothing else it should at least attempt to hold regular worthwhile discussions about every child with his [sic] parents (Tizard, Mortimore & Burchell, 1981: 207)

and justify this recommendation as follows:

> Almost all parents want to find out about their children's progress, and how best to help them, and almost all have opinions about the school, formed on the basis of their children's experiences of it. This concern for their own children can provide a focus for discussion about teaching methods, and school organisation, and for an exchange of information between parents and teachers, including parents who would be unlikely to be involved in any other way. Further, it is generally agreed that parents have a right to information about what the school is doing for their child, what he has accomplished and what his difficulties are, and that schools have an obligation to give them this information. (Tizard, Mortimore & Burchell, 1981: 207)

Research Context

The research took place in an 80-place nursery unit attached to an inner-city first school. First languages comprised Bengali, Cantonese, English, Gujerati, Hindi, Italian, Punjabi, Pushto and Urdu. About 10% of the children were of mixed race and around 20% from single parent families. The nursery was staffed by four teachers, including myself as team leader, and six nursery nurses. We were all monolingual, but received some bilingual support from a part-time classroom assistant, the deputy head of the school, and the home – school liaison officer.

Some of the changes in curriculum and organisation which we made during my first year as team leader had a close bearing on my subsequent research. A key development was to give the children access to a wider range of activities and equipment, encouraging them to become more independent in their learning, with the staff supporting and resourcing that learning, rather than always initiating and directing it. This new way of working quickly highlighted the need for an effective record-keeping system, which would chart children's development within an agreed framework based on the main aims of the nursery curriculum, celebrate each child's achievement, be useful to receiving teachers *and* be user-friendly enough to share with parents.

The new system incorporated files of work for each child, and 'pictorial tick lists' covering various curriculum areas, to be completed by teachers and nursery nurses working together, with evidence gleaned from systematic observations, supplemented by information from parents. Another key development which underpinned our record keeping was the introduction of pastoral groups. Universally welcomed, it gave each member of staff responsibility for ten children – home visiting, settling, building a relationship with the family, dealing with problems, maintaining their records and files of work (with nursery nurses supported in record keeping by a teacher).

So the findings of my pilot project – that parents wanted to know more about the nursery curriculum and what their children did all day – coincided with our new initiative on record keeping and records of achievement. We decided to move forward to parent consultations and assess the claims made by Tizard, Mortimore & Burchell (1981) for ourselves.

Methodology

I designed the research to start with 12 consultations to be undertaken by three teacher colleagues and myself. I would then interview the parents and teachers who participated, and present findings and recommendations to all the nursery staff. The nursery nurses would then each try one or two consultations and I would interview them for their reactions.

The first round of consultations and interviews went as planned, but the nursery nurses responded to our findings with such apprehension and raised so many important issues that the plan had to be modified to give time for discussion, meetings and training (see 'Staff Apprehensions', below).

Data were collected through semi-structured interviews with staff and parents and in field notes recording the chronology of the planning and implementation process and the discussion and debates which it inspired. Webb (1990b) identifies semi-structured interview as an appropriate method for teacher-research; at their best these did yield a wealth of data, with the respondents warming to the subject as they re-lived the occasion. I wanted to know what staff had learnt about the child and the family, what concerns parents had raised, what aspects of the child's development they had concentrated on, how much they had focused on the records and file of work, whether they felt well prepared, whether they felt pleased or dissatisfied with the consultation and what they felt the parents' reactions to be. Each interview endeavoured to cover these areas and to give respondents the freedom to raise new issues, which were then incorporated into subsequent enquiries. The fact that I too was trying parent consultations for the first time, experiencing similar mixed feelings about them, and was prepared to share these in the interview, contributed to the sense of a discussion between equals which the best interviews carried. Oakley (1981) identifies the power of experiences shared in common by interviewer and interviewee, and argues that this enhances rather than detracts from the quality of the data obtained.

The question of tape recording was problematic. Using a tape enabled me to concentrate on establishing rapport and covering issues with the respondent, and then to 'listen beyond' (Measor, 1985), when playback and transcription revealed nuances and layers of meaning which had passed unnoticed in the interview itself. However, comments from colleagues such as 'I've been dreading this all weekend' made me realise that tape recording can be counter-productive, and indeed I collected some of my best data after the tape had been switched off. I also found myself asking colleagues immediately after a consultation 'How did it go?' and getting such a vivid and succinct response that I would rush off to note down key points and phrases. Then, when we came to the pre-arranged interview slot, they repeated what they had told me already, and some of the spontaneity and point of the interview was lost.

The dilemma of 'to tape or not to tape' was minor compared with the question of how to conduct semi-structured interviews with a respondent whose first language I did not share. Similar concerns emerged in the consultations themselves (see 'We had a really good conversation', below): how do we ensure that the interaction by which we set such store is as meaningful as it would be if we shared a first language? I was interested to read how McCann (1990) in her study of Mirpuri infant pupils resolved the problem:

> Translators were avoided as past experience has shown that they were not averse to adding their own point of view to the interpretation, thus invalidating the data. Consequently Mirpuri families interviewed were selected because either mother or father spoke adequate English. Thus the data were skewed in favour of well-established families and did not cover the views of the few households where no English was spoken. (McCann, 1990: 187)

While I can identify with McCann's experience of interpreters, this line of action would not have been acceptable in this work situation. It would have excluded a sizeable minority of parents from the research – a group with whom staff, because of the language barrier, already communicated least, and whose needs we most needed to understand better.

I tried two strategies when interviewing parents for whom English was a second language about their consultations. One was to arm our bilingual home–school liaison officer with a list of questions, ask her to talk to the parent and give me a summary of the replies. The other was a three-way session, with the parent encouraged to use their home language as much as they wanted. The second strategy was more demanding but more effective; the crucial factors were establishing three-way rapport, and the interpreter's understanding of the issues being discussed.

Staff Apprehensions

Even the staff who were largely positive about the idea of parental consultations were well aware of the difficulties involved, and other staff were both apprehensive and resistant. The fears and feelings voiced enriched the research, offering different perspectives on some important issues. They weave in and out of the field notes and interview data, but I present them in summary form here.

We knew we wanted the consultations to be a two-way process, with a genuine sharing of information and concerns. But we also knew how lacking we were in the training in counselling and interpersonal skills to help us make that happen. We did organise a training session with guidelines and role play which staff found helpful but only a beginning. There are implications for initial training here.

If one of the aims of consultations is to deepen parents' understanding of the nursery curriculum, staff must feel confident in their own understanding of its educational value, and be able to articulate it. The nursery needs guidelines for each area of the curriculum which explain, in jargon-free language, what children will learn from the activities provided.

Even so, is it part of the nursery nurse's job to talk to parents about children's cognitive development? In addressing this issue we looked at the nursery nurse's job description, which requires them to contribute to record keeping; at the reality of their pastoral group responsibilities, through which they often develop a unique relationship with parents and a deep understanding of the child; at the close links between a child's intellectual, social and emotional development; at nursery nurses' own professional development, which would be enhanced by their full participation in the recording and consultation process; at the pay and conditions of nursery nurses compared with teachers, and their lack of a career structure; at research (Westgate & Hughes, 1989) which showed nursery nurses' interactions with children to be more cognitively demanding than those between children and teachers, although: 'their important contribution was not being fully recognised – even by the nursery nurses themselves!' (Westgate & Hughes, 1989: 58) The consensus that eventually emerged was that nursery nurses' involvement in consultations would be welcomed and supported, but not demanded.

Staff who expressed the most apprehension about consultations also felt that parents would find them threatening. While this could be seen as projection, it was also a valid concern – it took one parent four months to accept our invitation, and even then the consultation took place just inside the front door. Parents' evenings and 'going up to school' carry so many negative connotations, and we are all so used to professionals knowing best, that to be invited to take part in a more equal interaction can be discomfiting.

Past experience of open evenings also prompted the 'some parents just aren't interested' response. I find Wolfendale (1983) a good advocate here, stating firmly that:

> there is accumulating and possibly incontrovertible evidence that parents, irrespective of socio-economic background, are interested and concerned in their children's development and education; that apparent disinterest and remoteness arises from other factors (stress, anxiety, ignorance of educational processes, timidity) which explain but do not cause. (Wolfendale, 1983: 173)

Every parent invited attended the consultations, and several told us how pleased they were to have been asked.

Staff were anxious about knowing children well enough to talk in depth with parents about them. We tried to make regular observations, but other demands often intervened. Tizard, Mortimore & Burchell (1981) recognise the difficulties of monitoring an individual child in a large free-flow nursery, and suggest various strategies, including a system where:

> the teacher invited up to ten parents at a time to give a date and time during the following fortnight when they would be free to discuss the child. When the consultation was fixed, the staff concerned discussed

the child together and records were updated ... This method has the advantage that the consultations can be held as soon as possible after the appraisals of the child have been made, with up-to-date records. (Tizard, Mortimore & Burchell, 1981: 218)

The more record keeping and talking to parents we did, the more we appreciated, in the words of one nursery nurse, that: 'observations are really, really important – and so is feedback from other staff. You've really got to know that child.'

Some staff were worried that seeing the record sheets, which were designed to cover a wide range of likely development between the ages of three and five, would cause parents to put undue pressure on their child to achieve. This is a power-sharing issue. If we want parents to work with us as partners in their children's education, we have to give them the tools of the trade, and afford them the respect and confidence that they will use them properly. Athey (1990) shows how effectively parents respond when given a framework in which to observe their children's development. The key is to celebrate children's *individual* achievement within a wide developmental framework. (See below, 'She was outside the door with her file in her arms'.)

So how did the consultations work in practice and what were staff and parent perceptions of them?

Staff's and Parents' Perceptions of the Consultations

'I learnt ever such a lot I didn't know'

This was a common theme in all the staff's experience. We found out what children liked doing at home, what languages they spoke, whether they had started going to mosque, their eating and sleeping patterns, their relationships with brothers, sisters, grandparents, friends, family plans for moving house or travelling, problems of separation, divorce or absence of one parent. Without exception we listened more than we talked. This allayed our fears about not knowing everything we should about the child; it seemed that, by showing genuine interest, knowledge and pleasure in some aspects of the child's development, staff were giving parents permission and indeed encouragement to talk in a similar vein, and confirm or supplement our picture of the child.

'That was interesting, that they'd noticed it as well'

Much of the time we learnt about the child through an *exchange* of information, or 'comparing notes' between the parents and ourselves:

'Mum talked about C taking a book home, how she read it to her once and then heard her retelling the story, pretending to read the book, and using the same words. Mum said she was amazed. I showed her the "uses book language" bit on the records, and said how C was always pretending to be the teacher at nursery.' (Teacher)

'We both kind of related to his love of cars and how he knows everything there is to know about every car ... I mean, I've known from taking him out that he identifies them, but perhaps it's something we could pick up on more – it's worth knowing.' (Teacher)

Staff were pleased that the consultations were working as a two-way process which parents found useful too, checking to see if their perceptions of their own child were shared by school:

'Mum wanted to know if they were right in feeling that M was very bright.' (Teacher)

'I wanted to know what he was like in nursery, aggressive like, or tidying around, copying me. And everything Ms T said, it was him, everything was N. I knew that Ms T knew N – that there was one person who knew him. (Parent)

'We had a really good conversation'

The consultations which the staff rated the most successful were those where they felt a rapport had been established, and both they and the parents felt at ease:

'It wasn't like an interview, we just sat and talked like friends sort of thing. It was lovely.' (Teacher)

A factor crucial to the quality of this rapport was of course the language support available, when parents and staff did not share a first language. We found that consultations made greater demands than everyday communication does.

'It was difficult. I found that although she has a lot of very good English, she didn't have enough to carry exactly what she wanted to say. So she was finding it hard work, and I found that I was choosing my words, and the flow wasn't as natural as with say P's family ... You're not getting the spontaneous feedback – it limits it, and that's not fair to anyone.' (Teacher)

This parent subsequently confirmed what the teacher had felt, that she would have welcomed some bilingual support.

Working through an interpreter is a skill in itself – and one in which we had had no formal training. Where the interpreter was relaxed, knowledgeable and skilful, then the consultations were a worthwhile experience for all concerned:

'I really enjoyed it. I spoke to Mum in English virtually all of the time. K [deputy head of school] just reinforced what I was saying. And then at the end K talked to mum about the family. She's just so professional, and experienced. *And* she has a really lovely way of talking to parents.' (Nursery nurse)

'We could almost have managed without the interpreter but it was brilliant with him there ... I spoke to Dad in English and Mr B [PGCE student] clarified it when he needed it. Then Dad spoke to me in English and every now and then he turned to Mr B for some help ... They got into a really good conversation. Mr B kept turning to me and saying "I'll translate for you in a minute".' (Teacher)

This member of staff felt that the father had appreciated our efforts to find an interpreter, and that it had helped them both to admit their difficulties in everyday communication:

'Dad laughed and said to me "I know you don't always understand what I say to you; and other times I'm trying to tell you something and it comes out all wrong".' (Teacher)

This consultation was also a positive experience for the child, because for once she was hearing her first language being used by adults in school:

'R just sat there and *beamed*. She listened to them talking Bangla together and she looked at me and her eyes got big as saucers. I said to her "This is because I can't understand everything your dad says and he can't understand all that I say. But you're all right – you can speak two languages already, and you're only four".' (Teacher)

'She writes at home – not her name but some letters'

Mindful of the findings of Tizard, Mortimore & Burchell (1981: 212) that: 'unbeknown to the schools ... about half of the parents of three and four year olds ... were trying to teach their children to read or write, or both', I wanted to see how great an emphasis our parents laid on the three Rs in the consultations. They were clearly interested – listening while we explained about emergent writing and early maths, and contributing their observations to the records. One or two were more explicit about teaching:

'He talked about counting – "It's funny, if I ask her to get, like, three potatoes, she'll get them, but if I say, count them, she'll go 1, 2, 4 and when I say 1, 2, 3, she walks away." I tried to explain how clever she is to know what three is without counting, but you can't go on too much. Maybe we need a maths day for parents ...' (Nursery nurse)

'She was outside the door with her file in her arms'

Children and parents enjoyed looking at the files of work together. Staff sometimes helped to start with:

'I sat with them and talked about the first few pictures and sort of led it, initially ... P loved it, he really did. I think it was the highlight.' (Teacher)

'N was like puffing out. At dinner time I said to him "Your mum liked your pictures" and he was grinning from ear to ear.' (Teacher)

We often found the files more useful than the record sheets as a way into explaining the nursery curriculum to parents, because we could relate it to their own child's development:

'Mum asked all about her pictures and K [teacher/interpreter] explained about markmaking and how it's like the beginning of writing.' (Nursery nurse)

Parents' responses to the record sheets varied: some studied them closely, others were like the parent who:

'wasn't interested in plodding through, 'cos she'd other things she wanted to talk about. I think she was pleased to know we did have records though.' (Nursery nurse)

However, of the parents asked, a majority confirmed that they felt the record sheets were 'very important'.

'She had some things she really wanted to talk about'

Although the record sheets and the file of work gave some structure to the consultations, we found that many parents, once they realised that we were genuinely offering them time to talk, set their own agenda and raised their real concerns. Transition to first school loomed large; feelings about racial stereotyping came into the open; issues around bringing up mixed race children were discussed; fears about dyslexia divulged; relationships between children and staff questioned. Stierer (1991: 166) sees the hallmark of successful consultations as 'giving parents an opportunity to share with staff those aspects of their child's learning and development which *they* think are important'. We were pleased that parents felt safe enough to voice such concerns, and found that it broadened our understanding of the children.

Opinion was divided about whether children should be present for the whole consultation. Sometimes they were, and it seemed a very positive experience:

> 'M sat between us, very straight on her chair, with the records on her lap. She wanted to know what it all said, and gave examples to back up my comments! Perhaps consultation should be three-way, even at this stage?' (Teacher)

Some parents felt that children should be included 'because these things should not be hidden behind closed doors' but others said they were glad of a chance to talk without the children. This view was echoed by several staff:

> 'There are things I want to say to A's mum by herself – and maybe she'll tell me things if A's not there. Sometimes it's important children hear what's being said about them, but I want some time without him there.' (Teacher)

Conclusions

In terms of parental response, the consultations were 100% successful, unlike any parental involvement initiative previously undertaken. All the parents we asked said that they found the consultations useful and enjoyable, and suggested they take place, on average, once a term. Staff felt that a more realistic goal would be twice during each child's time in nursery. Staff learnt a lot about children and their families; parents gained some insight into the nursery curriculum, and children saw their work being respected and valued. Parents as well as staff admitted to feeling nervous, but interestingly some parents were noticeably more confident in their dealings with nursery after the consultation. Staff realised that training in counselling and communication skills, drawing up curriculum guidelines and a systematic approach to classroom observation are all prerequisites for effective consultations:

> 'Parents will hang on every word. I know I do when I go to the doctor or the dentist. You're the professional, they'll remember everything you've said. It's very important, what *you* say about *their* child.' (Nursery nurse)

Consulting with parents is a risky business. Staff are coming out from behind professional defences, inviting feedback that may be negative as well as positive, and acknowledging that parents are experts as well. On the whole we found the risk worth taking, and that power-sharing in this way enhanced rather than diminished parents' respect for the work we were doing in nursery and our commitment to their children.

The research does seem to bear out the claims made by Tizard, Mortimore & Burchell (1981). Clearly parents valued the opportunity to talk about their children, raise concerns and hear about their progress, while staff found it useful to exchange information and explain the nursery curriculum in terms of each child's individual achievement. We particularly valued the consultations with 'parents who would be unlikely to be involved in any other way' (Tizard, Mortimore & Burchell, 1981: 207) – often parents who are uneasy in a school environment or those whose first language the staff do not share. By recognising and providing for their needs, we established some two-way communication, hopefully signalling how important we thought it was to talk to every parent about their child.

6 Working Together: Parents, Staff and Children in the Early Years

JUDY ARROWSMITH

There is a substantial and well-documented literature on the importance of developing good home–school links, especially in the early years, where parental attitudes to education have an enormous influence on the extent to which children can benefit from educational opportunities. From Project Headstart in the 1960s onwards, research findings recognise the influence of the home on school learning and suggest greater parental involvement may make school learning more successful. For example, Mortimore *et al.* (1988) in the concluding chapter, say: '... parental involvement or at least some forms of it – was one of our key factors.' The nature and extent of that involvement, however, remains a contentious issue, as indeed is what exactly constitutes 'good home–school links'. Mortimore *et al.* continue by pointing out that teachers are often unsure how to proceed with activities to involve parents.

Some authors go further. As early as 1984, the conclusion to Tizard & Hughes' work is: 'Indeed, in our opinion, it is time to shift the emphasis away from what parents should learn from professionals, and towards what professionals can learn from studying parents and children at home' (p. 267).

Willingness to share responsibility for children's education requires informed and trusting partners. This involves time, hard work and patience and needs to be worked through with the people in a given school, since each school is idiosyncratic in interpersonal relationships. Exchange of information and honest views are vital if advances in working together are to be achieved. There should be, however, some fundamental principles which influence policy and planning, and some practical suggestions tried in schools, which are worth considering. These must be gathered.

Despite agreement on the importance of family and school co-operation there has been rather less research into how positive relationships can actually be fostered. Significantly, there is a firm determination on the part of parents and teachers to act on a sound knowledge base. Good habits of working together, established from the very first stages, are critical if there is not to be the typical 'tailing off' of interest towards the upper primary school. There is currently a thirst for new ideas of what can be done, what constitutes good practice, what strategies and techniques have been found to be effective.

The Project

The parent–teacher collaboration project was established at Moray House Institute, Heriot-Watt University after the urgent call for further research at the European Conference on Parent–Teacher Collaboration in the Primary School in Norway, 1984. It was intended to build up a clearer picture of the present position in Scotland, in a sample of schools, with a view to building on current good practice and improving the experience for the benefit of school pupils. After an initial phase of evidence gathering from staff and parents in a number of early education settings, the aim was to monitor in detail the step-by-step process of developing successful and positive working relationships in a number of Fife nursery settings and Lothian primary schools. Rapid feedback in the schools led to action for improvement and early findings formed the basis for in-service work and the development of workshop materials to spark off discussion in other schools and with pre-service early education students. At every stage more than one school in each category was selected, as a reminder that there is no 'correct' way to proceed in matters of partnership; each school is unique in the way it gradually negotiates working relationships between its members.

Stage A

From the early phases of data collection it became clear that the nature of co-operation is very difficult to prescribe since it depends so much on the people involved – their previous experience, knowledge and understanding of education, the characteristics of the neighbourhood and so on. For example, for some professional working parents, an 'appointments' system for parent–teacher discussion was preferred, so that a visit to school could be jig-sawed into weekly plans, whereas for some of the parents in an area of multiple deprivation, appointments were seen as threatening and a general welcoming 'open door' policy was much more likely to appeal. If the neighbourhood were one where baby-sitting was a known problem, it would be unrealistic to expect a whole-school meeting to be well attended. Parents who had a very negative experience of school themselves as pupils cannot be nursed into working with staff in the same way as those who are very keen to support the school in every way possible. Staff who had taught previously in schools where they worked closely with parents felt they had to change their approach with parents who were anxious and seemed unwilling. As one said, 'You have to expend an awful lot of energy to be really welcoming, whereas in my previous school we just got on as a team. It was expected.'

Each school's policy, though based on clearly thought-through principles, had evolved through interaction with parents. Personal contact and good communication became themes. There was a commitment to evaluation and constant modification in each school. One headteacher remarked: 'Good working relations don't just happen. You have to keep working at them and keep an eye on how people are coping.'

It seemed that the existence or not of a parent–teacher association (PTA) was no indicator of the state of relationships. In those schools where a PTA existed, it was an added bonus, but did not involve more than a minority of parents. It is clearly not the only, nor necessarily the first way of bringing about good parent–school communication or partnership. School premises still seemed to be the location for virtually all activities, despite research into the value of off-school premises meetings and home visits. Specific methods of shared working varied considerably with the confidence and life style of the parents, but it seemed that a general *willingness* to co-operate is more important than the actual 'ploy' undertaken, and this must be fostered.

Parents' experience of school visits was very varied. Nearly all had been at some point to discuss their own child (parents' evening) but beyond that, experience was individual. Some had been to school to help or give talks, others to accompany trips. Very few had done more than auxiliary-type work in school. The amount of father involvement varied.

General efforts by the school to radiate an atmosphere of welcome were important and the feeling that parents are valued. Once trusting relationships are established, there would appear to be no lack of ideas of how any one school might proceed.

Development work from Stage A

Development work in college and schools, as a result of the report was undertaken by Moray House staff. The most urgent recommendation was that immediate steps be taken to prepare pre-service student teachers for working with parents. Lectures, seminars and workshops were piloted with undergraduate BEd students and these now form a compulsory element in all pre-service teacher education courses. A staff-development 'slot' was offered to all staff and in-service provision made for teachers facing current demands for partnership. Visits to primary schools, lectures to primary school management staff and to the Lothian Branch of British Association of Early Childhood Education were undertaken, and the demand for in-service work continues to grow. Workshop notes and a video were completed for use with parents. Sessions were held to discuss methods of record keeping and ongoing evaluation, and parent discussions were offered.

Stage B 1991–92 – Action Research in Nursery Settings

Action Research was conducted in two nursery settings in Fife. It was designed to extend staff–parent partnership and to monitor the emerging critical approach developing in both staff and parents as they consolidated the working relationship in their own setting. It was clear from the earlier research that each school has to work through what is right for the particular people involved. It is a process of building up trust through personal contact and good communication. It was suggested that improvement depends on careful monitoring of what is going on, together with efficient recording of join action which has been tried and tested. The general aim of the Stage B research was to involve parents in evaluation and shared planning of learning in the nursery school. It was to allow staff and parents time to think critically together about educational issues and their joint responsibilities.

The nursery setting was a deliberate choice as a starting place. The nursery school is in a unique position in that parents or carers and staff meet each day. There is continuing and immediate contact, which however brief must go a long way towards breaking down the perceived differences between 'them' and 'us'. Parents talk naturally to staff about the child's current behaviour, achievements, nursery events and so on. Due to the children's enthusiasm to share what they are doing, families are drawn into nursery activities. However, if the working relationship is to be more than just casual exchange, there must be an attempt to involve staff and parents in deeper discussion and critical review.

The two nursery settings selected were quite different. One was a ten-place nursery class attached to a rural primary school and the other, a free-standing nursery school with 40 morning and 20 afternoon places. The catchment area of the school is one of higher employment although some of the employment is casual and seasonal. The facilities in the village are improving due to Urban Aid Funding.

Aims

There were ten aims underpinning the research in each setting. They were pursued sequentially over the period of study.

The aims were:

(1) To establish 'how things are going so far' from both parents' and staff's perspectives.
(2) To clarify present policy on parent–teacher partnership and the methods of implementing this policy.
(3) To examine current procedures for recording parental involvement.
(4) To identify current procedures for monitoring and evaluating initiatives involving parents and staff together.
(5) To identify areas for development or proposed initiatives from both parents' and staff's perspectives.
(6) To draw up an initial list of areas for development which should be addressed (ordered according to priority) and ideas to be tried.
(7) (If necessary) to re-negotiate the policy statement, recording and evaluation procedures.
(8) To address the first area for development or try the first idea.
(9) To record outcomes.
(10) To monitor and evaluate outcomes.

The purpose of each phase was always first and foremost for the benefit of the particular school. The question was clearly focused, 'How can we work together to make our children's experiences here during the nursery years, the best they can be?'

Methodology

The most complex task was to establish what parents thought about the nursery in general and how things seemed at the outset, before any 'action' could begin. Each nursery went about this in a different way. In the small nursery class, contact was frequent and speaking face-to-face was preferred. Staff rely to a great extent on oral communication. It was decided to tap in to parents' views first by group discussion at an invited coffee morning, which included a sale in aid of nursery funds. An important feature was that families were able to bring their under-nursery-school-age children with them, since baby-sitting is known to be a difficulty. Staff made the invitation very clear, reinforcing it when the family brought the child to school in the mornings and redirecting attention to the large, cheery posters advertising the occasion. Attendance was good although, as it happened, only women came, despite the fact that some fathers and grandfathers regularly bring and collect children. Perhaps a coffee morning was not as enticing to men as a pie and a pint in the local might have been (an improvement noted for next time!). The researcher led a semi-structured discussion on the nursery in general and expectations of parental involvement, making clear that there were no right and wrong answers and that it was important to share perspectives.

The group began by discussing education as a joint responsibility. Parents were asked what sorts of things they had taught the children before ever they came to the nursery. They went on to talk about their feelings about being involved in education during the nursery class years and indeed in primary school and about whether they felt welcome. They discussed whether parents could make much difference to what happens in the nursery and why some parents do not want to be involved. One parent remarked: 'Being involved doesn't mean you're always coming in.'

Practical issues such as how they first made contact with the nursery, the nature of their current involvement and the adequacy of communication were covered. They concluded with suggestions about useful ways forward. As a reminder of the whole context of community involvement in which the nursery class operates, a parent clarified: 'It's no a new thing, ken, this working wi the teacher. We've always helped oot wi the bairns and gone on trips: you jist get on wi it. No need to ha'e a carry on aboot it.'

In the nursery school, methods had to be a bit more formal, because of the numbers of families involved. Talking still seemed to be the most appropriate way with these parents since the nursery has taken considerable time to build up a positive face-to-face working relationship, so it was decided to interview the parents in small groups, using an oral modification of the nursery form given in SOED's *Using Ethos Indicators in Primary School Self-Evaluation* (1992). The researcher was involved in devising these and was familiar with their use, having piloted them in written form in Lothian schools. The suggested questionnaires are wide-ranging, covering topics such as children's enjoyment of and interest in nursery activities, different relationships both within the nursery and with parents, adequacy of equipment and facilities, communication with parents, children's behaviour, and the reputation of the nursery in the community.

The instrument was adapted into a set of questions, rather than statements, which could be posed to small groups. Two groups of ten families each were selected to represent the 40 children with morning places and all the families of the afternoon children were invited. Those selected were given a personalised letter, giving the background, dates, place and times. Although the 40 families were offered a specific invitation, it was made clear to other parents that they were very welcome to join a discussion group if they wished or else to take home one of the adapted questionnaires and return it, completed at the end of the week. Four completed questionnaires were received. To thank the parents for their co-operation, each one who took part was given a free raffle ticket with the chance to win a prize. The interviews were conducted by the researcher and two mature undergraduate students, although it was made clear to the parents that the questions were being asked with the full co-operation of the headteacher and staff and with the express aim of making the experience in this particular nursery the best it would be for the children. Parents seemed to know they did not have to agree in their answers, that there were no 'right' or 'wrong' answers. In practice, the parents did not turn up all together and so the discussion groups varied in size and several one-to-one interviews were conducted. Many stayed on for a coffee and more chat after the more formal interview was over. A good number of the parents had made special arrangements to be there, which seemed to signal their acknowledgement of the importance of the meeting.

In both nursery settings every member of staff was interviewed separately, so that each got a chance to give her own opinion. In the nursery class, a semi-structured interview schedule was used, with ample opportunity for expanding answers. The nursery school used a modified form of the SOED questionnaire, devised after discussion between the headteacher and the researcher. Again, the statement form was changed to interview questions. Members of staff did not see the questions before the interview to avoid discussion and sharing of responses. All members of staff were interviewed, including the caretaker and the dinner lady. It was felt to be important that everyone was fully involved throughout the project, since special effort was necessary and indeed special understanding, if only for the day-long presence of parents on the premises. In both nursery settings staff and parents welcomed the opportunity to take time to air their views – something which often gets neglected in the busy routine of 'getting things done'.

All the views were then collated, tabulated where appropriate, and illustrated with quotations.

Parents' Views on Involvement

Both sets of parents were enormously positive in their views of the nursery, very appreciative of the approachability and helpfulness of the staff. For example, in the nursery class, parents and relatives, including a granny whose association with the nursery went back 20 years, were enthusiastic about being involved with nursery school activities and point to the whole local tradition of parents helping out regularly with play, sewing, baking, story reading, accompanying trips and so on. Indeed they felt that in a small school such as theirs, this closeness, once established, was never lost and that the children reaped the benefit throughout the primary stage of education. The only problem they identified in this connection was that it made the transition to secondary school, with its seeming cold impersonality, the harder for children to cope with successfully. On the other hand, there was considerable debate about the definite need to be able to bring younger children along as well, if parents were going to come into the nursery, since there would be no one to mind them at home. The group suggested that in places where parents do not join in activities, it was not because they did not care or want to be involved but probably because they were 'a wee bit scared', 'they don't feel welcome', or 'there was not a nice feeling about the school'. (This has been experienced in other places.)

In the nursery school, the most contentious issue was whether most parents show support for the nursery. Such comments as the following illustrate this:

'Lots could do more.'
'Some do; some don't.'
'A few do.'

On whether the nursery explained what part parents can play in the child's education, parents were rather vague. More than half felt they had explained, but comments such as the following indicated that this area might need a bit of attention:

'Yes when the children were about to start.'
'In a group, they do.'
'Well once (I think).'
'Oh, don't think so.'

The 'No Smoking' ruling was grumbled about by several parents, who said it made things difficult if you needed 'a puff to relax'. Several mentioned that they would welcome rather more flexible hours so that the nursery morning could be a little longer. They explained that if you went to college, for example, which did not finish until 12.00, the parent had to make a short-time alternative arrangement, and it would be nice if the child could just stay on for the extra half hour. Among the many ideas for improvement parents suggested the outside playing area could be resurfaced:

'Astraturf would be nice!'
'It's amazing there have been no big accidents. The teachers have to watch them the whole time.'

Staff Views on Parental Involvement

Staff views in each setting varied especially on more controversial issues such as whether there should be home visits, or the extent parents should be involved in the group which includes their own child. For example, one nursery nurse remarked: 'Some children don't seem to do as much if their parent is on the premises, so maybe parent help in the classroom should be restricted to only *some* activities at specific times.' Another recognised the difficulties of dividing the finite amount of time available: 'If you chat too long with a particular parent, it means others have to slip away without a word. It's quite a balancing act!'

Some questions really spread the answers. For example, when asked, 'Do parents only get in touch if there is a problem or issue?' there was a very mixed reaction. The general feeling in the nursery school was that most parents felt comfortable enough to chat about anything, although one member of staff did say: 'A lot will only come if there's something special.' Another felt it would be 'about half and half.'

When asked about encouraging parents to come and chat, one nursery nurse said: 'I would discourage idle gossip when the focus of attention should be the child – indeed any conversation which does not directly affect the child is better left until after nursery hours – otherwise, loyalties are split.' Others said it would be very unusual to discourage parents.

Data Analysis

Making sense of the information and recognising areas for action was, of course, fundamental. The aim was to improve practice. It was here that the combination of those already involved, working with an 'informed outsider', was felt to be at its most valuable. There was distinct apprehension about what would be revealed. Even for relatively confident members of staff, it can be nail-biting, awaiting the evaluation of others. There was a tendency to adopt a defensive stance, to be too elated by hints of appreciation, or made desolate by a few rather stridently stated comments, without paying sufficient attention to the overall picture. Discussion was important especially with someone who had come to care about whether things improved or not. Getting it right mattered to everyone.

In the two nursery settings the analysis was tackled rather differently since the method was negotiated in each case. For the nursery class the researcher studied the data and presented emerging issues and comments, to the staff. They talked matters through with parents, and there was a 'Where do we go from here?' discussion all together. In the nursery school it was decided to take a two-perspective approach to analysing the data. The headteacher and staff picked out what they felt was important or needed discussion. The researcher operated independently and then compared notes to see if the interpretations differed significantly. Forward planning was undertaken together. The staff confessed how difficult it was to make any sense of the information and especially to see what was significant and what was not, what may be cause for concern, and what they could be pleased with. Often they failed to take sufficient note of the positive. The headteacher commented: 'We suffered the emotional impact of being asked our opinions, of learning the opinions of others about our dearly held practices and well-established routines. We felt vulnerable, exposed and insecure.' She revealed they all began to look forward to visits from the researcher because it tended to calm them about some things and actually energise them and fill them with enthusiasm leading to very positive feelings of being in control and *deciding* on how to progress. There was a distinct feeling of 'we're all in this together' and there was pleasure in things which were already good.

Plans for Action

After all the discussion in each nursery, a specific list of areas for development was drawn up and resource implications noted. Some of the issues were clear-cut. For example, in both it became obvious that there must be some provision for pre-nursery children if parents were going to be able to be at the nursery at all during the day. Sometimes there was a disparity of view depending on whose perspective was being taken: parents did not always agree with staff. For example, parents in one setting felt on the whole that staff did not tell them much about the child's strengths, and yet staff felt most of what they said was positive. Perhaps this might be because parents were looking for overall statements about character and behaviour (e.g. 'good at sharing toys', 'promising at art work') whereas staff tended to be very specific, as one parent pointed out: 'They tend to just tell you whether he's eaten up his dinner and things like that. I want to know how he's doing in general and where he needs a bit of encouragement.'

It was decided to spend some staff development time on giving more structured feedback to parents, reminding of strengths and areas for improvement.

In each school, there were some clear priority areas which had been noted by staff and parents; other issues which were selected for early attention and further ones deliberately set on the 'back burner' so that no one felt overwhelmed. It was interesting that in the nursery school one of the decisions was that each member of staff should negotiate her own way of working with parents and children in the nursery to suit herself and the relevant parents, and she would operationalise it the following term. Uniformity was deliberately avoided, since members of staff felt that their differences should be respected as long as there was ample opportunity to explore reasons and monitor progress. For example, one nursery nurse felt that she was not yet very confident about working with parents constantly in the room and at the moment felt she could only dedicate her time to the children, but would make very sure she chatted to parents about what had been done and how to extend the work at home.

Given the positive backcloth of satisfaction and indeed general enthusiasm for what was being done, identifying areas for improvement – or even simply bits of muddle and misunderstanding which could be cleared up – came to be seen as a spur to action rather than something to be feared. Ideas of how to improve were readily forthcoming. The process of selecting priority areas was reassuring since everyone was clear what they were going to attempt and no one felt overwhelmed by the impossibility of having to improve everything simultaneously. Fear gave way to determination.

Renegotiating Policy

Neither of the nurseries had a written policy on parental involvement, although both stressed the importance of parents in their information for parents and in their dealings with family members. Staff decided that the best starting place was to conduct a review of current practice, and share ideas regarding intentions. In the nursery class the teacher drafted a starter document outlining the aims and identifying ways of bringing about working together, giving details of why, how, when and where partnership is developed, how nursery activities are extended into the home, the importance of parent–staff exchange and so on. This was then discussed and modified. In the nursery school it was decided to share the process of formulation, so each nursery assistant was issued with a number of questions to set her thinking, in preparation for a brainstorming session. Armed with their notes, and having been duly prepared, the staff worked on each question, collating their answers to form the basis for the next discussion. The policy statement then evolved, under the headteacher's guidance, but was redrafted and modified, with the intention that these processes would continue. The staff also decided to produce a parallel illustrated 'deformalised' policy statement in parent-friendly terms.

Recording

The nurseries experimented with a number of ways of recording parental involvement, so that it was more formal than the 'How do you think it went?' level. While all nurseries keep records of work with parents, these are often intermingled with daily diary entries and files which include other information. This makes monitoring more difficult. Both nurseries started a loose-leaf file briefly describing nursery life, mainly using simple descriptions and photographs but with space for parent or staff to add a comment or for a child to draw a picture. Everyone was gradually educated to make constructive comment, so that while such things as 'Brilliant' were quite usual starter-comments eventually parents were beginning to be more precise as when, after a trip to the local supermarket a mum wrote 'Excellent demo of pizza-making'. Critical comments were particularly welcomed, for example 'Not enough time'. Staff reminded parents how these would be taken into account in forward planning. For example where a parent wrote 'Over the kids' heads' about a trip to the local butcher, it was decided that either the butcher would be given clearer guidance about what the children would want to be shown, or else an alternative venue would be sought.

In one nursery parents began to 'sign in' when they participated in nursery activities, with the date and activity noted, so there emerged a cumulative picture, from which to study numbers of parents involved, the types of activity undertaken, times of heavier involvement, whether it is always the same parents engaged in the same activities. The 'running record' kept by the teacher in the nursery class served a similar purpose. It allowed a picture to emerge of differing patterns of family involvement and in particular formed a check that no one was completely left out. It also became a pleasing, positive reminder of all the work done over the year, so helping to maintain enthusiasm and guide forward thinking. A drawback was that it was time-consuming – although probably not more so for the teacher than keeping the old staff diary – and the general comment column seemed a little self-evident in a small nursery, although it was recognised that it would be useful for students or to give continuity in case of absence or staff changes.

The use of Parent Chat Sheets at parents' evenings was piloted in the nursery school. Part of this was completed by the parent, or written by the member of staff or the parent during the chat. It became a record of the termly discussion, signed by both parties, and highlighted the child's achievements and progress, both at home and nursery. It identified strengths and areas where further encouragement and support were needed. Any further points made by parents at any time in the term – for example, concerns, questions, achievements – were added to the record by staff, as they arose.

Evaluation

Since one of the main aims was to involve everyone, and encourage a spirit of constant appraisal, the evaluation was a particularly important dimension. At the outset of the project, monitoring and evaluating was done entirely informally through chat between staff and parents. None of the feedback was recorded. Staff were determined to add to this since they recognised the importance of reviewing. In addition to continuing to encourage informal discussion, staff were required and parents invited, to write brief evaluative comments about each activity which involved parents. Parents could add an entry themselves or tell staff what they thought and staff would record the comments. At the end of each term's 'chats' with parents, staff discussed not only what was recorded about the child's progress at home and in the nursery but how valuable the term's work had been, bearing in mind how the goals on the recording sheet match general curriculum planning goals. General success was judged by monitoring informal feedback from parents, by parental contribution to the child's record and by staff judgement about willingness to share ideas, skills, equipment and observation. It was decided a more formal evaluation sheet of pupil progress in relation to set criteria should be completed by parents before the last profile is submitted to the primary school.

With the new recording and evaluation procedures in place, the nurseries began the long haul of tackling the specific issues identified. Of course what they actually did was appropriate only to the particular nursery. However, everything was in place for pulling together. By the end of the project, evaluation of each new step was beginning to become second nature and exchange was deeper than pleasantries or focusing only on the specific child. Parents and staff were becoming used to being asked for opinions and suggestions for improvement. Perhaps this was the most significant feature of the research. There was the realisation that there is no 'finished' state of affairs, only the continuing process of improving, evaluating and trying again.

Action

It was recognised that action was important if things were to keep improving. As Somekh (1993: 11) reminds us: 'The quality of educational research should be judged above all by its impact – or potential impact – on practice. If nothing changes in classrooms and schools as a result of research, are we justified in calling it educational at all? I think not.'

Each nursery worked towards targets appropriate to their own setting. For example, the nursery class started summer term coffee mornings where pre-nursery children could come and play, weather permitting, while parents chatted. They improved the outside environment with temporary alternative strategies, like planting up gro-bags, while awaiting permission for the more major alterations submitted, and exploring the possibilities of becoming a community nursery, with general under-five provision. They became enthusiastic about the illustrated loose-leaf folder with parent and staff comments, and planned to let it run for a term before discussing its value with parents.

The nursery school selected three areas for priority attention – better explanation of the part parents could play in the education of their child, further involvement of parents with children in the nursery activities, and improved and more detailed information to parents about their child's progress. They tried a variety of new methods, including a new section incorporated into the Parent Chat Record Sheet to guide discussion on activities in the home. They made a video, using children, staff and parents to illustrate aspects of the literary group's work, and held a 'Parents Come and Play' night. They also experimented with a new format for the once-a-term parent–staff discussions and agreed to run them for a pilot year before review.

1992–93 Action Research in Primary Settings

Similar action research was undertaken in primary schools, although the aims were modified to bring the work more usefully in line with current recommendations for school self-evaluation leading to school development planning. The baseline was to establish what parents, staff and pupils thought about the school in general, and the children's educational opportunities rather than only about home–school relations. SOED (1992) guidelines, *Using Ethos Indicators in Primary School Self-Evaluation: Taking Account of the Views of Parents, Pupils and Staff* were used and adapted forms of recommended questionnaires were administered. Improvements to policy, home–school communication and ongoing recording and monitoring techniques were made. Further improvements were planned together.

It was very noticeable that time in the primary school was at a premium; occasions which involved whole-staff discussion had to be planned into staff development time well in advance. The programme was carefully drawn up months before and so free-ranging discussion and constant updating as had happened in the nursery setting was impossible; a strict timetable had to be adhered to. Much of the discussion was limited to the headteacher with the researcher. Work on the policy, recording and monitoring procedures was mainly undertaken by the headteacher in each case. It was always felt to be important, however, that staff be involved as much as possible and even the decision about whether to go ahead was delayed until all staff had had the opportunity to hear what was involved and offer an opinion. In this way everyone was part of the same vision and understood the practical implementation.

It was felt that taking account of the children's views constituted a rich third dimension to the general picture of the school, what was satisfying and what was perceived to need improvement. The idea of pupils, parents and staff all developing their evaluation strategies together to improve the school was being encouraged. Even the youngest children were recognised as having a view worth listening to. An amazing number of pupils went out of their way to focus on the curriculum and to be balanced in their comments, what they liked and what improvements they wanted.

For example, some written comments were:

'I think it is good because our teacher doise not just hand over a book and say do page 89 she explains and helps us. Everything in our school is shared.' (Age 9)

'I think that children that can do there work faster are alwes the one's that get to do the more fun activities in class, like painting, drowing and other fun activities, this is not fair.' (Age 11)

'I get much homework that means I can not go out to play with my friends after school.' (Age 9)

By the end of the project, the schools had some targets to be incorporated into the school development plans. Some strategies had been thought through to help in the areas collectively identified as priority areas from pupils, staff and parents' perspectives. A spirit of ongoing evaluation by pupils, parents and staff was being fostered. They move forward together, knowing that the view of everyone matters and that they all have a share in the action. There is a growing sense of 'all being in it together' and a willingness to exchange views on school matters.

It is interesting that such a process of building up a shared working relationship lends itself well to collaborative research with an outside 'facilitator' or 'professional friend' working with those involved in the specific context. The facilitator can manage the considerable additional paperwork, which is often impossible to handle for busy staff, and so available time can be maximised. There is inevitably an emotional component which must be faced in changing relationships: being open to comment and possible criticism can cause apprehension. However, openness can be achieved; staff and parents do seem to grow in confidence as a result. The facilitator can act as support, at a practical level and as a sounding board for ideas, thus putting the project in context. The 'neutral' person can share enthusiasms, be a shoulder to cry on and help brainstorm alternatives. An enormous amount of staff and parent development was seen to take place as a result of working through a series of tasks together and this can only be of benefit to the children.

Although the staff and parents never used a term to describe the process they had lived through, their experiences measured up to the description of *Action Research* offered by Watt & Watt (1993):

It is pursued out of a desire or need to improve education knowledge and practices. It is accomplished through a recursive cycle of (1) identifying a problem area (2) studying it by gathering data and (3) reflecting on the data in order to make teaching decisions grounded in evidence rather than in hunches. Action is an integral part of the research and not an event which may – or may not – follow the study's completion. (Watt & Watt, 1993)

Each school began to address the issues in their own setting in ways they decided were appropriate for them. The emerging themes seemed to be restatements of the improved communication and personal contact of the first study; finding ways to ensure more constructive parent–teacher talk, better exchange of information, an emphasis on clearly focused meetings with individual or small group contact, rather than large open gatherings and better opportunities for staff development in relation to partnership with parents.

The Current Stage

The current phase of the study takes a much broader approach to the whole notion of education for primary age children, and rests on the fundamental belief that education does not occur at school but in the home and community as well. It shifts away from asking what schools can do by asking 'What is being done in an area to involve families in the education of their children' – with, of course, the supplementary question, 'What can be done to improve things?' The research recognises that although school is responsible for the formal aspects of education, home and community are essential influences on informal education, and on the extension of experiences initiated at school. In turn they influence school learning. The study examines the networks of support available to parents as they shoulder their prime (and legal) responsibility to educate their children, and it seeks to identify ways of improving the creation of a supportive total environment.

The research benefits from the addition of a social worker/researcher in addition to the teacher/researcher, and the team is supplemented by local field-workers; home-link staff, native minority language speakers and a native Gaelic speaking parent – all essential if families are to discuss in a relationship of trust and confidence. The focus of the research is particularly on families whom schools find 'hard to contact' for a number of reasons – those who are geographically spread, some who do not readily respond to school invitations, families who cannot or are not inclined to read questionnaire materials, who may not see the relevance of completing forms sent by the school, some of those whose first language may not be English or those for whom contact with school is seen mainly in a negative way.

The aim of the whole parent–teacher collaboration project was always to improve practice in the particular settings. However, the illumination for other schools is in demonstrating methods of eliciting the views of participants and in suggesting recording and monitoring procedures.

Such methodologies can contribute to the discussion of developing constructive relationships from existing baselines of experience. This chapter has offered examples of unique but appropriately evolved policy statements and ways forward, providing some insight into the complex process of building up relationships between parents and staff in their own settings. The study suggests that positive working relationships evolve over time. Each school, it seems, needs to address the issues themselves and together. However, some understanding of how others have proceeded, the range of approaches possible and some practical suggestions, are useful background for those determined to improve. Research into practice in specific settings stimulates discussions and encourages a sharing of ideas of what might be attempted elsewhere. It cannot, of course, offer advice about what will work in another school. That is for each school to grapple with for itself. It is often a hard process, as the schools involved in the research will testify, but it seems to be worth the effort.

7 Four Year Olds in Infant Classes in Small and Large Schools

ANGELA ANNING AND SUE BILLETT

Introduction

By law in the United Kingdom children are required to start school in the term following their fifth birthday. In reality most children enter the reception classes of primary schools at the age of four (Cleave & Brown, 1991a, b). Concern about the comparative under-achievement of summer-born infants in schools (Osborn & Milbank, 1987) has encouraged schools and local education authorities (LEAs) to adopt policies of starting all four year olds in the September of their fourth year, rather than operate a twice or three times a year entrance policy.

There is pressure from parents to get their children started in 'proper' school rather than 'play school', as many perceive nursery education. (See Bennett, 1987.) The anxiety of headteachers and classteachers to achieve good results in SATs (Standard Assessment Tasks) at seven puts pressure on early years teachers to start children on 'formal' schooling as early as possible. Finally, LMS (Local Management of Schools) constraints mean that even if headteachers are concerned about resourcing the education of four year olds in their reception classes, they are anxious not to lose 'clients' to a school down the road where four year olds are admitted early. More pupils means a bigger budget and more power.

Where nursery places are available, the knock-on effect to maintain buoyant school numbers results in the premature transfer of young four year olds, whose educational needs are better addressed in nurseries, into reception classes. The effect on nursery classes is the admission of large groups of young three year olds and an imbalance in the educational ethos of a legitimate 'pre-school' service catering for three to five year

98

olds. Overall the effect of these policy changes has been that although nursery education, mainly part time, has increased (a growth of 3.9% from 1989 to 1990) the increase in the number of under-fives in infant classes is greater (a growth of 7.2% from 1989 to 1990) (source DES, 1991b). Concern has been expressed by researchers about the appropriateness of the provision for the education of pre-fives in infant classes as the numbers of those admitted to schools has grown (Cleave & Brown, 1989, 1991a, b). At the same time policy makers have drawn up clear recommendations about the needs of four year olds (DES, 1986, 1989a, b, 1990). The clearest criteria for quality educational provision for four year olds are set out in the 1986 Report on Achievement in Primary Schools (DES, 1986). This report indicates that the most appropriate education provision for four year olds is a nursery class. If these young children are admitted to a reception class, a full-time ancillary worker should be employed if the number of four year olds exceeds six. (under statutory school age should be able to attend school pa Primary schools should be staffed on their expected summer ro 1986).

It was in such a context of concern and enquiry that the project described below took place. The features of small village school infant classes as the educational context for four year olds were a particular area of concern in the LEA where the research was commissioned; but the project was also concerned to contrast their educational experiences with children of similar ages in large urban classes within the same LEA context of policy and funding arrangements. This chapter can only report on some of the findings and details from the project, from the data produced. Further information on the findings is available from the authors.

Description of the Project

The LEA concerned had a significant number of both small village schools and large urban primary schools. Advisory staff wanted to identify and respond to the INSET (in-service training) needs of teachers who had four year olds in their classes.

However, it was a concern of the advisory staff that, previously, some courses for early years teachers had been based on assumptions of what was happening in the classrooms and what the teachers subsequently wanted as INSET. Teachers of four year olds felt that the courses offered had not addressed their concerns. The advisers wanted to involve teachers of four year olds in identification of key issues. There was also a belief that, in being involved in the project, by observing children in a range of situations, collecting and analysing data and working intensively with higher education (HE) researchers, teacher-researchers would develop and extend their skills as early years practitioners and could then share their insights with others via INSET.

GEST money was used to fund a grass roots project whereby classteachers, the primary advisers and HE staff involved in early years Initial Teacher Training and INSET worked together to investigate the educational experiences of four year olds in village and urban schools. The project was designed to collect and analyse information about what was happening to four year olds in infant classrooms, with the focus on small and large schools, and to collect information and opinions from classteachers, headteachers and parents. The insights gained would be used to generate a programme of in-service, and to inform LEA policy on the education of four year olds.

Methodology

The methodology for the project was designed and costed by a working group of two LEA advisers and two HE staff.

The data was collected by questionnaire and interviews adapted from those used in Bennett & Kell's (1989) study of four year olds in infant schools, with the authors' permission. The follow-up interviews included closed questions to check on the accuracy of factual data given in the questionnaire responses (such as admission policies, staffing details, resources), and open questions to examine more complex issues such as philosophy and curriculum provision. The important features of the enquiry were the problems identified in having four year olds in schools, and the resources and facilities felt to be necessary to meet their educational needs.

The Bennett & Kell study addressed the professionals' responses to the educational needs of four year olds. In the project described there was also a concern to record parents' views. There was no structured interview schedule for parents as the researchers wanted to establish a 'conversational' dialogue with them. However, agreed issues were raised. These included the ease of the child's transition to school, information received from schools, their views on appropriate education for four year olds, and any general concerns about their child's first year in school.

Four teachers were seconded by the authority, each for two days a week for six weeks. These became the teacher-researchers. They observed a sample of 32 paired four year olds, the youngest and oldest four year old on register, in 16 infant classes. They also interviewed the headteacher, class teacher and parents. The seconded teachers were selected by the LEA advisers on the basis of proven abilities as reception classteachers, recent personal professional development and their 'people' skills. Two of the teachers taught in small village schools and two in large urban schools. These teacher-researchers each observed in four schools similar to their own working contexts. The HE staff trained the teachers in the use of child observation techniques and data collection and monitored their progress. The teachers undertook a short pilot study to work through procedures and anticipate problems. The teachers were each allocated two further days' secondment to analyse data and draft reports. The HE researchers compiled final reports for LEA staff and the Education Committee. Eight small village schools and eight large urban schools were identified by the teacher researchers and LEA staff as representative of LEA contexts for small and large school provision for four year olds. The headteachers and staff were approached and agreed to take part in the project.

Questionnaire and interviews

The questionnaires were sent to the headteachers and classteachers to focus their thinking and ensure that factual data was available before the teacher-researchers visited the schools. In a pilot study, the teacher-researchers had found that the most successful strategy was to check the factual questions first, but to concentrate, in the interviews, on the more open-ended questions which many teachers had found difficult to articulate in their questionnaire responses.

Observations

The original intention was that the researchers would be trained to use the target child observational schedules designed for the Oxford Pre-School Project (Sylva, Roy & Painter, 1980). The teacher-researchers undertook a pilot study. They worked in pairs in a classroom and cross-checked observations. They found the schedule unsatisfactory for the purpose of gathering information about the curriculum offered to the four year olds in infant rather than nursery settings. At a further training session HE and teacher-researchers worked together to design an alternative observation instrument. It was decided to track each of the target children throughout one school day, using field notes to record contextual classroom data and to record the role of adults and peer group in the learning episodes observed. With such a small sample of children, comparisons made between children on the basis of systematic observation instruments would be of limited value. We wanted to look at the quality of the children's experiences rather than to monitor the activities in quantitative terms. However, a common format for the collection of field notes and contextual data would allow comparison across children and contexts.

School contexts

Small village schools

The eight schools were village primary schools ranging in size from 36 to 131 children, in old buildings, apart from one in relatively modern premises. They were in isolated parts of the county. Some children who lived a long distance from school travelled by taxi or school bus and these children had long days in school. In fact, some four year olds were spending eight hours a day away from home.

All the small schools had two intakes – in September and January – but they had individual arrangements for the length of time four year olds spent in school. For example, some schools had children attending for one session per week in the half term prior to their registered intake and then arranged for part-time attendance for the first few weeks. This allowed the children to have a gentle introduction to school routines and get to know staff and pupils. All the four year olds went into mixed age classes. Class sizes ranged from 8 to 26 pupils. Three class teachers were junior-secondary trained, four trained to teach five to eight year olds, and one trained for threes to eights. Experience ranged from 18 years as an infant teacher to a probationary teacher. Except for one teacher, the preferred age ranges for teaching were given as 'middle' or 'top' infants. Additional part-time teaching support varied from 0 to 17 hours a week. In most cases a part-time teacher took older children out of the classroom for additional help, leaving the classteacher to concentrate on the needs of the younger children. NTA (non-teaching assistant) help depended on the commitment of the headteacher to providing such support. Hours of NTA involvement varied, from one hour to full time – in this case to support a child with special educational needs. In one case the NTA was covering full time for clerical staff absence. All schools encouraged parental help, but this could be unreliable, and some concern was expressed in teacher interviews about parent helpers' 'gossip'. Children from local high schools were also encouraged to come as helpers and again could be as much a liability as a support.

Large urban schools

The eight schools were all close to a city, with locations varying from housing estate, to dormitory town and inner-city areas. School size varied from 165 to 375 pupils. Children either walked to school or were brought by car; none relied on school transport. The general tendency was for two intakes, in September and January. Children attended part time or full time depending on their age, but were all full time by the summer term. All the schools arranged for the four year olds to visit their classrooms once or twice in the term prior to starting school. Parents were invited to coffee mornings or evenings to meet staff. The age range in classes varied from a single four-plus age range to 4.1 to 5 years and class sizes ranged from 20 to 29. Some parallel year group teachers also responded to the questionnaire as well as those in classes where the four year olds were observed. Two of the teachers had been trained to teach four year olds, nine had been trained for the 5 to 9 or 5 to 11 age ranges, and the rest for 7 to 11. Experience of teaching reception classes varied from one to eight years. Six teachers claimed to prefer working with four and five year olds, and the rest preferred older infants or younger juniors. The average hours per week of NTA support in these classes was between four and eight. Most teachers used parent helpers in the classroom to compensate for lack of NTA support. Parents were used mostly in baking, sewing and art and craft supervision. A range of students – Trident, BTEC, NNEB or ITT – were also used as an 'extra pairs of hands'.

Comments

It was noted that the young children attending small schools generally had longer days than their contemporaries in urban schools. The village children often had to rely on school transport which extended the day and gave little flexibility to parents about taking and collecting their children.

Both the small and larger schools had similar intake patterns giving some flexibility over entry to school, although the village schools in general advocated a more gentle introduction to routines, procedures and curriculum when the children were at school.

There was strong support for the mixed-age classes in the village schools by the parents whereas parents of children in the urban schools preferred single-age classes. Perhaps this was a case of parents supporting the system their children were in as the only one they knew. Both small and large schools encouraged parental involvement in the classroom, but it was often more difficult, logistically, to have consistent help in the village schools.

Questionnaire and Interview Responses – Small and Large Schools

Philosophies

In the small schools, the headteachers emphasised the importance of schools as 'an extension of a caring home atmosphere'. The development of social skills, confidence and independence in the children were given as priorities. A wide variety of stimulating, meaningful activities, preferably practical/play based, were advocated as the preferred mode of learning. Adult interaction with the four year olds and space for physical movement were also stressed as vital. Numbers in reception classes should be kept low – ideally to 15 in mixed-age classes. In the large schools headteachers' views were sharply polarised. Those with nursery experience were adamant that nursery was the most appropriate education for four year olds, and anxious that they did not have the preschool resources, space or ratio of adult to pupils to provide for them. They were more aware of national concern about four year olds, citing HMI and NFER (National Foundation for Educational Research) evidence in one case. Other headteachers believed that four year olds were just part of a 'continuum' and were 'covered' by the general philosophy of 'their' school.

In the small schools the classteachers acknowledged the importance of a happy, secure learning environment and the need for children to have a gradual phased introduction to school. They emphasised the importance of providing practical, play-based activities; the key role of language development; the importance of access to adults 'so that time should not be wasted' and the need to foster social skills. In the large schools the classteachers also emphasised the need to 'create a cosy feeling' so that children are 'happy and excited about coming to school' and the importance of giving 'love, care and attention' so that the children will develop a feeling of worth and success at the start of their education. They emphasised the need to provide 'stimulating, first-hand learning experiences' for four year olds and access to play facilities, especially space and large apparatus, at regular intervals during the week.

Curriculum

In the small schools, the curriculum priorities were broad, and identified by classteachers as language – pre-reading and basic vocabulary; practical maths and basic number work; manipulative and physical skills; social and communication skills; and creative activities.

Interestingly, in their questionnaire responses, the small schools' teachers were more skills oriented than the large schools' teachers. The small schools' teachers emphasised the importance of sound basic skill work as the foundation for all later learning. Given the fact that four year olds were often in small numbers (two or three coming into the class) these young children had to be absorbed quickly into mixed age groupings and assigned parallel, but less complex, tasks than those for older children. The older children were seen as providing models of what to do. Play activities were available to four year olds, though constraints on space meant that role play, natural materials and construction play were often sited in classroom corridors or the school hall where adult interaction was necessarily limited. In the large schools, however, four year olds were usually taught as a separate group when they began school and were eased into general classroom organisation and activities. They were assigned 'appropriate' tasks related to the current topic. Early literacy and number skills were mostly introduced through commercial schemes on an individual basis. Role play areas (houses, shops etc.), sand and water and construction play were always available to the four year olds in the large schools. This was not the case in small schools.

Problems

The headteachers of both types of schools shared a common concern over the lack of funding for suitable resources for four year olds and also for the appropriate adult/pupil ratios in the classroom. At this time there was no LEA funding forthcoming for children until they reached the term in which they were five, and this was a cause for concern. Both small and large school headteachers identified inappropriate parental expectations for their four year olds as sometimes being a problem. One headteacher said: 'We try to explain to parents that they shouldn't expect their youngsters to be reading War and Peace by the end of the first half term.'

It is not unexpected that the problems identified by classteachers were classroom based and different in kind from the headteachers' problems. There was also a commonality of concern among the classteachers across school types. The most significant problem for classteachers was lack of trained adult help in the classrooms to support the learning of the four year olds and to take on some of the 'house-keeping' tasks. The teachers felt acutely that they lacked the time to talk with and listen to the youngest children. They were also concerned that they did not have enough play-based equipment and resources, particularly in the small schools where capitation was so limited. Of particular interest was that classteachers generally were concerned about lack of outdoor play time, space and equipment.

The small school headteachers who had mixed-age classes felt that the family groupings could alleviate potential problems, particularly as the older children were encouraged to help settle in the new children. A problem associated with mixed age classes was that classteachers sometimes had less time to devote to the younger children and the older children were often devoting their own 'learning time' to helping the younger ones.

In the large schools, the teachers' main concern was that the school routines – assemblies, hymn practices, playtime and lunch-time arrangements – were generally inappropriate for four year olds. Teachers in the large schools, in common with their headteachers, were concerned about national pressures for accountability, and pressure to return to the three Rs and basics. In the small schools the needs of the local community figured more prominently in teachers' interviews and they seemed more sheltered from national pressures.

Parents' views

There was general agreement from parents in both samples that preschool liaison and admission arrangements had been satisfactory. They commented that some sort of preschool provision – play group, nursery or toddlers' group – was important as a prerequisite for a successful start to school. They spoke highly of their children's teachers.

There were some interesting differences in parents' responses from the two groups of schools. Parents from large schools wanted to know more about what their children were doing at school, particularly in relation to reading. Most parents from large schools believed that their children would make most school progress by early entry to a reception class. They were not keen on vertically grouped classes. Two highly articulate parents in the large school sample stood out from all the others. They were aware of the importance of structured play and the learning needs of under-fives. They had each visited several schools before selecting one for their child. In general, parents from large schools chose schools by 'local reputation' and their proximity to home.

Parents of children in the small schools felt that they were already well-informed about what their children were doing in school. These parents expressed pride in the village schools and felt that both the institutions themselves and the teachers were important to the local community life. Parents from the small schools liked the mixed-age-range classes. They felt that mixed-age classes benefited the children both academically and socially. However, they were worried about the lack of space, both indoors and outdoors, and lack of resources for the children. This was a concern that they shared with the teachers. Two parents expressed concern that the National Curriculum testing at seven would place too much emphasis on formal schooling for four year olds.

Observations in Schools

Both the youngest and oldest four year olds in each of the 16 classes were observed for a day in their classrooms, including playtime and lunch-time. The teacher-researchers took notes of classroom layouts, the space, equipment and resources, the organisational patterns of the day's activities and adults available to the children. They recorded the curriculum experienced by the children and the roles of adults and peer group in their activities. This data was then examined in relation to stated philosophies and preferred curriculum models offered via the questionnaires and interviews with class teachers.

Some contextual features

In all the classrooms teachers were having to improvise to overcome lack of space for active, play-based learning for the four year olds despite the emphasis that headteachers and classteachers had placed on its importance at interview. In the small schools the hall space was sometimes used for teaching activities for periods of the day. In the large schools five of the eight classes shared play areas between classrooms in order to maximise space. Access to supervised outdoor play was a problem in all schools. One of the small schools had a particularly dangerous sloping and slippery small playground. Only two of the large school classrooms had direct access to outdoor play areas. It was noticeable that in the small schools older children took an active role in supervising the four year olds at playtimes. One of the large schools had an ambitious and very successful programme to enhance the quality of play behaviours at playtime. All the classrooms were short of basic storage space and had to 'make do'. In three of the large schools, windows were too high for both adults and children to see outside, and this gave an enclosed feeling. All the schools were equipped with basic play resources, though with small sums available for capitation, staff in small schools complained that it was difficult to replace broken items or to invest in large-scale play equipment. This was also influenced by the proportionally small numbers of younger children who would have regular access to the equipment; spending priorities were clearly elsewhere.

The four year olds in both small and large schools were grouped by age and/or ability for formal, seat-based work, and free choice/friendship groups for 'play' or practical work. This was largely to 'keep the peace' as children moved from formal to what was seen as 'keeping them busy/occupied' tasks. In general, where children were seated in groups for language, mathematics or science work, they worked on individual but parallel tasks. It was noticeable that any collaborative behaviour observed was limited to pairs of children on practical or play-based activities. The usual patterns of boy only and girl only preferences of both activity and friends and rejections of those trying to 'intrude' upon these patterns were observed. Observations revealed that boys favoured active, construction, natural materials activities; girls favoured table-top activities, role play and art and craft activities.

Curriculum Experienced

Tables 7.1 and 7.2 summarise from the field notes some of the curricula experienced by the youngest and oldest four year olds in four small and four large school classrooms. They show similar patterns of routine and teacher–pupil activity across the two types of schools. In each setting opportunities are provided for first-hand experiences for children along with teacher-determined tasks and child-determined activities. Overall, observers' comments suggest potential for purposeful and motivated action were sufficient and appropriate. However, looking in more detail at the experiences of individual children offers a somewhat different and less reassuring perspective.

The extensive field notes from which the summaries were taken (Tables 7.1 and 7.2) gave insights into the particular behaviours and learning experiences of each child observed. The following extracts from small and large schools, reveal a somewhat desultory pattern of curricular experience and pupil responses.

In Small School B, Jane's episode at 10.24 involved her Ginn mathematics book. Observational notes offered the following detail:

> Teacher tells her to get the number book and asks her how many things are in the picture on the page. She counts 1, 2, 3. Teacher tells her to put rings round the correct number next to the pictures. She starts to count herself, but loses concentration and chews her pencil. Says to the boy next to her, 'I can count these'. He counts the stars too. She continues drawing rings round correct numbers without enthusiasm.

In Small School C at 10.00 Richard's episode in the Shop Play is described further in observational notes:

Table 7.1 Small schools – Summary of child observations

A (Mixed infants) Tom*(Y) Daisy**(O)	B (Mixed infants) Anna*(Y) Jane**(O)	C (Mixed infants) Jack*(Y) Richard**(O)	D (Mixed Infants) Terry*(Y) Rachel**(O)
8.55–9.30* Mat activities flash cards, interest cards *Language Imaginative* 9.50** Dot writing, joking, free writing, laughing (I) (T) *Language* Much spasmodic conversation with the teacher who encouraged development of work 10.30* Free choice of reading book (I) *Wandering* 11.00* Collecting numbers sets (C) (T) *Maths* 11.30** Big/little hand sizes, lots of discussion (C) (T) *Maths* 11.50** Singing and pantomime discussion (C) (T) *Music Drama* 1.00 pm** School assembly (S) (T) *Procedural* (S) (T) Mat-story/photos** *Language* Child is tired 1.40** Painting *Art/Craft* Leading on from discussion with photographs	8.55–9.45* Mat activities counting, number rhymes, singing, registration (C) (T) *Maths/Music/Procedural* 10.00–10.24** (I) Colouring and gazing, fiddling with pencil. Child appeared unwilling to proceed with this activity *Pencil Play* 10.24** Number book (I) (GIN–scheme) *Maths* 11.00* Snack (drink and biscuit) *Procedural* (C) 11.20–12.00 PE in Hall – lengthy (C) (T) *PE* 1.15 pm** Arrival of new infants. Class nursery, rhymes on the mat (C) (T) *Language/Music* 1.30* Cutting & sticking *Art and Craft* (G) 2.05** Shop *Role Play* (G)	8.55* Book corner exchange of news (C) *Procedural* 9.15* School assembly (S) *Procedural* 10.00** Shop, with teacher. Structured shop play (I) *Maths* 10.10** Home Corner (G) *Role-Play/Domestic* 10.20** Sand Matching game (I) (G) *Imaginative Maths* 11.00* Drawing Christmas Stockings (I) *Art/Craft* 11.30* Counts objects in stocking, shows teacher (I) *Maths* 1.15 pm** Drawing a gingerbread man collage (I) *Art/Craft* Activity continues until 2.00 pm 2.00* Child holds and examines guinea-pig; reads a book about guinea pigs *Science/Language* (I) 2.30* Tidying up *Procedural* (G)	9.00* Maths activities sorting/ matching (G) *Maths* 9.15* Reads to teacher (I) *Language* 9.20* Shape jigsaw clixi pegs *Manipulative Maths Construction* (I) 9.30** Discussion on Christmas decorations, preparation for helicopter visit *Language* 10.00** Sentence Maker (Breakthrough of Literacy) (G) *Language* 10.10** GIN–scheme number books, colours/shapes (I) *Maths* 11.00* Lego Construction (G) 11.20* Blocks *Construction/Social Interaction* (G) 1.00* Helicopter arrival – stimulus *Science/Language* (C) 1.30** Class discussion about helicopter *Language* (C) 1.45** Christmas mobiles/shapes *Art/Craft Maths* (I)

Table 7.1 *continued*

Large, well equipped classroom. Good variety of activities. At least two adults present at all times. (Part-time teacher and voluntary help) Children occupied at all times. This appeared too much for one child who was very tired in the afternoon. Vigilant teacher.	Morning emphasis on 3Rs except for PE. 3Rs work formal. Class mat activities occupy much time. Little variety of stimulating experience.	Relaxed, contented atmosphere. Both four year olds appeared to be involved in purposeful tasks at the right level.	Very good variety of stimulus provided. Helicopter visit a great success – children animated and intensively involved. Excellent atmosphere. Home/school co-operation much in evidence.

Key:

(S)	School	(O)	Oldest	(P)	Parent helper present
(C)	Class	(Y)	Youngest	(St)	Student present
(G)	Group	(T)	Teacher present		
(I)	Individual	(NTA)	Non-teaching assistant present		

Table 7.2 Large schools – Summary of child observations

A (Reception) Sally*(Y) Harry**(O)	B (Reception/Middle) Timothy*(Y) Flora**(O)	C (Reception) Christian*(Y) Marcus**(O)	D (Reception) Andrew*(Y) Naomi**(O)
Rehearsal 9.00–11.15 Infant classes to a dress rehearsal for Joseph and his Technicolor Dreamcoat (S)	*Natural Materials* 9.45* Sand – with two boys. Mountains and tunnels. Boisterous play 10.09 Told to wash. Parent sweeps up sand from floor (G)	*Maths* 9.10** Recapping work done (C) on cylinders/cubes – new cuboids 9.20** Assigned to construct straw + pipe cleaners with 5 ch. to make a cuboid. (G). Leads and succeeds	*Construction* 9.40* Playing independently with plastic construction bricks (I) 9.50 Takes pieces from two girls – model – argument – he wins. Taunts them about their 'inferior' model, threatens to smash theirs
Playtime 11.15** Playing with two boys in playground – coat around shoulders – laughter and horsing around (I)	*Procedural* 10.51** Mat time class discussion about bird's egg	9.32 Show to teacher next door teacher + parent helper 9.40 Tackles making a cylinder rolling pipe cleaners around toilet roll middle	9.59 Teacher sends two boys to replace girls in construction area (G) 10.00 After initial boisterous play, three boys work together
Science 11.30** Weather chart on mat in classroom (C). Hangs around at back – standing sucking thumb. No responses	*Art/Craft* 10.55 Chooses – 2 craft table. Teacher demonstrates zig-zag snake, helps her complete task (G)	10.55** After playtime, follows up drawing with writing (I). Teacher helps. Also supports his drawing of the wolf which is in difficulties	10.08 After dispute he throws down a plank. Teacher intervenes – tells them to put bricks away 10.09 Reluctantly lines up for assembly
PE 11.40** Choosing time. Bats and balls with boys (G)	11.16** Goes to hang up apron – goes to carpet to play with potato men (I) 11.20** Writes letter in Post Office	11.05 Interrupted to look to orange plant – colour table – wide class attention	*Language* 9.00** Teacher reads Jack and The Beanstalk. Listens (C)
Language 11.45** Told to come and do some words. Flash cards. Team game (G)	1.30 *Hymn Practice* (S)	*Language* 9.30* Drawing part of Three Little Pigs story, told by teacher, acted with puppets day before (G)	9.20 Yawns. Sent to writing table by teacher (G). Teacher helps her write sentence; corrects letter size, pencil grip
Wanders 11.55** Wanders – polydron, plasticine (I)	*Procedural* 2.00 Mat time – assigning tasks (C) 2.03** Chooses house corner, three girls, going to bed' (G). Dressing up. Taking the dog for a walk	*Art/Craft* 11.23** Goes across to make viewer cylinder – with his mother (parent helper today)	9.32 Told to draw picture 9.34 Told to go and choose
Maths Watches group with student 12.00** Joins next game (G)	*Wandering* 2.16** Wanders around classroom – picks up and plays with plasticine (I)		*Table Toys* 9.36** Jigsaws and small blocks (I). Joined by a friend – girl 9.39 Work together
Procedural 1.30* Mat time, finishing off work but S. can choose			

Table 7.2 *continued*

Maths
* Matching game – 2gs + 16 (G). Teacher intervenes when argument starts
1.44 Changes to a counting game. Three children
1.53 Tidy up time
PE
1.55* Changes on mat
2.00 Music and involvement in hall (C)
2.30 Playtime
Story
3.00 Story time

Three parallel reception areas
Large L shaped room. Light from large windows. Well equipped
Access to patio area in good weather
Children purposefully employed – quiet, relaxed atmosphere
Well-equipped playground and grassed area for playtimes

2.25 As they tidy she and friend giggle and try on hats (G). Plays telephones
Story
2.30 Playtime
3.00 Story time (C)

Three parallel reception. Middle three classroom areas with team teaching – small rooms.
Age specific groups in morning mixed in afternoons
Large play area from cloakroom supervised by parents
Outdoor play for groups of children supervised by NTA
Small grassy area with logs and trees in playground
Toilets out of sight of teacher

Maths
1.39** Mat time – Teacher explains task – sets of circles – colour differential in circles (C). Teacher questions and demonstrates display work on white board
1.45** Nominated by teacher to work with five children on colour patterns worksheet (G). Works with sporadic attention – occasional teacher prompts; very interested in felt tips and stapler rather than task
Maths
1.20* Working on colouring (G) cubes in workbook. Tunes in to painting table discussion of colour mixing and experiments with crayons
1.29 Turns to watch children with play dough
1.38 Watches children in water
1.42 Completes task and shows teacher pointing out his mistakes – done on purpose? Asks to go to water but diverted to play dough
Art/Craft
1.45* Rolls out dough – uses cutter (I)
Natural Materials
1.50* Shows shapes to teacher. Elects to go to water

Procedural
1.10 Assigned tasks from mat time (C)
Art/Craft
1.12 Tracing (I)
1.15 Crayoning (I)
Maths
1.26** Called across by teacher to join largest and shortest sorting activity – ribbons – making sets. She succeeds
1.40 Teacher instructs them to draw snake – then a shorter one – correct response
Language
1.25* Task is to complete worksheet (I) – six words to write and join to correct picture. He has to be summoned by teacher from construction area
1.31* Letter shapes – with teacher practising 'a' – called across
1.37 Parent helps him complete worksheet. Colours carelessly standing up
1.41 Asks to go back to 'village' to play
Construction
1.44* With other boy tips out 'village' sets and plays. Boisterous. Rejects girl who tries to join. Lots of arguments
1.50 Sent by teacher to parent helper for letter information. Breaks other boys model as parting gesture

Table 7.2 *continued*

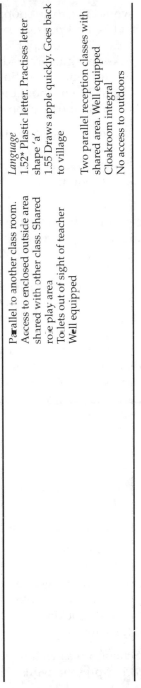

Parallel to another class room. Access to enclosed outside area shared with other class. Shared role play area. Toilets out of sight of teacher. Well equipped

Language
1.52* Plastic letter. Practises letter shape 'a'
1.55 Draws apple quickly. Goes back to village

Two parallel reception classes with shared area. Well equipped
Cloakroom integral
No access to outdoors

Key: (S) School
(C) Class
(I) Individual
(G) Group

Teacher asks Richard if he would like to go shopping. Richard goes into the home corner to collect a bag and purse. Teacher asks him what he would like to buy. He chooses a lolly for 2p. He gives 2p to the teacher and takes it to a table. He picks up a gingerbread man and joins a queue for the teacher's attention. He counts the buttons, and fingers the decorations. The teacher talks with him about the gingerbread man, she asks him what he would like to do and he chooses the sand.

In Large School D, Andrew's letter formation activity at 1.52 reveals an experience perhaps concerned more with the 'mechanics' of the task, than with learning. It also poses questions about the role parent helpers can have if they lack information about the educational purposes of an activity:

Parent helper gets Andrew to run his finger over the plastic letter 'a' tray. 'Now you're going to have a go at writing "a".' Andrew runs his finger over the 'a' shape again. 'What begins with "a"?' 'Andrew.' 'Yes, it does, and so does apple. We're going to draw apple. Let's write it first.' Andrew picks up a pencil. 'Start at the top.' Andrew has problems. 'No, watch the ball again.' She puts the ball on the tray and Andrew watches it run. 'I know which way.' 'No, not like that, at the top, like the ball. Put your pencil on the dot.' She guides his hand. He tried hard, but he has real problems with 'a'. He copies the other letters in apple. Some correct, others not. Parent does not intervene. 'Can you draw an apple?' Quickly draws an apple and colours all over with a red crayon. He stands up and moves back towards the block play. 'Put your work in your tray, Andrew.' Ignores parent and goes to play with the 'village' bricks.

It is worth recalling that both small and large schools reported how much they valued parental involvement, but other research (Bennett & Kell, 1989) indicate the importance of helpers being well briefed in infant classrooms.

In Large School B Flora's 'letter' writing at 11.20 is described as:

Goes to the Post Office, collects paper to 'write' a letter. Moves chair around to sit next to a friend. Draws with a blue felt pen for a few seconds. After exchange with her friend goes across to teacher and asks for an envelope. Once letter is finished she folds the paper and puts it in the envelope. Cannot cope with sticking the flap down. Tucks it in instead. Tidying up time. She helps.

A child like Flora in Large School B was well motivated to persevere on seat-based tasks with the teacher present, whilst Timothy (see Table 7.2), also highly self motivated, selected tasks where he could 'do his own thing' and rushed through teacher-directed, seat-based tasks in order to get back to his self-chosen learning activities as quickly as possible. Observational detail revealed Flora building on a variety of skills during the day; Timothy practised manipulative play behaviour and skills mainly with other boys. The extent to which these children benefited from the curriculum on offer seemed to rely as much on their already established skills as it did on teacher structure and intervention.

These extracts, along with Tables 7.1 and 7.2 offer only a small part of the extensive observational data gathered on the curriculum experienced and its context. However, the extracts and interpretations (above) go some way towards illustrating how, in both large and small schools, the potential for teacher-directed activities to require minimal concentration and to evoke low levels of motivation in children, was clearly evident. Parent helpers may fare no better. In both settings, there was little adult intervention in children's free choice times.

The observational evidence indicated that the *quality* of educational experiences offered to the four year olds in both the large and the small schools depended on the expertise of the classteacher in organising and resourcing the day. It also depended on the availability of other trained adults in supporting children's learning and on the attitude/maturity of the children in using their own time constructively. Teacher or other trained adult interventions could have helped children to achieve higher levels of maturity.

The variations in teacher expertise and children's behaviours ranged across small and large school contexts equally. One significant difference was that in small schools four year olds spent longer sitting with whole class groups for discussion on topics, stories, etc. This was simply a management of time issue, with one teacher and a small but wide age-range class to manage. A positive finding for small schools was that the children appeared to go about their tasks in a more unhurried and relaxed way. Playtimes where the 'family' atmosphere provided security were less stressful than for children thrown into the hurly burly of large, hectic urban playgrounds.

On conclusion of the research, the teacher-researchers maintained that they had benefited from the opportunities for gathering and analysing the detailed field notes in that this knowledge could inform and illuminate their subsequent INSET provision as well as their own practice. Tracking individual children and examining the data in the context of breadth and balance of curricular experience, over a day, had revealed the often low level of demand of the child's activities with clear implications for learning opportunities lost. The implications for planning and provision was something they subsequently addressed with their colleagues, via INSET provision.

Discussion

The project highlighted a range of issues general to research in schools and some specific to the experiences of four year olds in infant classes in small and large schools. There appears to be real potential for research which involves LEA, HE and school collaboration. However, in the current climate of financial devolution from LEA to schools, there are concerns about how such initiatives might now be fostered.

The general issues include:

(1) It was an insightful decision of the LEA primary advisory teacher to use GEST funding to investigate the in-service needs of a particular group of teachers through a teacher as researcher approach. It was significant that the headteachers and class teachers spoke frankly to the teacher-researchers instead of offering a defensive stance perhaps because they felt that they were dealing with fellow professionals with an evident understanding of the challenges of educating four year olds. All the teacher-researchers noted that the project experience had significantly affected their own classroom practice. They had also become more reflective and analytical in their work with very young children. The declining opportunities for LEAs to continue acting in this capacity seem highly regrettable.

(2) It was the teacher-researchers who challenged the method of collecting data within the original research design. They found that the systematic coding observation schedule restricted the kind of data they felt would be useful in assessing the quality of educational experiences in which their colleagues would be most interested. They also learned how difficult it was to analyse and draw inferences from data collected in a less structured way.

(3) An important feature of the project was the follow-up meetings for headteachers and class teachers organised and fronted by the teacher-researchers. With great sensitivity and professionalism they explained what the data had revealed about the educational experiences of the four year olds in the schools. They shared insights, provoked frank and open discussion without any sense of them (the researchers) and us (the researched) polarisation. This sense of shared responsibility had important consequences for

shaping their professional pressure on LEAs to modify policies for provision for four year olds.

(4) The meetings gave all those involved the opportunity to discuss in-service needs of teachers confronting some of the difficulties raised and had a direct bearing on identifying INSET priorities.

Issues specific to the project:

(1) The most significant effect of the project for the schools was that, after the report had been summarised for the Education Committee, the LEA changed its policy and agreed to fund four year olds in schools and other related initiatives. This represented a considerable financial commitment and had clear implications for the resourcing difficulties for educating four year olds in an appropriate way that headteachers and classteachers had identified. There was more funding given for NNEB and NTA support for four year olds in small village schools and a 'peripatetic' pre-school was funded to allow access to some nursery education for children living in isolated, rural areas.

(2) With threats to the survival of small village schools, the project evidence reflected strong community commitment to their schools. Evidence from the project made it clear that the quality of educational experiences depended not on school size but on appropriate teacher expertise and on headteacher commitment to resourcing the educational needs of young children. Common to both small and large schools were the pressing needs for capitation to buy resources and increased staffing budgets to pay for teaching assistants. Both these needs were recognised and addressed by the subsequent LEA policy changes.

(3) It was evident that parents in both urban and rural settings were very supportive of the teachers of their four year olds. They argued strongly for appropriate support for them, both with resources and staffing.

(4) Sadly, although INSET needs for the teachers of four year olds were clearly defined by the teacher-researchers and recommendations made in the final report, LEA cutbacks resulted in the loss of a designated early years adviser. A network of teachers has since set up self-help groups to co-ordinate early years issues with a series of half-day authority-wide conferences and related regional meetings in order to sustain an in-service programme. More recently the LEA has responded to the repeated demands of early childhood staff for professional support and has made two new appointments of advisory staff with early years expertise

8 From Home to School – Do Children Preserve their Counting Skills?

ANN MACNAMARA

It is not immediately obvious that many children of three and four years of age have well-developed mathematical skills even before they start school. The ability to recognise these skills would enable the nursery and infant teacher to build on them. Failure to do this has two results. First, the child has to relearn something that they can already do – clearly a waste of effort. Secondly, the child may believe that these skills are not valued in the school environment, which could serve to alienate the child by suggesting a divide between home and school. In its ultimate form, this attitude reappears in the later years of the secondary school in the commonly held notion that mathematics is important, that it is done in school but that it does not really affect everyday life as it is separate from it. It is a school skill.

Research by MacNamara (1990) focusing on a specific mathematical ability, supported this notion. This research involved working with 90 children aged four plus to six plus years of age from nursery and infant classes in two schools in the north of England. These children were asked to undertake a simple task as a precursor to some further work on addition (which is not reported here). It was during this research that evidence of these children's abilities and their beliefs about school mathematics began to emerge. In order to set the context of the argument, the theoretical background and the initial experiments will be described in some detail.

Theoretical Perspectives

The research reported here asked children to look at a computer screen displaying sheep for a brief moment and to say how many there were. This ability, to say how many there are in a group without counting, is known as 'subitising'. It was first described by Jevons in 1871 although the first rigorous experiments did not take place until Taves' (1941) work on adults' ability to recognise the number of 'blips' on a radar screen as part of World War Two research. This ability is not limited to visual perception but is also found in the recognition of a number of sounds heard and is also found in general memory span.

There appears to be two distinct mechanisms for deciding how many objects there are at a glance; the first is subitising and the second is estimating. The boundary between the two occurs with adults at about seven objects. Kaufmann *et al.* (1949) found a statistical difference in the time taken between estimating for more than six objects and subitising for six or less objects. Subitising was more accurate, more rapid and done with more confidence.

Klahr (1973), working with adults, also found that the time taken depended upon the number of objects in the group. When the group size was five or less, the relationship between the reaction time, measured in milliseconds (RT) and the number of objects in the group (n), was given by:

$$RT = 421 + 66n$$

Thus reaction time was a function of the size of the set and not a constant as had first been thought. This had implications for the model proposed to explain the results. An initial suggestion was that a group of objects was labelled with its numerosity – its size – in much the same way that it would be labelled with its colour. This would have led to a fixed time for recognition of all small groups of objects and not to a situation where the reaction time depended upon the size of the set of objects. Klahr's work implied that there was a different mechanism at work as the length of time taken did increase, although slowly, as the size of the set grew.

Klahr & Wallace (1976) suggested that the very small amount of extra time taken was necessary as the person matched the perceived set with the corresponding set held in long-term visual memory. A set of five would take longer than a set of three as more time would be needed to match the extra two items. Klahr & Wallace (1976) suggested that for sets of more than five objects, some other mechanism such as counting or estimating was used. This work was all undertaken with adults and there was no evidence to suggest whether the ability to subitise came before or after the ability to count. Most of this work depended upon the accurate measurement of the length of time that it took for the subject to answer the 'How Many?' question accurately.

Subitising in Babies

Work with very young babies (Antell & Keating, 1983; Starkey & Cooper, 1980) suggested that this ability is found before children learn to count. The babies' ages ranged from a few days to a few weeks old; the test of whether they could recognise a difference was if they spent more time looking at a picture if the number of objects in it was the only thing that changed. It appeared that the babies did this with groups of objects up to three. In this case, the conclusions could only be concerned with whether the babies could recognise whether something was the same or different if the numerosity was changed.

Subitising in Children

Studies of young children's abilities to subitise (Schaeffer, Eggleston & Scott 1974; Chinlund, 1988) showed that young children aged two years to five years could correctly label small sets. However, in both these pieces of research the children were allowed up to four seconds to report on their findings and, although instructed not to count, it is difficult to see how the researchers could be certain that the children were not counting silently. Accordingly, it was decided that children in the study reported here must not be given the opportunity to count the objects but that the research must be constructed so that the children had to make a decision without the time to count.

Experimental Design

The children

The children who took part in this study came from the nursery and two parallel infant classes of one school and Class One and Class Two of another school. At the beginning of the study, the children's ages ranged from four plus to six plus years of age. The staff were very welcoming; the researcher had taught in both schools which made liaison with individual members of staff relatively easy and informal. Work was done with individual children by withdrawing them from their class at times convenient to the class teacher. In most cases, the computers were situated outside the classrooms in the communal areas and the children had to work with the distractions of normal school activities. Almost all the children in one school had been taught by the researcher and some of the older ones in the other school. They, and their teachers, were used to working with other adults.

All the children from both schools took part in the exercise. One child's results were not used; he has cerebral palsy and, though he enjoyed working with the program, he did so with help from his nursery nurse. Two children showed some signs of anxiety about the exercise despite gentle encouragement; they were allowed to do as much as they chose and then they returned to class. These incomplete results were not used. The numbers of children in each age group are shown in Table 8.1:

Table 8.1 Population structure

Age	Boys	Girls
4+	10	9
5+	28	13
6+	23	7
Totals	61	29

Total number of children involved = 90

The sample was heavily weighted in terms of the numbers of boys participating; as the intention of the research was to find children who were accurate subitisers, this was not, at this stage, considered significant. The intention was to use the program with the largest number of children available. One result of this, however, is to make it very difficult to draw conclusions based on gender. Future work will consider more evenly balanced groups. Only two of the children were second language speakers; their first languages were French and German.

In order to assess whether children could subitise, it was decided to use a limited time exposure of a variably sized group of randomly arranged objects and assess subitising ability in terms of accuracy of response. A commercial computer program was used (I-Spy by Holmes McDougall) which presented a number of sheep on the screen in random formation for variable lengths of time. The nature of the program meant that the format of the presentation could not be varied and, in this part of the research, the presentation was in random form. There is evidence that spatial arrangement has some influence on the ability to recognise set size (Beckwith & Restle, 1966; Potter & Levy, 1968), but this was not a variable.

Decisions about the length of time that the sheep were to stay on the screen were limited, to a certain extent, by the availability of choices in the computer program. Research on visual perception (Sedgwick, 1982) refers to saccadic eye movements which change the point of fixation of the eye three or four times a second. This implies that the exposure of a stimulus for between 250 mseconds and 330 mseconds would enable it to be seen 'at a glance' without any eye movement. Klahr & Wallace (1976) measured the time taken to report set size without eye movement by filming the eye during an experiment. They found that the mean reaction time for one eye fixation varied from 342 mseconds to just over 400 mseconds for set sizes from one to four. This is slightly longer than the length of time that the eye stays still, but not long enough for the eye to move from one item in the display to another which would be expected if counting were taking place. The computer program allowed the minimum exposure time to be 500 mseconds and this was the time used.

The program was designed to show ten groups of sheep in random order with each group requiring a response from the child. The display appeared on the screen, then, when it had gone, the numerals 1, 2, 3, 4 and 5 appeared in a line at the bottom of the screen. An arrow moved continuously across the screen underneath these numbers. The child was told to press the space bar when it was under the correct number. If this was done, the machine made a 'ting' and moved on to the next display. If the child made a mistake, the machine noise was less positive – rather more of a grunt – and the child was shown the same display again. Further mistakes resulted in the machine showing the display in a static form with the number beside it. The results used in this research were taken from first attempts only.

The children were told that they could press the bar themselves if they wished or the researcher would do it for them. They did not have to be able to recognise the numeral as they could just say how many there were. The interest of the researcher was in the ability of the children to recognise and label correctly the groups of sheep.

It was decided to limit the maximum number of sheep to five as this was the maximum size of the set most likely to be subitised. In a typical session, two sheep appeared twice; three sheep appeared twice; four sheep appeared three times and five sheep appeared three times. Accuracy of response was the dependent variable and thus considered the guide to whether or not the child was subitising.

Results

Although most of the children had more than one turn with the program – it was very popular – all the results were from their first attempt so there was no element of practice in the performance. The use of the computer eliminated observer bias or influence as there were no subjective judgements made, just the recording of whether the child had answered the question correctly. In the interpretation of the results, there has been no allowance made for chance as it was thought that this would be spread evenly across all cases. There did not appear to be much guessing made by the children; most of the replies were made instantaneously in a firm, decisive manner. A record of the children's responses was made and an analysis of the number and type of error carried out.

Number of errors

Table 8.2 Error scores on zero, one, two, three and four numbers across the age range

	Errors on: Zero numbers	One number	Two numbers	Three numbers	Four numbers
Age 4+					
Boys n = 10	0% (0)	40% (4)	40% (4)	20% (2)	0% (0)
Girls n = 9	11% (1)	11% (1)	44% (4)	22% (2)	11% (1)
% of total n = 19	5% (1)	26% (5)	42% (8)	21% (4)	5% (1)
Age 5+					
Boys n = 28	18% (5)	43% (12)	29% (8)	7% (2)	4% (1)
Girls n = 13	15% (2)	46% (6)	23% (3)	8% (1)	8% (1)
% of total n = 41	17% (7)	44% (18)	27% (11)	13% (3)	5% (2)
Age 6+					
Boys n = 23	48% (11)	35% (8)	17% (4)	0% (0)	0% (0)
Girls n = 7	29% (2)	43% (3)	29% (2)	0% (0)	0% (0)
% of total n = 30	45% (13)	37% (11)	20% (6)	0% (0)	0% (0)

Table 8.2 shows the percentage of errors that were made and on how many numbers; the figures in parentheses are the raw scores.

Twenty-one of the 90 children made no mistakes at all on the program; a further 34 made mistakes on only one number; and so, overall, 55 of the 90 children made errors on one number or none. Of the errors that were made, only 5% of the total errors that the four year olds made were more than one away from the correct answer; as were 6% of the errors that the five year olds made and only 3% of the errors that the six year olds made.

Overall, six year old children were more accurate than five year old children, who were more accurate than four year old children. There did not appear to be any gender bias although the sample of children was weighted in the direction of boys, especially with the five and six year olds. In all cases, errors were more common with set sizes of four or five objects. The older children made proportionally more errors on groups of five than on the smaller set sizes.

Extension of the Research

The younger children were in the nursery classes of the two schools; the older children in reception or vertically grouped infant classes. The purpose of the study was to find a group of children who were 'good' subitisers to take part in some further research on addition. However, as the research took place over the spring and summer terms, there was an additional opportunity to follow up some children who had moved at Easter from a nursery class to a reception class.

A small group of these children were offered the opportunity to repeat the experiment with the sheep program during the first half of their term in the reception class. They were very enthusiastic about doing this. The five children who participated in this were those who expressed an interest in so doing.

The results were surprising. Some of the children who had been the most accurate subitisers in the earlier research showed no evidence of the ability and complained bitterly that the sheep were not displayed on the screen long enough for them to count them. When it was suggested that they should just say how many there were as they had done before, they were not able to do this. One of the boys, who had made no mistakes at all while in the nursery, became quite distressed and said: 'I can't count them because I can't see them to count them'cos it makes them go away too soon.' He then tried to use his fingers on the screen to touch each one as he chanted the counting numbers. The researcher suggested that he should just say how many there were as he had done previously, but he insisted, saying that this was the way that they had to do it now they were in the reception class.

The ability to subitise was apparent in children aged five plus and six plus who were already in reception classes and many had performed very well on the sheep recognition task. The behaviour described above was from a few children in particular circumstances who were recently admitted to the reception class from the nursery and so were still finding their way in terms of the cognitive and social demands of the classroom situation. It may be that, at this particular time, the social constraints and the desire to please the class teacher led the children to behave in a way in which they thought that they should.

Discussion

There appear to be two interrelated issues. The first is the role of subitising in the development of early mathematical skills and the second is on the effect of school mathematics teaching on the abilities that children bring with them from home and the nursery class.

Role of subitising in the development of mathematical skills

The debate about whether subitising precedes or follows counting is not resolved. One view is that the child recognises the whole group and then labels it with a number word, without necessarily understanding that it is composed of separate parts. On the other hand, there is some evidence (Gelman, 1977) that recognition of number patterns develops after practice in counting objects. It is clear that the children needed to know the number names to offer them as labels. Whether they needed the ability to count accurately is another matter.

There are possibly important implications for the development of conservation skills. If a child can label a group of objects with its correct set size, regardless of the disposition of the objects, there is the implication that the child can conserve that particular group size. This was evident with children of four plus, who in Piagetian terms, have not reached conservation. This was also evident in work done, among others, by McGarrigle & Donaldson (Donaldson, 1978) – the Naughty Teddy task, and Gelman & Gallistel (1978) – the 'magic' game. However, the ability to subitise appears to be evident only with relatively small numbers of objects.

An interesting by-product of the activity arose when two boys, aged seven plus, who were not part of the original group of children, were working with the program. They found no difficulty with set sizes up to five and asked to be allowed to try with bigger groups of sheep. They were accurate with set sizes up to nine and ten, with improvements in their scores with practice. When asked how they did it, Mark replied: 'I always count some ... I remember some and then I count the rest.' It seemed as if Mark could see some and label them with their size through subitising, and then (possibly) count and add on the rest.

Into formal schooling

The children in this study who had transferred from a nursery class to a reception class had transferred from one classroom ethos to another which was very different. They had moved from a classroom ethos attendant upon a relatively well staffed nursery class with a teacher and a nursery nurse for 26 children, into a classroom with 30 other children and one teacher; from an informal, setting where the child was responsible for the direction of much of her/his learning to a more teacher-directed, formal setting. This served to emphasise the group and conformity to the group. Thus there appeared to be social pressures upon the children to behave in a certain manner and to conform to particular kinds of teacher expectations, particularly as noted, to count where counting was not required.

As has been noted elsewhere (Barrett, 1986; Bennett & Kell, 1989), there is evidence to suggest that much of the work in reception classes does not offer a good match to the children's abilities or experiences. As Bennett *et al.* (1984: 214), say: 'Many mismatches in demand occurred because the teacher did not ascertain that the child was already perfectly familiar with the task content.' There certainly seemed some evidence of this for children involved in this study in connection with their subitising skills.

In looking for explanation for this mismatch, it would seem to be appropriate to consider the records that the children from the nursery class took with them into the reception class. In all cases, however, there was adequate documentation of the children's abilities in subitising, so the mismatch was not due to lack of available information on transfer.

In this particular reception class, the teacher taught mathematics only through a commercial scheme of work. On entry into the class, the children started at the beginning of the scheme. Most of the activity in the first few weeks involved counting and colouring in. This particular scheme emphasised the gradual introduction of set sizes and their labelling and reinforced the role of counting in answering 'How many?' questions. The teacher, although very experienced, admitted that she did not enjoy mathematics and she allowed the ownership of the mathematics taught in the classroom to remain with the writers of the scheme. As she had no ownership in the class mathematics, it was not surprising that the children had not either. As Desforges & Cockburn (1987: 102) point out, the scheme can be taken to be the whole of what is meant by mathematics in the children's eyes, as it is 'the only overtly assessed part of the mathematics curriculum'. Understandable then, if the child begins to take the view that particular skills are not valued and thus ceases to use them.

In this class, neither the teacher nor the scheme used the rich informal mathematics – of which the ability to subitise is but a part – that the children brought to the school setting. This was also found in work done on addition and subtraction by Romberg & Carpenter (1986). This is an issue that has implications for the teaching of mathematics throughout the age range; attitudes to mathematics are formed in the early years at school and a system of teaching mathematics that denies recognition of an early ability in one aspect must accept the possible consequences in terms of an alienation of children.

Acknowledgement

I would like to thank Len Frobisher, my tutor at CSSME, who supervised the work reported in this chapter.

9 The Nature of Teaching Mathematics Subject Matter in Reception Classrooms

CAROL AUBREY

Introduction

This chapter will provide a detailed analysis of one exemplar lesson from each of two teachers which is illustrative of on-going research work established at the University of Durham. This work is studying reception teachers' mathematical subject knowledge. More specifically the focus of the wider study is pedagogical subject knowledge as it is developed both in the course of teaching particular topics by different teachers and in the course of teaching different topics by the same teacher.

It was Shulman (1986) who noted that the role of subject knowledge in teaching was a neglected area of study. In so doing he both reflected and provided an additional momentum to an increasing research interest in the learning and teaching of subject matter content. Moreover, he stressed the particular importance of pedagogical subject knowledge, which is concerned less with teachers' knowledge of the subject than with knowledge of teaching particular subject content areas, gained through the experience of teaching these areas to children. It influences the teaching goals which are set, the particular content which is chosen and the way it is presented. It guides the design of the teaching tasks as well as the means by which these are introduced, supported and assessed. The implications of this for the class teacher are that knowledge of the way young children gain understanding of these topics and knowledge of their common misconceptions are required, as well as a means for accessing the prior knowledge that young children possess.

The Broader Context of the Study

The first phase of the Durham project (Aubrey, 1993) concerned the construction of assessment tasks designed to incorporate both areas of informal competence that young children are known to bring into school and content compatible with the National Curriculum attainment targets in mathematics. The aim was to examine the mathematical knowledge, strategies and representations of one reception class at school entry. The next phase of the project (Aubrey, 1994a) involved an investigation of the mathematical competences of 48 young children and their class teachers' reported planning and implementation of the mathematics curriculum. The aim here was to consider the extent to which account was taken of children's informal competences, through an examination of the nature and sequence of topics taught and teachers' reported encouragement of children's own construction of knowledge.

Both of these phases identified mathematical competences brought into school in a range of areas: counting, recognition of numerals, representation of quantity, simple addition and subtraction and social sharing, appropriate language of measurement, position in space and on a line, and in selecting criteria to sort objects. Reception teachers reported they planned integrated topic work, emphasising the importance of play, flexibility and choice, with opportunity made for practical activity in areas where children had already demonstrated competence. The content and sequence of the curriculum seemed to be derived from published infant schemes which provided a rational analysis of subject knowledge. Little account appeared to be taken by their class teachers of young children's developing knowledge of mathematics gained in out-of-school settings and little evidence of its consideration in infant mathematics schemes could be found.

The third phase described the way mathematical knowledge was presented and how it was understood by teachers and children in classroom contexts. Teacher and pupil interactions were continuously recorded in four reception classes across children's first year at school (Aubrey, 1995). The focus was on the gathering and coding of data and the derived patterns of interaction. The emerging lesson structure comprised repeating segments, with sub-segments providing the 'warp' of lessons. A segment usually consisted of a small group activity which had its own specific goal and actions. Further analysis of the lesson segments and sub-segments into components which defined teacher and pupil actions, provided access to recurrent patterns of moves which formed the 'weft' of lessons. Individual teachers had their own styles of working. The amount of time in which there was opportunity to engage in mathematical tasks varied as did the number of children involved and the overall quality of experience provided. Rich pedagogical knowledge appeared to be reflected in the content and structure of lessons, in varied and well-integrated verbal and concrete representations, with links made to pupils' existing mathematical skills and understanding, as well as support provided for children's actions.

A subsequent Economic and Social Research Council (ESRC) grant provided the opportunity to repeat and extend the previous phase of the project, following a larger cohort of children and their reception teachers through the first year of school. This chapter will examine in depth a specimen data-handling lesson carried out early in the year for each of two teachers who took part in the project: one novice teacher in her second year of teaching, and one 'expert' teacher in her twentieth teaching year (her seventh with reception-age children). While this method may allow the consideration of some of the ways pedagogical subject knowledge develops with experience, as Brophy (1991) noted, experience is not the same as expertise and a future, full-scale report of the data will allow the subtler comparison of the ways a number of different experienced teachers introduced and developed a range of mathematics topics in children's first year at school.

Theoretical Background

As yet few research attempts have been made to investigate teachers' pedagogical subject knowledge through the detailed analysis of classroom discourse. During the 1980s, however, the teaching of a number of elementary school mathematics topics was extensively investigated by Gaia Leinhardt and her colleagues at the University of Pittsburgh. These topics included fractions (Leinhardt & Smith, 1985), two-digit subtraction problems (Leinhardt, 1987), functions and graphing (Stein, Baxter & Leinhardt, 1990). Comparisons of expert and novice teachers, typically with grade 4 (ten year olds), were made through the use of interviews and analyses of series of video-taped lessons by Leinhardt (1989).

This led to descriptions of lessons in terms of the teacher's *agenda*, or overall dynamic mental plan for the lesson with its goals and actions, the *script*, or outline of content to be presented, carrying the sub-goals and actions built up through teaching the topic, *explanations*, including what the teacher says, does or demonstrates and *representations* of the mathematical concepts procedures or idea, whether physical, verbal, concrete or numerical (see Leinhardt *et al.*, 1991). Included in the agenda would be the main activity structures or 'segments' such as checking homework, presenting new material and carrying out reviews, guided practice, monitored practice, drill and tutoring.

The characteristics of these activity structures have much in common with a summary of key instructional behaviours of Good, Grouws & Ebmeier (1983), in particular, those associated with the teacher's attempts to induce understanding of a mathematics topic which they termed the 'development portion'. Here the teacher would use demonstrations and the manipulation of material and concrete examples to identify salient features and stimulate class discussion. Next the teacher would increase questions to assess comprehension, provide additional support if necessary and initiate controlled practice. At this stage teacher monitoring and feedback would still be available.

It is interesting to note that the structure provided by these two models, which focus on effective teaching behaviours, bears some resemblance to the sequence of stages through which the more recently developed cognitive strategy instruction passes. This, however, is derived from a quite different knowledge base, in psychological studies of cognitive and metacognitive processes underlying knowledge and skill development, and carries quite different, and explicit intentions to encourage learners to take an active role in learning, enhanced by cognitive strategies. Cognitive strategy instruction (for a review of this area see Wang & Palincsar, 1989) consists of a sequence of stages: *assessment*, where the teacher observes and questions to identify current knowledge and strategies; *introduction*, where the teacher makes explicit what strategy is to be learned, when and why; *guided practice and modelling*, where the teacher demonstrates and models; and independent *application*. Teacher modelling has been used extensively by Schoenfield (1985) in cognitive strategy instruction for mathematics problem solving. Of significance, too, is the degree of similarity between guided practice and 'expert scaffolding' of Wood, Bruner & Ross (1976) where an adult, usually the parent, offers temporary support to the young learner according to his or her particular learning characteristics and fades this as independence is gained. I have noted elsewhere (Aubrey, 1994b) there is some evidence that young children's early, preschool construction of mathematics in the context of their social and physical world is enhanced by what Wells (1985) described as a 'supportive' parental style which provides another example of expert scaffolding.

Educational research, however, has shown that more than cognitive processing is involved when classroom tasks are being undertaken.

Appreciation of the wider social context underpins children's understanding and beliefs about the nature of classroom tasks and school performance. Doyle (1983, 1986) has shown that while tasks may vary in demand from *memory and procedural*, to *comprehension and opinion* or interpretation, children are very aware that tasks are set within the overall assessment framework of schooling and as such carry ambiguity (the extent to which a correct answer can be determined in advance), and risk (the extent to which the criteria for judging success can be ascertained). In striving to maintain task engagement and classroom control as children seek to make tasks explicit, teachers appear to respond by lowering the cognitive demand. Empirical studies of British classrooms (Bennett *et al.*, 1984; Desforges & Cockburn, 1987) have shown how prevalent are practice tasks in primary school classrooms.

Aims

The overall aim of the on going project has been to investigate teachers' subject knowledge, in particular in terms of its influence on the content and processes of mathematics teaching in reception classes. Two main aims were set for the ESRC phase of the project:

(1) to observe and to analyse the content and style of classroom discourse of seven reception classrooms over children's first year in school, as well as classroom organisation, taking account of practical and pedagogical considerations
(2) to consider the educational implications of these findings for learning and teaching mathematics in reception classes.

Participants and setting

As noted above, this chapter compares and contrasts two reception teachers involved in a data-handling lesson. Teacher A, the novice teacher, was a main scale teacher in a small infant school. Teacher B, the expert teacher, was head of the infant department of a large primary school. The intake for each school was from a local, private housing estate with a similar socioeconomic background for each of the two groups of children. The novice teacher had 19 reception children. The expert teacher had 15 – nine full-time September starters and six 'part-time' children, due to commence full-time at Christmas. Relevant to the current chapter were three-data handling tasks: selecting criteria for sorting a set of multi-coloured figures/people, sorting Smarties to a given criterion, and devising a simple means of representing this.

Classroom observations

One day each week, at a time agreed with each reception teacher, the researcher observed and recorded the classroom interactions. Teachers were aware that the focus of the research was mathematics but it was stressed throughout that no change to existing practice was required, much less desired. The researcher was present to record what normally took place. Data collected were of two kinds:

(1) teacher–pupil interactions were continuously recorded through the teaching period by a small Aiwa tape recorder worn by the teacher in a 'Walkman' belt with a small microphone attached to her collar.

(2) As field notes had accumulated in the previous phase of the project, patterns emerged which had led to the production of a standardised format. This included a plan of the class showing the main activities and areas, with sections to comment on lesson segments observed, deployment of adults,pupil grouping, the role of adults and pupils, activities undertaken, mathematical content involved, classroom management and any additional comments.

Teacher Interviews

Both teacher A and teacher B had been interviewed once, towards the end of the school year. Questions had been grouped under a number of headings:

A *Teachers' mathematical knowledge*, concerning the teachers' own attitudes towards, beliefs about and sense of competence in mathematics at their own level (subject knowledge and beliefs).
B *Mathematics that young children should learn*, related to what teachers regarded were key concepts, knowledge and procedures to be taught to young children (pedagogical subject knowledge).
C *The way young children learn mathematics, in school and outside* and concerned with the way teachers' accessed this knowledge, dealt with misconceptions and challenged more able children.
D *Planning and organisation*, concerning daily, weekly and half-termly planning carried out by the teachers in the course of reception teaching.
E *General*, including questions about advice which might be given to a student teacher, and what the reception teachers would regard as useful continuing professional development in mathematics teaching.

Analysis

Overall a minimum of 18 lessons were observed and recorded for each teacher over the period end of September 1992 to the end of May 1993. Earlier work had allowed the generation of suitable categories, grounded in observational data, for analysing the classroom activity; and these categories with some minor refinements were confirmed by further work in the current phase.

It was found that a structure of mathematics lessons emerged which, on the one hand, supported lesson organisation and which, on the other hand, served classroom instruction. The basic unit of instruction, or segment, normally consisted of small group work which was typically repeated once, with a second group of children. Each segment had a general framework with specific goals and actions and a specific duration of around 15–20 minutes. Each segment would be introduced; then normally children would be required to display knowledge, skill or understanding as they carried out a small task, and some coaching and guiding would commonly take place, where necessary, as teachers monitored and assessed individual performance; finally, some comment would be made on the results. Individual teachers had their own set of routines consisting of both what they said and did and what they expected children to do or to show. Experiences provided ranged from the structured and teacher-led to the more open-ended and exploratory. Generally teacher-led activities were fairly tightly structured as some choice in independent practical activity was usually available for the groups not working with the teacher.

Accordingly, analysis of lessons took the following form. Lessons were transcribed on to the left-hand side of A3 paper, and the right-hand side of the paper was divided into a number of columns:

Group	Discourse	Mathe-matical content	Materials used	Teacher activity	Pupil activity	Comments

From observation field notes the researcher noted under 'Group', who was involved in the activity. Indication of 'Materials used' provided the basis for consideration of the concrete representations of mathematical ideas used. Under 'Mathematical content' attainment targets of the National Curriculum were identified, as well as the level and the specific statements of attainment. The column 'Pupil activity' allowed for additional comments on children's non-verbal responses, which the researcher observed but which might not be apparent from reading the transcript. Under 'Teacher activity' main task components were noted, as well as more detailed points under 'Comments'. These components provided a systematic way of describing the teachers' inferred sub-goals and the verbal strategies they were observed to use to reach these goals, such as informing, questioning, repeating, eliciting or 'talking aloud'. Additional comments were intended to indicate whether or not prior knowledge in key areas of mathematics was being used to provide a foundation of connections among concrete experience, language, pictures, diagrams and symbols upon which future learning could be built. Discourse was, thus, the means of mediating the task structure and content by utilising a range of strategies, determined by the goals set and the materials used and which monitored at key points pupils' response and the impact of teaching. Specific illustrative examples from the transcriptions could be noted under 'Discourse'.

Teacher interviews were transcribed. Responses of particular interest to the present chapter were the two reception teachers' reports on (a) their own attitudes towards, as well as experiences and knowledge of, mathematics, (b) their own, often similar, views about the way children learned mathematics, and (c) their planning and organisation. The interviews allowed some opportunity to consider relationships between their own explicit intentions and actual teaching observed in classroom settings. The following section now presents and examines the data.

Results

Mathematical content

Tables 9.1 and 9.2 show deployment of content within the segments of the lessons described in terms of National Curriculum attainment targets. Although the negotiated focus for the study was mathematics the structure for the whole lesson of teacher A, including English attainment targets, is provided since it typified this teacher's observed practice over the year of placing greater emphasis on, and providing more opportunities to engage in, English than mathematics.

For teacher A, the novice teacher, the introductory segment, or 'carpet time' for the whole class involved recognition of initial letter sounds c, a, o (English attainment target 2, level 1). As the children moved into groups, one group had an English reinforcement activity related to the introductory segment: drawing objects beginning with the same three letter sounds and practising letter formation. A number of other children chose practical activities, such as painting, building or sticking. Five children worked on a teacher-directed, mathematics activity. The children had done many sorting by colour tasks and it was the teacher's intention to introduce classifying by a different criterion (selecting criteria for sorting a set of coloured, plastic people and applying consistently). After the children had sorted by colour and, prompted by the teacher, by different multi-coloured people/figures, a second activity was prepared. This involved drawing a set of apples and a set of balloons (recording with objects or drawing and commenting on the results). In the course of the first segment the teacher introduced and applied the mathematical term for a 2-D shape (the set hoop was referred to as a circle), and the language of set (all the dolls inside the circle were the same, or a set).

Mathematics provided the content for the teacher-directed activity in which five children took part. Of the total recorded lesson one-third of the

Table 9.1: Deployment of mathematics content in lesson segments for teacher A (novice)

(19 Reception-age children)	AT 2 Number L1 a) b)	AT 3 Algebra L1 a)	AT 4 Shape and Space L1 a) b) c) L2 a) b)	AT 5 Handling Data L1 a)
Teacher A: Segment 1:Whole class Recognition of initial letter sounds Eng 2 L1				
Segment 2: Group Draw something with specified initial letter sound c, a, o and practice letter writing Eng 2 L1 Eng 4 L1				
Segment 3: Groups choose from Construction, Painting, Cutting and Sticking, Sand, Water or Shop play				
Segment 4: Group of 4 Set hoops and coloured people a) Sort by colour;	/		/	/
b) Sort men, ladies, boys and girls				/
Segment 5: Same group Draw a set of apples and balloons, then colour them	/		/	
(Introduced terms: set, circle)				

Table 9.2: Deployment of mathematics content in lesson segments for teacher B (expert)

(9 Full-time and 6 'Part-time' Reception children)	AT 2 Number L1 a) b)	AT 3 Algebra L1 a)	AT 4 Shape and Space Ll a) b) c) L2 a) b)	AT 5 Handling Data L1 a)
Teacher B: Segment 1:Group of 6 (The rest choose activity)				
a) Recognition of initial letter sound in SMARTIES (Eng 2 L1) and count letters in SMARTIES	/			
b) Using mathematical terms to describe common 2-D and 3-D shapes (circle, cylinder, cuboid)			/ /	
Comparing and ordering objects without measuring using appropriate language (tallest, shortest)	/		/	
c) Sort a set of objects by colour. Count each set	/			/
Using language of number (most, least, full)	/			
d) Recording with objects and commenting on results				/
e) Drawing objects and commenting on results (Teacher draws 'Smarties' graph, using one-to-one correspondence. Children check by counting				/
f) Children colour own photocopied 'Smarties' graph and count different columns	/			/
Teacher reminds them a tube is a cylinder, *not* a cuboid. Total Smarties counted.	/		/	
Segment 2: Whole class Later in the day graphs of different groups are compared. It is noted that the number for each colour differs from tube to tube	/			/

discourse related to mathematics. While engaged in the structured mathematics task Teacher A was interrupted by, and attended to, the English reinforcement group as she monitored and assessed their work and steered them on to the next activity.

Teacher B the 'expert' teacher started with a small group of six children engaged in a data-handling activity. This was repeated through the day with the remaining groups in the class and led to a final, follow-up whole class review which allowed discussion and comparison of the results obtained for each group. While she was engaged in group work the rest of the class was given considerable scope in choice of activity and worked independently of the teacher.

Before the lesson started teacher B produced for the researcher her agenda for the lesson:

Maths from a tube of Smarties

1. discussing shape of box – cylinder
2. sorting by colour
3. counting and comparing
4. recording
5. sharing
6. repeating with another group with another tube of Smarties

   – do both tubes contain the same quantity of each colour?
   – compare.

While the first sub-segment of segment l also involved the recognition of the initial letter sound in Smarties this short routine served as an introduction to, and was an integral part of, the Smarties theme and was followed by the counting of the letters in the word Smarties. Although embedded in her lesson was the same core, colour sorting activity as teacher A, teacher B incorporated counting within l0 (and within l00 for appropriate children) as well as using and applying language of number ('full' and 'most'). In addition, with teacher B children recorded and commented on the results with the same objects (Smarties). Supported by the teacher's drawing they were able to represent the results another way by colouring and counting the columns of Smarties. Finally, later the same day, the whole class compared the various graphs of Smarties and speculated on the reasons for the differences observed. Furthermore, consideration of the Smarties packet led to recognition of 2-D and 3-D shapes: it was stressed that the tube of Smarties was a cylinder, *not* a cuboid and it had a face which was a circle. A collection of cylinder shapes by children, from the junk modelling box as well as the solid mathematical shapes box, provided more discussion, comparison and ordering. The rich variety of routines within sub-segments, composed of teacher's moves and children's actions, were carefully interwoven to produce a seamless lesson. Applications of counting and language of number and measurement, classification and ordering of 3-D shapes, within the main activity of sorting to a criterion, recording with objects and drawing, and commenting on results allowed meaningful cross-referencing across mathematics attainment targets of number, shape and space and data handling. It also allowed the teacher to cross-reference across sub-segments within the lesson.

The data-handling lesson under consideration, thus, involved all of the children in two mathematics activities. In contrast to teacher A, once working, teacher B received no interruptions and except for occasional explanations offered to the researcher which, in any case, were related to ongoing work, all of the teacher discourse was focused on the mathematical task being carried out.

Task components

Teacher A introduced the teacher-led mathematics activity clearly gaining the assistance of two children in opening the set hoops:

'These are tricky to open ... into a circle ... Now I tell you why we use these. We use these so we can sort things out. So that we can put them in different places. I was going to ask you how you could sort these [differently coloured people] first. With colour, like Scott said?'

She explained the use of the set hoops, using different verbal representations ('sort things out; put them in different places') as well as telling children what they would do. As children sorted, she tutored and guided, 'talking aloud' to children's actions – 'Now look, Christopher has put red in here, so are you going to decide where you want to put red, Nina?' – and informing – 'anybody who's got red put it in here'. She observed and monitored, correcting – 'Oh, that's in the wrong place' – and prompting – 'Scott is that yellow?'. Finally, she commented on the results:

'So we've put ... all the red ones in this circle. This circle is what colour? We've put the yellow ones in this circle. What colour? We've put yellow ones in yellow. Put blue ones in blue ...'

First she summarised for the children then she required a repetition in unison. As noted, the children had already sorted by colour and the main purpose of the lesson was to introduce classifying by a different criterion.

This time teacher A did not tell the children how to sort but tried to elicit from them the different criterion, which she had already determined:

'I noticed that when you were putting them in colours Scott said I've got a little girl and Christopher said I've got a little boy. Did you notice there were different types of people? All these people are different?'

As this did not work, another cued elicitation was provided:

'Right, let's think. We're not thinking of colours now. Forget about colours. Doesn't matter what colours they are. Think. All these people are different. How many different types of people have we got? We've got a man and lady, a girl and a boy – so we've got four different types of people. Do you think you could sort them into different types of people now?'

Eventually teacher A simply told the children what to do:

'Girls can go with girls and the boys can go with the boys. Right, let's take all the people out of the circles. Who are we going to put in this circle? [Eventually a single, closed question.] Right, men in that one ...'

She corrected – 'Now Scott said men in that one, Christopher ... Who goes in here? Ladies, good, Emma' – and commented on the results. This provided the opportunity to reinforce and apply the term 'circle' and introduce the term 'set', needed for the next segment:

'We've sorted them. Let's check that all the people are the same ... We've got a circle full of? Boys, and a circle full of girls ...'

'So what do we call this? There's a funny name for this ... We call it a set. Can you say that word? Set? So we've got a set of boys, a set of girls, a set of men and a set of ladies.'

So, on to the next segment, where children were asked to draw a set of balloons and a set of apples. Here, children were simply told what to do. Where necessary, help in executing the task was provided:

'Right, can we go back and sit at the table ... Right, what it says is this ... It says draw a set of, what's this? Balloons, so what you do is draw balloons inside the circle because that's the set. Like the sets over there in the circles. Do you see, Nina? Do you see what we're doing? That's right. Brilliant. Set of balloons in there and a set of apples in there.'

Again an alternative verbal representation was provided – 'inside the circle because that's the set'. The rest of the time was spent assisting children:

'Can you draw balloons, Christopher? ... Shall I show you? ... You hold the pencil and I'll hold the top. You just do a round. Can you do a round like an 'o' and then a string? There, you've done it.'

By the time the children were sorting by different people the language group had finished and were bringing work to be checked. There were five interruptions during this part of the lesson. As children moved to drawing sets there were more interruptions:

'So what we call this ... there's a funny name for this. Stand back for me just a minute while I talk to these children. We call it a set. 'Right, this is what it says, is this ... Are you listening? That is beautiful. If you listen I'll tell you what you do. Cheryl go where you are working ...'

Teacher A's intention was for children to classify by a different criterion and to complete the prepared worksheet. This resulted, first, in cued elicitation where, as Edwards & Mercer (1987) describe, the teacher asks questions while simultaneously providing heavy clues as to the information required. When this failed, she simply informed children what to do.

On starting her lesson, teacher B had explained to the researcher:

'This is all sorts. It's almost, well, it's pictoral representation, counting, it's a multitude of things. It's shape. Its logic, in a way.'

Focusing, here, specifically on the data-handling aspect of the lesson, the teacher poured the tube of Smarties on to a large sheet of white paper. At this point the first goal was set:

'I wonder how many different colours there are?'

The children made various suggestions: 8, 15, 13. Then the children were provided with a purpose for the first sub-segment:

'Shall we try and sort the Smarties into colours? What colour would you like?'

The children were told what to do and each child was nominated a colour to sort: red, pink, orange, blue and green, with purple and yellow left for the teacher to sort. Throughout purposes were made clear and there was surprisingly little cued elicitation. The children sorted and the teacher moved on to commenting on the results. How many did each child have and, consequently, who had the most? One child gave the wrong answer so the teacher asked each child to count again and then repeated the question to the same child. This time he was right so the teacher repeated the answer, blue has most, and moved on.

She took the large sheet of paper and drew a base line. This time she was introducing a new procedure for recording, so first she demonstrated with her purple and yellow Smarties:

'I've got three yellow, like that, right, and I've got three purple and I'm going to put them on like that.'

Her 'talk aloud' procedure meant children had a verbal, physical and concrete representation. The task continued as the teacher supported each child to produce a column of different coloured Smarties and to count them again. At all times the teacher's verbal representation was linked to the child's actions. Now teacher B was ready to move on to the next stage:

'Oh this is a lovely pattern, isn't it? Now that makes a lovely picture of all the Smarties ... I want to put a picture up on the wall of those Smarties.'

Having recorded with the Smarties and commented on the results, the Smarties would be drawn:

'I don't know how to draw Smarties' (said one child). 'I do' (said another).

'We could draw them (repeated the teacher) ... Somebody said you could draw them, right, now this is going to be quite difficult.'

Felt-tipped pens were collected and, again, the teacher used 'talk aloud' strategies:

'So I would have to draw round all those ... so this is blue. How many to draw for blue? Can you remember?'

Links were made to the previous sub-segment and the purpose for counting became clearer. As the teacher moved each sweet aside she drew it so the children could see the one-to-one correspondence between the sweets and her drawing of them:

'One, two, three, four, five, six, seven, eight ... Right take them off and I'll draw.'

Again a verbal representation of her actions was given – 'right, that is blue seen to, shall we take them out of the way?' The children were asked to help – 'How many do I have to draw for green?' When the pictorial representation was complete the Smarties were put back in the tube:

'Now we can eat them after dinner, can't we, because we've got a picture, haven't we? Right, we'll put them back in this.'

The teacher went off to photocopy her sheet so each child would have a personal record of the activity which could be coloured and counted:

> 'Now this is a copy of what I did, except it hasn't got the colours on. This is what the Smarties were like. So if I put on the bottom here [she marked each column with a colour code for the children] you can go off and you colour them in, can't you.'

Children were supported and coached as necessary:

> 'What's after pink, Sarah?' [And in response to a child's query] 'It's on the bottom, pet, brown, do you remember how we put them in rows?'

Again, different sub-segments were cross-referenced. Prompts were provided – 'now colour them and count them while you colour them in.' Finally, in summary, the teacher commented on the results:

> 'Now that's what this tube of Smarties, or cylinder of Smarties looked like, isn't it? That's the picture of what we've got inside here, isn't it?'

For the researcher, she explained:

> 'Here you've got colouring, you've got pencil control. It's so there's language built up there, there's shape, there's the number. There's pictorial representation which is abstracting ... so much involved here ...'

For the children:

> 'These are beautiful. We are going to put all these up on the wall [and setting the scene for the afternoon] ... I wonder when we open another cylinder of Smarties or tube of Smarties that we'll find that it's got eight blue and five green and five orange and five red and three yellow and three purples. Do you think they will be the same pattern? ... Do you think if I open this one, and we'll open it this afternoon, ... do you think we will get the same?'

The activity of one group was summarised and the purpose of the next was set. There was still time for yet another challenge to one child's comments – 'I've done blue, green, orange, pink, red, brown, yellow, purple.' 'How many Smarties were in the tube altogether, William?'

Teacher interviews

Teacher A confessed to feeling uneasy about mathematics herself because of the way she had been taught. This was why, she explained, she tried to ensure children did not feel under the pressure she had felt under in school:

> 'I don't know why but you had to get it right ... I think that has gone right through my life and in secondary school ... I was always ... don't look up because they might ask you the question ... so I think that, really, if you start, it should be fun with no pressure and I have this thing about putting ticks and crosses ... I don't like putting crosses ... I would rather say, can you check that one again ...'

> 'It was fear. I still feel intimidated by maths, people who are good at maths. I don't feel I can do it. It is probably from infant school but especially from secondary school I was panic-stricken.'

> 'It took two goes to get my O level and that was just through fear.'

In contrast, she reported feeling more confident in language, her main subject of study at polytechnic.

> With respect to children's learning, the most important things were:

> 'Things they discover for themselves but you can build in a structure so they discover it ... the classroom should have opportunities where things can be found out ... you have to have some structure. They don't just learn because it happens to be there. You organise your classroom so you have a structured activity which offers the children the opportunity to learn.'

In terms of content, number, shape and measuring were important and the National Curriculum provided a framework which was very helpful because it identified the different areas of experience all children should have. Number, she felt, children found easy but measurement:

> 'The abstract things ... language of maths ... they find quite confusing ... words like more and less ... very difficult ... the same ... they understood ... longer and shorter and lighter and heavier were difficult ...'

In terms of organisation, teacher A described how 'carpet time' was used for whole class introductions, as well as explanations about classroom tasks, so 'they had an idea what was going to be happening that day' before they moved into group work. Normally she had two groups working with her:

> 'One group on a reinforcement-type activity and one group on a teacher-directed sort of activity, just supported really ... a structured activity ... which offers the children an opportunity to learn.'

A mathematics and language activity would commonly be running each day: one might be consolidation and the other exploration. Alongside these subjects, science and technology might be introduced. If something 'came up' mathematics might not be done but some activity using mathematics would take place. Assessing took place through working with a group, through observation and talk and asking why something had been done. The staff devised termly topics but the reception teachers planned the maths activities weekly. Teacher A reviewed, on a nightly basis, whether children needed more reinforcement, more practice, or whether to move them on. Teacher-led work took place in ability groups but activities set up for exploration would be undertaken in mixed ability groups, as would pair problem-solving activities.

Teacher A had never used a mathematics scheme but thought such material was useful as a source for ideas and for providing the stages to follow when creating personal worksheets. Under general comments, the most important advice she felt she could offer to a student teacher would be to have patience and a sense of humour, to 'make things lighthearted and positive'. Making things fun for children so they saw what they were doing not as work, but more like a game and doing practical activities, is essential. Above all, building up confidence so children could come and say if they did not understand. In terms of her own continuing professional development, in-service that offered problem solving, that was practical and that provided new ideas and ways of doing things would be the most helpful.

Teacher B had always liked mathematics, as had her father before her. She had passed the Eleven Plus and gained an O level in mathematics. She, too, believed that mathematics should be fun. This she had learned from rearing her own children. In her view, not everyone would become a professor of mathematics or even get a GCSE Grade A–C, and in any case, we had to educate the rest as well. In a reception class everyone should have a chance to learn. Number was important, the language of mathematics, symbols and numbers and, eventually, operations on those numbers (addition, subtraction, multiplication and division). Pattern, sequencing and ordering were also important and measurement, to an extent, though much of this was, in fact, learned out of school. She herself had learned to tell the time from her grandmother. Like teacher A, she thought the National Curriculum provided a useful framework for planning and providing balance. It was a 'wonderful checklist ... AT1 was basically what Cockcroft was saying', together with number, algebra, shape and space. With respect to children's learning, Plowden had been misinterpreted:

'Children and their needs are first and then you match and that's where the message that you didn't teach the children came from ... that children must discover for themselves. You have got to teach them how to learn. You have got to teach children something just for them to go on to discover. Unless you've got a repertoire of certain things you are not going to learn anything. ... Teach them how to learn, teach them facts and methods as well as how to do things ... Learning is like an apprenticeship, isn't it? We are further on in life so we pass on what we've learned by showing, speaking, explaining, talking, getting something back, you know, and this is exchange.'

This was why, teacher B explained, teaching every day in small groups was so important. The only way to get the 'core' right was to give more time and to explain it more fully to everyone. In terms of organisation, there were two 'maths days' each week: one a computation, 'skills sort of day', and one a maths games day. In addition teacher B introduced mathematical investigations to the whole class approximately once a fortnight, though sometimes once a week. These were left set up in the classroom for open exploration.

Assessment consisted mainly of daily recording in a spiral notebook, noting down what had happened, who had been seen, who had not, or anything else important. This could alter radically the plan for the following day. Most of it, however, was 'in her head'. Daily planning took place in the context of fortnightly reviews of half termly plans.

Most of the content, too, 'was in her head' drawn originally from commercial schemes:

'I have been through Ginn, SPMG and Peake. I have done them all. Found fault with them all. Nevertheless, we need them for a variety of reasons: when you are inexperienced, for instance, the school needs continuity and some teachers do need them ...'

Teacher B, however, 'just knew it now': she knew the ideas and the sequence of these. Children learned in a small group situation: groups of five. For the first term the groups would be mixed ability, mathematics games would remain mixed ability grouped. After the first term there would be a certain amount of ability grouping, on a flexible basis. Investigations would be mixed ability grouped. Now and again she would want to see how they operated, what they really knew and then she would put five of similar ability together and see what happened. A teacher could work with children at different levels and present things within the task to stretch the more able:

'You have got to think through what you are going to do, to want from it and know you are going to have William in your group and what can I add to this for him. Or for Sarah, or for whoever ... I know Sarah ... can't do much ... to send Sarah on her own would show her up too much and would embarrass her and would switch her off. We have five minutes as a class, revisiting ... most of the time I "hit" most of them.'

It would depend on what she was doing, the purpose, what she was wanting to find out and why. In conclusion, teachers were different and there was no one right method. She could not, much as she would like to, affect the practice of other people. This was not an easy thing to do.

It is interesting to note at this point, as in an earlier phase of the project, the finding that published schemes play a powerful role in shaping teachers' views on the content and sequence of reception class mathematics instruction. There is the suggestion, too, that the National Curriculum may take over this function by providing a supportive framework for early years mathematics teaching.

With respect to children's prior knowledge, teacher A noted that measurement was confusing to young children, while, teacher B suggested that much measurement knowledge was acquired in out-of-school contexts. It is significant to note, at this point, that analysis so far carried out for the wider project indicates more misjudgements on the part of teachers of young children's existing understanding of measurement than of other areas of the mathematics curriculum.

Under general comments, while teacher A mentioned problem-solving as a desired topic for in-service training, teacher B in similar vein mentioned investigation:

'I think coming to grips with AT1, the ideas behind it and the way you would manage it within a classroom ... making it workable in your classroom.'

These comments served as a timely reminder that if the teacher's primary task is to impart new knowledge this task is constrained by the multiple demands faced by the teacher in organising this knowledge and making it accessible and engaging to diverse groups of young children. Both teachers accessed children's existing knowledge in the context of small group work and, in fact, comments made by each teacher, on organisation and grouping, served both to reflect observed practice and to place this within the broader framework of teachers' intentions.With respect to providing support for a student teacher teacher B's concluding comments in many ways exemplified her own approach to teaching:

'I think that it really must be an apprenticeship ... you can learn so much from other people.'

Expert scaffolding was seen not simply as a temporary support to a young learner but, equally, a means of guiding a young teacher.

Conclusions

Analysis of the two lessons in terms of the structure and content of segments and sub-segments, as well as in terms of task components, provided access to differences between the novice and expert teacher at a number of levels. In terms of structure and content, the main lesson segment of the expert teacher was complex, comprised of six interlinking sub-segments with much forward and backward referencing, cross-referencing across the areas of number, shape and space and data handling and grounded in children's prior knowledge. The expert teacher offered coherent and related activities of sorting, leading to recording with objects and drawing, which provided the foundation for future construction of simple block graphs and from which conclusions could be drawn.

Overall the novice teacher's lesson was simpler in structure and less rich in terms of content introduced. Her second segment involving the drawing of sets of apples and balloons did not relate directly to the previous sorting of coloured, plastic people/figures and may, thus, have had less meaning for the children, though appropriate verbal and concrete representations were offered. The interruptions from the English group led to some attention being diverted from instruction to management and to some lack of clarity in instructions given for the second segment. For the novice teacher only one-third of the transcription related to mathematics. For the expert teacher, all discourse related to instruction in mathematics. Opportunities, thus, to engage in mathematics activities differed in the two lessons, as well as in the range and quality of experiences provided.

Prior knowledge of sorting to a criterion was accessed and used by both teachers, though the way it was applied and extended differed. Teacher A, while attempting to elicit children's ideas, in fact, first provided clues to which children did not respond and, finally, informed them of what was required. Individual children were prompted and corrected as appropriate.The expert teacher started the lesson with a clear 'agenda' or mental plan of the segments which she was able to supply to the researcher both in written form at the beginning of the lesson and in the form of a commentary offered at key points in the lesson. Seven years of reception experience had provided her with 'scripts' drawn from her previous experience of teaching such lessons. Goals for each segment were clearly stated and children were told what to do. Inaccurate responses to teacher questions led to the repetition of the question with additional relevant information being made available to support the pupil concerned. Through teacher demonstrations and modelling, 'talk aloud' strategies, and teacher-produced support material children were 'scaffolded' to carry out an activity beyond their independent means. Throughout, children were provided with appropriate verbal and concrete representations of ideas being introduced.

Teacher interviews revealed contrasts in the teachers' reported knowledge of, liking for, and confidence in mathematics. In terms of children's learning, both teachers discussed the role of discovery in reception class mathematics teaching and both teachers recognised the limitations of discovery as a basis for moving children forward. Teacher B believed it was essential to teach children how to learn, to provide them with strategies, knowledge and procedures to carry out independent work. Teacher A described how the teacher should build in a structure which offered children the opportunity to learn. The interviews, thus, allowed some consideration of the ways teachers' own mathematical knowledge, their views about learning and teaching mathemtics might influence their observed practice.

This chapter has provided an intensive focus on one lesson of one expert and one of a novice teacher. The aim has been to show the potential in recording such detailed information for the light that is shed on the processes of teaching. Data from these two lessons can be indicative only of the wider pattern of findings which emerged over the year. In fact, over the year, teachers were observed to spend most of their time assessing and observing, coaching, guiding and correcting in small group situations which encouraged active learning. While they did not have time for lengthy diagnostic interviews the tasks they presented allowed them to assess the extent to which children could answer questions about content and apply knowledge strategically. This suggested the dynamic process of knowledge development in response to particular tasks, in other words, that task demand *changed* in the process of tutoring and guiding and in the scaffolding of responses from individual children. It suggested, furthermore, an awareness of the interaction between assessment of prior knowledge and instruction and of the need for the teacher to model cognitive strategies and to provide support to children's early efforts.

'Initiation-response-feedback' interaction sequences, used by teacher A, were observed over the year to serve a variety of purposes, for instance, to check knowledge, to remind, to invite involvement, to model, to support and to review. On occasions where such questioning became unhelpful it usually arose from gaps in the teacher's own subject knowledge or, perhaps, in the case of this young, less experienced teacher the lack of access to a repertoire of similar, previous 'case' lessons upon which to draw. In the case of the expert teacher previous 'case' experience provided the basis for the assured movement through a series of related segments with clear goals and efficient planning.

By attempting to make more explicit the nature of, and growth in, teaching expertise, it is hoped that student and novice teachers may be helped to appreciate better the development of teaching through and beyond the 'survival' stage, and be provided with some explanatory scaffolding themselves, as they reflect on their own developing performance and that of their pupils.

10 Evaluating National Curriculum Assessment at Key Stage 1: Retrospect and Prospect

DIANE SHORROCKS

It could be argued that the introduction of the National Curriculum and its attendant assessment system represents the most significant change to occur in schools since 1944. This is especially the case in primary and infant schools, where prescription of the curriculum has been minimal and where accountability, in the form of externally acknowledged assessment outcomes, has not figured large since the virtual demise of the eleven plus exam. In infant schools and departments, the notion of formalised assessment has been even less familiar.

However, it is worth pointing out that assessing children of seven or younger is not a new activity in our educational system. In schools up and down the land children are assessed and tested informally by their teachers in spelling tests, 'review' pages in maths workbooks and by hearing them read etc. On a one-to-one basis, many children are more formally assessed by educational psychologists and teachers if problems are being experienced. But another trend is also obvious, the use of more standardised testing procedures by local education authorities (LEAs) at various age points and in various subjects. Caroline Gipps and her associates (Gipps, Steadman & Blackstone, 1983) carried out national surveys of the extent of such testing. They found that 82 of the 104 LEAs had some kind of official testing programme. Of these, 31 were formally testing children's reading by age seven and three were testing in maths and IQ at this age. By the time children reached eight years, 41 LEAs were testing their reading, 14 their mathematical progress, and 12 their IQ. In the study of reading tests results, carried out by NFER (1992), many LEAs were regularly using a reading test for seven year olds, most often the Young Group Reading Test.

It would be wrong to suggest, therefore, that formal assessment is unknown in most infant and primary schools, but what is new is the fact that it is now carried out in systematic ways over the three core subjects and is scored according to the agreed system of levels.

We have now several years' experience of the implementation of the curriculum and the assessment system at Key Stage 1, so it is an opportune moment to step back and reflect on the process and implications for teaching and learning in the early years. This is a need that has been appreciated by central government, too, resulting in the major review carried out by Sir Ron Dearing. Such a review was not generated out of thin air, however: it was the result of considerable protest on the part of schools and widespread expressions of disquiet in broader educational circles.

In this chapter I will seek to evaluate the outcomes and effects of the implementation process so far, with the focus on the assessment system. This is a task in which the School of Education here at the University of Leeds has been particularly involved, having carried out major evaluations of the Key Stage 1 assessments in 1991 and 1992 (Shorrocks, 1993; Shorrocks *et al.*, 1992, 1993).

Retrospect: Origins and Principles

The move towards a National Curriculum, including an integral assessment system, was brought about by the perception that standards in education were falling, and that this decline should be halted forthwith. In reality there was little clear evidence that standards were indeed on the decline, but the political judgement on this was supported by many powerful voices (Moon, Isaac & Powney, 1990). However, it does not require an argument of declining standards to justify wishing to improve the quality of teaching and learning in our schools.

It is probably worth reminding ourselves at this point that the basic approach to the assessment system was outlined in the TGAT report (DES, 1988), following the DES suggestion that there should be 'nationally prescribed tests done by all pupils'. To the relief of many, the proposals made by the TGAT group seemed benign and progressive in character, stressing cross-curricular assessment tasks at Key Stages 1 and 2 and a variety of modes, practical, oral and written. They did, however, advocate and retain traditional 'subject' areas, with the curriculum for each being specified in detailed ways within Levels, and Attainment Targets (with the additional layer of Profile Components originally).

The proposal was that the assessments at all ages should be *criterion-referenced, formative, moderated* and should relate to *progression*, despite the fact that no other assessment system had ever been put in place which met these four criteria. The argument for the emphasis on formative assessment was that, although such an approach requires very detailed investigation, the scores could be summarised and aggregated in a variety of ways in order to serve other assessment purposes, most importantly *summative and evaluative*. The results were to be shared with the children themselves, so generating increased motivation and involvement.

The assessments were also to have two facets, the Standard Assessment Task (the SAT) and judgements made by the teachers themselves, Teacher Assessment (TA). Both kinds of assessment were to be carried out by the teachers, in order to ensure continuity of experience for the children and so give rise to more valid assessments. For reasons of time and resources, the Standard Task could not cover the whole of the curriculum or the whole of a child's work, hence the need for broader teacher assessments alongside. The original purpose of the assessments at Key Stage 1, was 'to identify children in need of help which is exceptional for a child of that age, whether because he or she is making so little or so much progress' (DES, 1988: para. 147).

The assessment system is curriculum-based, where the curriculum is specified in two ways; through detailed general requirements (the Programmes of Study, the non-statutory element) and through precise listings within Attainment Targets and Levels (the Statements of Attainment) which set out what children should know, understand and be able to do. Most importantly, the levels, although charting progression, are age-independent. The assessment system is also classroom-based, with children being assessed by their teachers (in both facets of the assessments) in the context of their normal learning environment, with all the positive and negative aspects that this might imply.

The result in many Key Stage 1 schools and classrooms has been the adoption of a more subject-based approach to curriculum delivery, with the radical changes in planning strategies and organisation that this implies, together with related changes in the recording of attainment for each child, backed up by evidence. A great deal of time and effort has been invested in putting in place not only new recording systems, but also in carrying out the statutory testing requirements. These are indeed far-reaching developments, and appear to have influenced infant classroom teaching in positive ways, at least according to reports by HMI (1990) and OFSTED (1993). They suggest that there have been improvements in particular areas of the curriculum, notably in English and science, and in the quality of planning. They also suggest that primary teachers have become more confident in their assessment and monitoring of children's work. These are clearly claims that bear further examination.

Prospect: Outcomes and Issues

The basic principles beg further comment, and need to be related to the actual findings of the various evaluations of the Key Stage 1 assessments. To do this, I will take each of the major characteristics in turn and use these as a vehicle for raising significant issues.

Criterion-referenced assessment

Assessment is about making informed judgements based on good evidence and using these judgements to make appropriate educational decisions. It serves important functions in many ways if the results can be shown to be valid and reliable for their purpose and generally trustworthy. It is also salutary to remember that there will always be *error* in any assessment: the perfect system has not yet been devised and is probably not possible. We are essentially making inferences about what the behaviour or outcome really indicates and how validly and reliably any task is tapping what a child knows, understands or can do.

Even when we have come up with a result or score for any task, this is meaningless unless it is given significance by comparing it, either with the results from other people or with a specified set of behaviours or knowledge. This is the basic distinction between *norm-referenced* and *criterion-referenced* assessment. The first attempts at systematic measurement of human psychological characteristics were early this century and were essentially norm-referenced in character, developed for purposes of screening or selection. The 1960s and 1970s witnessed a move away from the complex work on norm-referencing, toward criterion-referencing, an approach which allows us to discover in more precise terms what a child can do and understand (Thorndike & Hagen, 1977).

The national assessment system, recognising this, is criterion-referenced and attainment-based: the results are descriptions of what a child knows and can do, not predictions of what that child will be capable of in the future, as most tests of ability imply. The outcomes are reported in some detail, so that such categorisations as a 'level 2 child' should not exist. We are being encouraged to detail attainment, not categorise and label children, and this is especially significant with young children in their early years of schooling.

In any assessment or testing process, it has first to be decided exactly which attributes, knowledge and skills are to be measured, then activities have to be devised which allow these to become 'visible' in order to judge the performance or understanding of the child. One potential criticism in this situation, is that because some knowledge or qualities are easier to measure than others, we may be in danger of choosing a narrow (and maybe irrelevant) range of outcomes and missing out on some central ideas and qualities which are difficult to pin down for assessment purposes.

This is not necessarily a criticism that can be levelled at the specifications in the Attainment Targets: there has been a fairly clear attempt to incorporate some quite complex and subtle kinds of knowledge and insights, perhaps too subtle in some cases. However, they do not all seem to have been devised with assessment in mind. Even in their revised versions (as in mathematics and science) they still contain a great deal of ambiguity and imprecision. The paradox here is that the qualities that make them credible in curriculum terms are the very qualities that make them so difficult as starting points for assessment. In the revised mathematics and science Statements of Attainment, fewer Attainment Targets and Statements have been achieved by building even more content into many of them and by making others very general. Neither of these is helpful in terms of assessment, and Key Stage 1 teachers have clearly found enormous difficulties coming to terms with the Statements, in all their versions.

To give more detail, the evaluation of the 1991 assessments showed the following (Shorrocks et al., 1992);

- Teachers were confused about the meaning of such terms as 'sight vocabulary' and 'fluency' in reading and the idea of a 'particular' or a 'generalised' statement in science.
- They were also unclear about the range of a child's work (best, worst, at what point in time etc.) they should take into account in making their final, summative judgements.
- They were unclear how frequently they needed to collect evidence of a child's attainment (some were applying a 'three occasions' rule).
- In science, they were confused about how they should treat evidence collected some time before, when a particular topic was being covered.

It is clear therefore that the 'criteria' in this criterion-related system have proved a little intractable, which has compromised the dependability of the scoring outcomes to a very considerable extent so far.

Moderation

The above comments indicate both the need for, and the difficulties of, moderation. A national assessment system that is criterion-referenced or criterion-related requires effective training procedures and the means for teachers to reach agreed definitions and interpretations of the criteria (the Statements of Attainment) and apply the same mastery standards. The detailed evaluations carried out so far have indicated that these have been far from satisfactory, if a valid and dependable national assessment system is the aim.

The particular findings in relation to the 1991 and 1992 assessments were as follows;

- Wide variation existed in the extent and quality of the training, moderation and support programmes, although most teachers received some training in SAT administration; only 7% of the sample thought their training had been adequate.
- Too much of the training focused on administrative matters rather than on classroom organisational aspects.
- Teachers said that the kind of training they had found most professionally useful had been attendance at agreement trials with colleagues from their own school or from other schools, but only 65% of the sample had any experience of them.
- In the second year of the assessments (1992), one quarter of the teachers in that sample had received no training for administering the SAT, and only 58% of those who did receive training thought it was adequate.

The clear finding from these evaluations was that training and moderation procedures (in terms of quantity and quality) left something to be desired, and of course, training and moderation are the bedrock of an assessment system such as this. Any assessment system is only as good as the people who put it into practice. Appropriate materials and training are a significant way in which the national assessments could be better moderated and calibrated.

Progression

A central plank of the original TGAT proposals was that progression in all the Attainment Targets should be demonstrated via a ten-level, age-independent scale, covering the school years from age five to sixteen. This has been reviewed, but the original idea was arrived at by looking at other scales used in assessment systems, here and abroad, and discovering that for a single age cohort (for example, all eleven year olds), a five or six-point scale was most common. Averaging this across the four Key Stage assessment points, ten levels seemed appropriate.

In practice, especially at Key Stage 1, this has provided only a few very gross categorisations (Levels 1 to 3/4) with not enough differentiation at the lowest levels to do justice to the attainments of slow-developing children or children with special educational needs. The steps between the levels have proved rather uneven, and over time it might not be easy to demonstrate to parents exactly how their child has progressed, given little change in the levels awarded from year to year. To add to the problem, the combining of scores across Attainment Targets (aggregation) loses information and produces even more of a generalised grading.

The merit of the system, of course, is that it provides a common framework for the discussion of a child's progress across schools and phases. Its age-independence also allows children to be monitored at their own rate, irrespective of their chronological age. But once again this has not proved so ideal in practice. It is not immediately evident that we should expect exactly the same performance from children of different chronological ages who are deemed to be at the same level. This is a matter that will no doubt need much more attention as all the Key Stages come on stream and the same children reach a second and subsequent Key Stage assessments.

Teacher assessment and SAT assessment

It has by now become almost a cliché to say that effective teaching is based on accurate assessment of what children already know and can do and where any 'gaps' exist. Teachers aim to achieve this by a judicious use of observation, questioning and analysis of the child's 'products' and errors. These, ideally, are carefully recorded and each child's progress monitored. This represents formative assessment at its most valid and useful and it is this quality that the national system appeared to encourage in the original proposals. Of course, these ongoing assessments made by the teacher can be summarised as required, in order to provide a summative score or level, so in the context of teacher assessments, both possibilities exist.

But how should the summative scores arrived at in this way be related to the summative scores reached via the SAT? From the beginning, it has always been suggested that the two sets of scores can be combined (DES, 1988) and that the extent of the curriculum to be covered in fact required this. The summative assessment of the SAT provides a 'snapshot' of a child's performance at one point in time and is clearly of a rather different nature to the teacher assessments.

Teacher Assessments (TAs) are based on long-term, detailed consideration of a child's performance in a wide variety of contexts, a quality that is likely to be especially important with young children. When they are summarised into a summative score, it could be argued that this makes such assessments more trustworthy and valid than a single Standard Task administered at one point in time. This argument would only hold for the national assessments, if it could clearly be demonstrated that all teachers were applying the same interpretations and mastery criteria in all their assessments. Questions raised earlier throw considerable doubt on this, at least in the short-term.

So what is and what should be the relationship between the two kinds of assessment in presenting overall profiles of a child's performance and progress? The original proposal in the TGAT report was that the two could be combined. In 1991, when the fuller and more detailed Orders were involved for the core subjects, the SATs at Key Stage 1 addressed only a small proportion of the possible range of Attainment Targets (ATs). TAs filled in the rest, as it were, and there were considerable discrepancies between many of the TA and SAT scores. In the ATs where both TA score and SAT scores were available, the SAT score prevailed, unless the teacher made a case for this not to be so, an event that happened rarely.

Close analysis showed that the influence of the SAT was different in the different Profile Components (no longer applying in the core subjects) and subjects, although the overall trend was for SAT scores to be higher than TA scores, so the resolved and combined scores were better than those based on TA alone. In English, agreement between the two measures was not high, and the SAT increased the final score for many children. In mathematics, where SAT scores were again higher over most ATs assessed, a careful choice of ATs within the SAT could noticeably improve the final scores. In science, the SAT had an enormous impact on the final scores, purely because Sc1 (the infamous 'floating and sinking' activity) dominated and scores were high in this activity (see Shorrocks *et al.*, 1992).

In the 1992 assessments, significant developments occurred. Whereas in 1991 the SAT served to raise overall scores, a rather different pattern of influence emerged in 1992. Table 10.1 shows the outcomes for the two kinds of scores, for the ATs where all the comparative information was available in both years. The 1991 TA and SAT scores are derived from the sample of children in the schools who took part in the 1991 evaluation, which was reasonably representative of the national population of seven year olds. In Table 10.1, the percentage of children awarded the levels 1–4 are listed, as well as those awarded 'W' ('working towards' Level 1).

Table 10.1 Percentage of children attaining levels W – 4 (TA scores and SAT scores) in selected Attainment Targets, in 1991 and 1992

				Levels		
AT/Year	*TA/SAT*	*W*	*1*	*2*	*3*	*4*
En2						
1991	TA	4	34	50	13	*
	SAT	2	30	50	17	*
1992	TA	1	22	54	22	1
	SAT	1	22	54	22	1
En3						
1991	TA	2	35	58	5	*
	SAT	2	20	67	11	*
1992	TA	1	25	61	11	0
	SAT	1	27	61	11	0
En4						
1991	TA	4	35	57	4	*
	SAT	2	27	57	14	*
1992	TA	2	23	59	15	1
	SAT	1	22	57	18	1
En5						
1991	TA	1	32	62	4	*
	SAT	0	27	67	5	*
1992	TA	0	20	70	9	1
	SAT	0	20	70	9	1
Ma3						
1991	TA	4	30	63	4	*
	SAT	3	51	36	10	*
1992	TA	2	23	61	14	0
	SAT	2	30	49	18	0
Sc6						
1991	TA	3	28	60	9	*
	SAT	1	7	52	41	*
1992	TA	1	15	51	33	0
	SAT	0	9	44	46	0

Note: * indicates this Level not used in 1991

Before discussing the information in Table 10.1, it is important to make the general point that with information such as this, based on samples of children that are deemed representative, there will always be a degree of error in the outcomes. Differences of 1–2% may not be of great significance in terms of considering trends and relationships. However, in so far as they have credibility, it should be remembered that 1% of the national population of seven year olds is over 5,000 children!

To take the information AT by AT, starting with the English ATs, in En2 (Reading), the 1991 results in TA were considerably lower than the SAT scores that year. The scores were lower in that more children were awarded the lower levels and fewer were awarded the higher levels. By 1992 however, the two sets of scores were exactly the same. In En3 (Writing), the 1991 scores were again lower in TA than in the SAT, but by 1992 they had become marginally higher. En4 (Spelling) and En5 (Handwriting) showed a similar kind of trend in the two years. The one mathematics AT that was common across the two years was Ma3 (Number), and here the trends were not as easy to see. The distributions over the two years show a similar kind of pattern to the other ones listed, but in 1992 there was an overall increase in the scores, a strange finding since the mastery requirements in the SAT were harder in 1992 than in 1991! In the science AT, Sc6 (Types and uses of materials), the scores were very discrepant in 1991, with TA scores being very low and SAT scores very high. By 1992, however, the TA scores had increased dramatically, but the SAT even more so.

The conclusion to be drawn from this kind of comparison, is that Key Stage 1 teachers have proved to be fast learners. The standards exemplified in the first SAT in 1991 were different from those apparently applied by the teachers in that year, for reasons that have been discussed. 1992 saw this situation rapidly rectified, to the extent that in 1992, teacher assessment scores in many of the ATs were high, increasing the overall outcomes.

The ATs that were new in the 1992 SAT (namely Ma12, Ma14 and Sc9) showed a similar trend to the ATs in 1991, when the effect of the SAT was to generally raise the scores by producing higher results than TA. However, in the ATs that had also been addressed in the previous year (the English ATs, Ma3 and Sc6), the effect of the SAT in the second year was to lower the resolved scores or to maintain the status quo, except for Sc6, where there was again the tendency for the SAT to raise the overall scores. When the patterns of scores are examined in this way, the SAT can indeed be seen to be acting as a kind of national calibrating and moderating device, although with some odd results for some ATs.

However, this analysis covers only the ATs addressed by the SAT in the two years: TA scores as a whole in 1992, in the remaining ATs, showed some interesting characteristics. Across the ATs, very few children were awarded a 'W' score (working towards Level 1) except for Ma6 , where 13% were awarded this score. Ma6 also presented other interesting problems, since 2% of the teachers in the sample awarded Level 1 scores when there are no Level 1 Statements! This clearly points up an important training issue.

The teachers' scores in some ATs showed a tendency toward the lower Levels, while others showed a very definite tendency toward the higher ones. Of the 37 ATs where the teachers had to supply their assessment (including Technology), broadly speaking 12 fell into the first category and four into the second. Interestingly, all the Technology ATs showed a tendency toward scores at the lower Levels – predictable perhaps as they were new ATs coming on stream for the first time. Table 10.2 below gives some flavour of the distributions for ATs at the extremes: the remaining ATs showed average kinds of distributions.

Table 10.2 Percentage of children awarded each Level in Teacher Assessment scores, for selected Attainment Targets in 1992

AT			Levels			Number in sample
	W	1	2	3	4	
Lower scores						
En5	0	20	70	9	1	1466
Ma4	1	13	80	6	0	1494
Sc16	2	16	75	7	0	1496
Te2	1	14	78	6	0	1431
Te4	2	24	63	11	0	1401
Higher scores						
Ma14	1	14	57	26	2	1465
Sc2	0	4	53	42	0	1496
Sc3	0	5	50	45	0	1495
Sc4	0	4	53	42	0	1496

It is not easy to see any obvious pattern here, except to comment that the AT scores that showed the tendency toward the lower scores in 1992, were in the main ATs that had not figured compulsorily in the SAT in 1991 or 1992 (the 1992 SAT materials were available to the teachers as they made their TA judgements that year), although three (Ma5, Ma8 and Ma13) had appeared as optional ATs. Neither is it possible easily to explain the very high scoring outcomes in the second category, except for Ma14, where it was clear that some of the Statements at the various levels were inappropriately placed, so that children could legitimately be awarded the higher levels because of the ease of the Statements (see Shorrocks et al., 1992). It is certainly not clear why these science ATs should give rise to such high scores, since another (Sc16) showed much lower scores: the argument is not simply one of teachers erring on the side of caution in ATs where they had come across little previous assessment guidance.

Overall, then, the relationship between TAs and the SAT assessments has not proved to be a straightforward one. The evidence on which the two are based is somewhat different in character, but summative judgements are possible on the basis of either. Both, in principle, are appropriate for certain purposes and it is important to remember that it is the same children being assessed against the same criteria, by the same person and at roughly the same point in time. These are forces that should make for similarity. However, the differences in the character of the two kinds of assessments are forces for dissimilarity. The issue of the *purposes* for the two is still unresolved and the question whether and how the two should be seen in relation to each other, is still an open one.

Conclusions

In this chapter I have sought to summarise some of the important issues and implications of the Key Stage 1 assessment system. We have travelled a considerable way since the original proposals from the TGAT group and the first years of implementation. Along the way some subtle and some not so subtle changes have taken place. The scope and timings of the assessments have reduced considerably, and while this has eased the task of administration and reduced the overall impact on wider school activities, it has undoubtedly been at the expense of the validity and appropriateness of the enterprise for children of seven years having now much more of a 'pencil and paper' character. A very uneasy path has been trodden trying to achieve this balance between manageability, validity and reliability, and it is by no means clear that an appropriate solution has been reached. The National Curriculum (with its assessment system) requires teachers not only to consider what should be *taught* and in what ways, but also to ask the vital question of what children have *learned* and the evidence for this. This should in theory improve the quality of both teaching and learning in schools, but only to the extent that teachers see the point of the enterprise and are properly trained and supported.

11 Assessment: Is it an Art or a Science?

SHERIDAN EARNSHAW

This research investigated how Year 2 teachers were planning and assessing science in the infant classroom. As a Primary Science Advisory Teacher working with teachers in a local authority for six years, I had been involved in training teachers not only in developing their science teaching but also in organising assessment and SATs (Standard Assessment Tasks). I felt I needed some clearer insights into how these teachers were subsequently putting this training into practice within their own classrooms. How were they now planning science activities and how were their judgements about the children's learning in science being formulated? In looking at these issues I was concerned with overall levels of effectiveness in the management of these activities and felt it would be useful to know more about these aspects.

Teaching science at Key Stage 1 had been enforced by National Curriculum Orders in 1989. Prior to this, science had been taught in some infant classrooms but in a relatively *ad hoc* way, depending largely on the knowledge and interest of the teacher and whether or not science was perceived as a priority subject. In the 1960s the philosophy of Plowden (CACE, 1967) was interpreted as advocating first-hand discovery – science activities had seemed to be an excellent way of 'discovering' and were seen as lending themselves to a child-centred approach. Unfortunately the somewhat *ad hoc* approach was sustained by the continuing lack of an accessible and cohesive scientific knowledge base, appropriate to the infant age range. It was Harlen (1985) who, recognising this deficit, initially outlined the content of what might constitute a science curriculum.

About this time and before the introduction of a National Curriculum, HMI (HMSO, 1989) had acknowledged that the teaching of science was improving but that there was clearly still a need for greater 'breadth and balance'. The introduction of the Science National Curriculum brought considerable breadth, and it was with communicating this breadth and with endeavouring to maintain some balance that I became concerned in my capacity of Advisory Teacher for Science.

The question, then, that this research examined was: What factors influence the effectiveness of teachers' assessment of science at Key Stage 1? It investigated how science was being planned, organised and assessed and how teachers were making judgements about matters of attainment. A further related question concerned how teachers were using assessments once they were made.

The Research

The research was carried out in a North of England authority. It involved 15 teachers in 15 different primary schools ranging from small rural village schools to large urban schools. The sample included children from a variety of backgrounds including a number of ethnic minority children, many of whom had English as a second language. The class sizes ranged from a village school with a class of 13 children to an urban school with a class of 33 children. The research sample was limited because of relatively limited time available, but it seemed important to include a reasonable range of types of schools within the sample for the findings to be suitably broad-based.

The teachers involved had a wide range of experience and skills between them, including some with up to 30 years' teaching experience and some with considerably less. All the teachers in the sample had some Year 2 children in their class. The majority of teachers were already known to me through the science courses or SAT training I had offered. Also included in the sample were three teachers of whom I had no knowledge but who had received some science training.

The teachers had varied science backgrounds, as far as in-service training was concerned. Two had attended DES-20 day science courses; seven had taken part in Authority INSET run by the science team. The remainder had received SAT training but no specific training concerned with scientific knowledge.

To invite participation I wrote to the headteachers of the target schools asking for permission to carry out research with a Year 2 teacher. The head was asked to nominate the teacher. I then spoke to the class teacher by telephone and wrote several further letters outlining what would occur on the proposed half-day visits to each teacher. It came as an enormous surprise that all teachers welcomed my visits and went out of their way to be extremely helpful. Despite this, however, some were clearly nervous at the presence of someone relatively unfamiliar to them in the classroom, studying aspects of science. This was evident in comments such as: 'It's like being on teaching practice all over again' and 'Thank goodness that's all over, I feel as if I've just taken an exam!'

Prior to the half-day visit, each teacher was asked to complete a questionnaire giving information about the size of class, the age range, and their training background in science and assessment background. The questionnaire asked teachers to identify:

How many years have you been teaching?
How many children do you have in your class?
What age groups do you have in your class?
What science training have you have had if any?
What assessment training have you had if any?
Do you have an assessment policy in school?

This information provided an initial and clearer picture of relevant aspects of each teacher's background, training and current class.

The next step was to visit the teachers and observe a pre-planned science activity with a group or a class of children. I had prepared an observation sheet, to ensure a clear compatible focus across all cases. This focused upon how activities were introduced, the interaction between individual children and the teacher, and how children worked with and reacted to their peers. It also noted aspects of whole-class management and effects upon the science activity, for example the number of times the teacher was interrupted while talking to the children. A note was made of any assessment opportunities identified by the teacher and of possibilities for assessment not identified by the teacher.

Trying to be a 'fly on the wall' in an infant classroom is by no means an easy task and it was difficult not be distracted. When I was addressed by the children I gave as little comment as possible, so as to avoid interaction I sat as far away from the science work as audibility allowed. I had a mental image of my hands being tied in order to stop myself intervening in the ongoing science work.

Each teacher was interviewed, prior to the observed science activity in order to ascertain the following:

• the focus for the following science activity

- what considerations the teacher had made in planning the activity
- how the science activity would be organised
- how many groups of children were involved in the activity
- what assessment opportunities had been identified and planned.

I identified also where the teacher intended to be during the session and how much time would be spent with the science group(s). I also included a question concerned with identifying any potential problems they were anticipating. This question received a variety of replies, such as: 'I think it will be chaos!' and 'My greatest problem is that the children want immediate feedback, they are so enthusiastic. So I say go and discuss it with your friend, but that's not good enough for them. There will be umpteen interruptions.'

A second interview took place following the activity to ascertain:

- the perceived success or otherwise of the planned activities
- the nature and range of any assessments that had been made
- any overall views the teachers had concerning the teaching of science
- any views teachers had on carrying out assessment.

The pre and post-activity interviews were thus designed to give some indications of a match between the intended and the perceived outcomes of the activity. It would also be useful to compare the teachers' observations about the children's perceptions of this aspect of science with my own observations of the children at work.

The Planning of Science

The science activities planned by the 15 teachers covered a range of topics, including investigating electrical circuits, investigating wind power, observing different sugars dissolving, sorting waste materials, investigating light and investigation of the absorption of materials.

The science activities were, in general, suitable for the age range of the children. In general, the planning was done from the Programmes of Study; this was consistent across the 15 teachers but from this point there was some considerable variation in the planning methods utilised across the sample. Only three of the 15 teachers planned in some detail. For these three, this detail consisted of matching the science activity to their knowledge of the children to be involved, of identifying the Statements of Attainment (SoA) to be assessed, of planning an appropriate method of assessment from a range – this might be observation, question or product-based – a piece of written work to be assessed after the activity, or a mixture of two or more. For these three teachers, it also included planning suitable activities for the rest of the class if not all children were participating in the science activity. Other teachers, but still a minority, demonstrated that they were clear about their own role by being able to anticipate where they would need to be at any particular time, as this pre-activity comment reveals:

'I'll let them go and test things themselves but when they are in the shared area I will go and eavesdrop ... because if I'm there on certain occasions there might be something to record which will go in my jottings.'

Two other teachers had planned assessments but had selected a SoA that did not correspond with the focus for the activity. Three teachers had planned minimal assessment and one teacher had seemed rather vague about assessment at pre-activity interview:

'There are various little science tactics they are going to be working on. In fact there's a lot of AT1 in this work as I see it.'

This teacher did not identify any specific skills to be developed nor did she explain what these 'tactics' were. When a teacher was able to offer a greater level of detail it revealed a more strategic and coherent approach to planning and to associated links with assessment:

'I write out all my tasks for the week and the objectives because I sometimes find that when I write down the objectives that I'm actually doing, it isn't right so it makes me re-think what I've planned. Then I look at the ATs, the general ones and then the more specific, that I'm looking for when I want to assess.'

The HMI Report (HMSO, 1991) on *Assessment, Recording and Reporting on the First Year 1989–1990* refers to the factors that lead to successful assessment as follows:

The two most significant factors which lead to successful assessment practice are detailed planning of curriculum provision and teaching approaches in relation to ATs and also effective classroom management. (HMSO, 1991: 14)

The findings from this research would seem to endorse this view as far as planning and its relationship to assessment is concerned. The next section looks at classroom organisation (what HMI call 'management').

The Organisation of the Activities

The organisation of the activities and of the class was invariably linked to the planning. In most cases the science activity was carried out by a group of about six children, and in two cases it involved the whole class.

The observational schedule facilitated data gathering in relation to the following areas:

- whether appropriate equipment was available
- the roles of any other adults (other than the teacher) in the classroom
- how teachers used questioning in relation to assessments.

The following illustrates a difficulty that one teacher, with many years of teaching experience, was having with science on this particular occasion. She had organised a number of activities for investigating 'eyes'. The resources she had allocated were inappropriate, having given the children concave mirrors for looking at their eyes and different timers for timing blinks. The children were given no guidance in fair testing when carrying out an eye test. Her planning had consisted of 'looking for some AT1' and did not involve any other SoAs, revealing that there was no clear indication of what children might learn about their eyes nor how the resources would support this. The children changed to different activities at leisure, with no check on findings thus far. At the end of the session this teacher had not made any assessments.

HMI (HMSO, 1989: 10) pointed out that although teachers were able to identify worthwhile activities, they were not clear about the potential they had for children's learning and that teachers 'seldom showed how the activities would progressively develop the children's scientific knowledge, understanding and skills and consequently this limited their value'. This seemed borne out by the 'eyes' work.

In direct contrast to this, however, this next teacher planned activities in detail and had anticipated organisational aspects by instructing the children not to interrupt her when she was carrying a red file. On beginning the observation, I was interested to see how the children would react to this instruction. The time she spent in discussion with children was in every case without interruption. She was able to question each child individually; this seemed to assist the children in effectively carrying out the activity, as observation of children after she had moved on revealed. This organisational strategy seemed to have real potential for enhancing the quality of the learning experience for these children.

Other adults observed in the classrooms consisted of parents, language assistants and support teachers, assisting with a wide range of activities. Support teachers tended to assist in teaching other areas of the curriculum such as mathematics and English. On the other hand, parents tended to help children who were sewing or baking. In general these adults appeared not to participate in the planning and organisation of the science tasks nor in the assessments, according to information acquired from interviews and observations. There was, however, one exception, when the class teacher and the support teacher planned science activities together, and each of them made assessments during the activity. They then came together at the end to share information. The class teacher remarked at post-activity interview:

'We plan together, you put more into it and you are more enthusiastic, we spark each other off. Sometimes you get stuck with just one of you.'

They both spent time talking to groups of children while they were working and, as with the teacher who used the red file method, there was ongoing, well-focused interaction between class members and the teacher. It seemed that joint planning and a team-based approach to organisation had some potential for promoting the learning, through well-focused opportunities for adult–child interaction.

Thus there were a number of problems arising from interruptions by children and other adults. An earlier example has already illustrated some benefits from uninterrupted discussion between teacher and child. On one occasion a teacher was observed to be interrupted no less than 23 times by children, teachers and the headteacher. Instances were also observed of the teacher not always being in an opportune place at an appropriate time and thus missing opportunities to assess children's knowledge in relation to particular SoAs at particular points in the activity. This is an organisational and planning issue in that in order to take advantage of such opportunities the teacher perhaps needs to be aware of when they are likely to occur and try and ensure attendance. Asking questions at the end of an activity was observed to provide some teachers with information about children's understanding. The depth of that information seemed directly related to the strategies the teacher used as the following two examples illustrate. This first teacher was questioning a group of children who had made spinners so as to create an optical illusion:

Teacher: When you spin, can you see the bird in the cage?
Children: Yes.

Teacher: Well done.

No immediate follow-up from this question was observed nor did the teacher persist with further questions to find out what the children had noticed or learnt. Other teachers were observed to elicit better discussion by asking appropriate, probing questions. In one classroom a group of children were testing materials to find out which one absorbed the most water:

Teacher: Can you explain why the sponge has more water in it?
Pupil: It has big holes in it and holds more, it's soft.
Teacher: What did you find out about the plastic?
Pupil: It's too slippery to hold water and it's hard, water can't get inside.

In organisational terms, then, the dilemma seemed to be when to teach and when to assess. Should assessment occur immediately after something had been taught or should learning and understanding be assessed at a future point?

Assessment and its Outcomes

All the teachers were observed making some kind of assessment of the children. However, the assessments varied depending on aspects of the planning and organisation of the activity and on attention to related detail. We have seen already something of the variety in the quality of the assessments made. The majority of the 15 teachers made more assessments in AT1 than in any other AT. The reasons for this were possibly twofold. One was that there were perhaps only one or two suitable SoAs that could be assessed through any observed activity, and another that the teachers were finding it far more difficult to assess children's knowledge than to assess process skills.

During pre and post-activity interviews, some teachers had expressed a view that assessment did not tell them anything they did not already know about the children's understanding. However, somewhat at odds with this, all the teachers, without exception also remarked that they had gained some information about individual children over and above that anticipated, once the activity had taken place. Many revealed that they had been surprised by the responses of certain individuals and also that the children had demonstrated prior knowledge which had not been taken into consideration by the teacher, when planning. Satterley (1981) describes this tendency to be over-confident about one's knowledge of children as a 'halo effect'. In the following example, however, this teacher revealed in the pre-activity interview that she had anticipated the children might have some difficulty with recording temperatures. The post-activity interview revealed that the children's difficulties perhaps went deeper:

> 'Owen couldn't read the thermometer; that surprised me and Anna was confused. She understood what we were doing yesterday. She surprised me the most, perhaps I take it for granted she understands and she doesn't.'

Here was an example of 'negative' surprise – a lack of understanding on the children's part, not previously anticipated and clearly affecting outcomes.

The extent of the recording of assessments varied from teacher to teacher. Where teachers said in pre-activity interviews that they would make jottings or notes during the activity they were seldom observed doing so. The good intention to take notes while assessing was evidently difficult to carry through into practice, largely because the teachers were either involved in asking questions and talking to children or they were organising the rest of the class. As one teacher admitted:

> 'I'll be trying to jot things down but I don't think this is easy to do at all. I find there is so much going on in the classroom, it's almost impossible to write anything down.'

This teacher did not take notes or make jottings but spent time with the group discussing their ideas. The kinds of interruptions noted earlier, made by children and other adults, also seemed to leave many teachers with little time to make such notes. However, those teachers who wrote down the criteria they were looking for beforehand, alongside children's names, were observed ticking these off as they were evidenced. This gave these teachers some evidence of learning.

The teachers were asked about subsequent steps they should take once they had made assessments. Suggestions were tentative on the whole. One teacher remarked:

> 'Those children I was doubtful about I suppose I would talk to them again and see if I could get anything out of them, but that's an ideal situation. The way things are, it's finding time to look at it again. The topic effectively ends next week.'

Such developments were suggested when teachers had diagnosed children's problems, as was the case of the child having difficulty reading a thermometer. This teacher had subsequently remarked that time needed to be spent improving this skill and intended to plan for it. Some teachers considered developing elements of AT1. They felt that children needed more help with recording or more activities requiring them to hypothesise. Formative assessment was rarely referenced, often, it seemed, because teachers associated assessment with coming at the end of a particular topic and thus would not be focusing again on that area. In general, they were unsure where to go next and made vague suggestions for future planning:

'Maybe in another activity we'll do recording in a different way and pick up on some areas of AT1.'

During observation and interview, it was noted that none of the teachers used children's self-assessments as part of their overall strategy for information gathering. Children were not informed beforehand if they were being assessed, neither were they asked to comment on either their own performances nor on what they had found out during the activity except in those cases identified above. Alexander, Rose & Woodhead (1992) suggest that this is an important part of the assessment process, remarking that, 'Pupils should as far as is feasible be involved in the assessment of their own work' (p. 33).

Knowledge of Science and its Assessment

Four of the 15 teachers involved in the research had a related science-based background and all 15 spoke of trying to come to terms with the science document. As one teacher pointed out:

'I find some of the statements a bit vague. If you think about them a bit too deeply you do realise some are not straightforward, don't you?'

Those teachers who had some prior knowledge still experienced difficulty in interpreting the SoAs and were unsure of the concept paths within the ATs. Those teachers who had received some science INSET were still making conceptual mistakes. The lack of conceptual understanding presented difficulties which affected assessment opportunities:

'We did an experiment with cabbage and we put cold water on and it turned blue and we put vinegar on it and it turned red, I was as amazed as the kids and that worries me all the time. I don't really know what I'm talking about.'

The sample, as a whole, experienced difficulty in teaching physical science having had no previous experiences themselves:

'It's my own knowledge really, I don't understand. I don't understand forces until you explained it on the course. I couldn't see it for myself. I did biology at school, that's all. It's the physics side of science I feel very unsure of. I'm glad I just teach Key Stage 1 and not higher levels.'

Although some teachers commented that they had enjoyed the activities they also admitted that they lacked confidence in teaching the subject:

'It's not an area that's ever interested me, isn't science. Although I quite like doing the activities with the children I'm not confident myself in teaching scientific facts.'

Several teachers remarked that they had turned to reference books when trying to plan and find answers to certain questions but as one long-serving teacher explained:

'When I'm planning I get some books so I can look for activities and swot up, but some of the children ask really hard questions. Like today, I was caught out by the metals because I've no idea why some metals are attracted to magnets and some aren't.'

Overall the 15 teachers found science difficult to teach and difficult to assess.

Conclusions

This research gave me useful insights into how science was being taught in the classroom and how these teachers were putting assessment procedures into practice. Teachers' anxieties concerning science and assessment are understandable and clearly there will be no easy solutions post-Dearing. The content remains as challenging as ever. However, there are no statements of attainment to support assessment, only level descriptors for assessment at the end of the Key Stage. This is likely to make the teachers' task even more difficult. All of the teachers involved in the research were trying hard to overcome the problems of taking on board an avalanche of new information and related assessment procedures. I concluded that there were a number of factors which influenced the effectiveness of teachers' assessments relating to the planning and provision of the activities. Many of these were also recognised by HMI (HMSO, 1991) who stated:

Good assessment practice involved a carefully balanced combination of the established procedures for judging young children's progress – observation, questioning, discussion and marking – and the use of ATs against which to measure those judgements. Teachers used the evidence of written and other tangible work together with occasional notes of their observations and discussion, in judging children's attainments. (HMSO, 1991: 13)

Planning for good assessment means planning activities in detail and recognising in advance what learning outcomes to expect. Each activity needs to have a detailed breakdown with a manageable number of developmental concepts and skills identified. If the planning was done carefully beforehand and in detail it appeared, from my observations, the more successful the activity would be and the more fruitful the assessments gained from it. By using the word 'success' in this instance I refer to the quality of the activity and the associated learning outcomes. The lack of teachers' knowledge of scientific skills and concepts, inhibited this detailed planning of suitable activities and their assessment in many cases. In general these teachers lacked confidence when planning science activities. However, there was some variation in teachers' planning and organisation of science and assessment. This variation raised a number of issues:

- What is the minimum required from teachers?
- Are some teachers unaware of how to plan effectively?
- Are there some teachers who will never be able to plan effectively?

Satterley (1981) remarks that knowledge of the results of pupils' performance provides information which is potentially capable of improving teaching. Lacking this knowledge implies a diminishing of the likelihood of effective planning. Even when assessments had been made by the teachers in the study there was little evidence to suggest that they were being used to inform further planning by the teacher or to consider whether or not they had met their original learning objectives through the provision of the particular activity.

Integral to the learning process is a requirement for teachers to evaluate the effectiveness of the activities they plan. They need to be able to look closely at the type of activities they plan and how these activities affect learning outcomes for a range of children. It would be useful for teachers to consider the assessments they have previously made when planning. The teachers who had planned in detail, and who felt confident in the science they had taught and had also used their assessments in subsequent planning, were the ones whose activities proved to be well organised and from which information was gained.

Some teachers made use of collegial support when planning, such as planning and assessing with colleagues in the same year group or alongside support teachers. The teacher who did the latter found it had many advantages in that ideas could be exchanged and encouragement was given.

Efficient organisation is an essential element of assessment. The teacher needs to be able to organise and manage the class while maintaining a focus on the assessment activity. A lack of organisational skills can lead to a chaotic situation as Bennett *et al.* (1984) noted:

> It had been shown that teachers typically adopt what has been termed a crisis management style. This requires that they be all things to all pupils at all times. The consequences of this style include constant interruptions, divided teacher attention, lack of adequate class supervision, lack of opportunity for diagnosis and explanation and, in many instances, teacher frustration. In short, a learning environment which is far from optimal for teacher or taught. (Bennett *et al.*, 1984: 219)

Similar situations were observed in two classroom where teachers were constantly interrupted by the children. This seemed to minimise potential learning outcomes and diminish qualitative aspects of the activity. Signalling clearly, even to very young children, that the teacher does not wish to be interrupted, was observed to fulfil its intention. This management strategy had resulted in the teacher having time to make notes and collect evidence without constant interruptions. Observations revealed that potential assessment opportunities were missed because of the heavy demand on teacher time. Many children had not been taught to be self-sufficient. This could have saved the teacher valuable time. Asking appropriately framed questions after the activity was giving a small number of teachers further useful information.

Concerns were expressed by the teachers about the lack of time available for the development of science-related assessment skills. No sooner had the three core documents arrived than teachers were asked to incorporate other National Curriculum subjects into their teaching. Many teachers felt it would take time to develop overall assessment skills. A further consideration was concerned with how learning is affected by the passage of time:

> 'What worries me is, it's all right, they know it today but will they know it next week? You write it down and give it to the next teacher but is it really a true assessment of what they will know by the time they get to the next teacher? If they've done it today it doesn't mean to say they will understand it next year.'

The relatively new learning position that teachers are in is noted by Sutton (1991) who remarks:

It is worth noting, right from the start, that assessment is a human process, conducted by and with human beings, and subject inevitably to the frailties of human judgement. However crisp and objective we might try to make it, and however quantifiable may be our 'results', assessment is closer to an art than a science. It is, after all, an exercise in human communication. (Sutton, 1991: 2)

Teachers require support in their efforts to teach and assess science and this can, to some extent, be provided by in-service training in the form of extending the designated courses for science and providing further core knowledge training. There is clearly a need to continue locally based training in applying the assessment process. However, teachers need time to assimilate information and improve upon their assessment skills and five years of promised stability may help if continued support and opportunities for professional development are forthcoming.

The information I have gained through the research will influence both my planning of in-service provision for teacher and work undertaken in the classroom in support of teachers.

12 The Teaching and Learning of Science in the Infant and Lower Junior Age Ranges

KEITH BARDON

Introduction

Ten years ago the Department of Education and Science (DES, (1985) published the document Science 5–16: *A Statement of Policy*, in which it made the following critical comments:

> It is still the case that too few pupils in primary schools are systematically introduced to science. The task for all concerned is to define policies for the development of science in primary schools, and to plan and implement strategies for putting those policies into effect. (DES, 1985: 6)

Since that time the profile of science in the primary classroom has greatly increased; however, viewing the subject as an integral part of the primary curriculum is still relatively recent. For some teachers, adopting this view has been a developmental process. As the world has become increasingly science-oriented so their teaching has needed to change to accommodate this shift in emphasis. Some teachers have found science thrust upon them by a range of DES/DfE (Department for Education) and LEA (local education authority) initiatives and, of course, the introduction of the National Curriculum. The implementation of the 1988 Education Reform Act has undoubtedly accelerated the rate of educational change in primary schools with evident impact in infant and lower junior classrooms as they bore the brunt, in the primary sector, of the introduction of these statutory requirements. It was for this reason that this particular age band was chosen as the subject of this study.

The intention of the study was to look at the classroom practices of a small number of teachers for the purposes of identifying the principle features of the science they were teaching and the factors influencing its delivery. It is in keeping with the type of research described by Engelhart (1972) as a 'classroom climate study' in that it examines teaching methods, influences upon them and their effects on the pupil population. An approach was thus adopted which enabled the teaching programme as a whole to be studied. To some primary practitioners the task of teaching science as an integral part of the curriculum was, as stated above, something of an innovation. Without doubt the intensity of National Curriculum science made new kinds of demands on all those involved in the education of the pre-12 year olds. As those teachers now address a purportedly 'slimmer' science curriculum it seems timely to review lessons learned from the initial implementation. Thus it was within a climate of change and development that this research into the teaching and learning of primary science was carried out.

This study does not attempt to assess the impact of the National Curriculum on the teaching and learning of science, although it is inevitable that some related references will be made. Other initiatives such as the Educational Support Grants and changes made to Initial Teacher Training may have played a part in raising the profile of primary science and it could be some time before the levels of influence of these initiatives can be determined. The project focuses on the classroom climate relative to the teaching and learning of science in the infant and lower junior phases of primary education. The study itself is ethnographic in nature in that it strives to illuminate rather than simply describe situations and events, that is, it aims to 'penetrate beneath surface appearances and reveal the harder realities there concealed'. (Woods, 1988: 91)

Research Sample

The nature of the research question suggested that it would be more appropriate to place the emphasis on depth of information rather than breadth; time constraints did not allow for both. It was decided therefore to look in detail at the work of five teachers. With this relatively small initial sample size, it was impossible to include a substantial number of permutations of teacher age and experience, pupil age, school size, socio/economic mix of intake etc. The sampling was subsequently based on the type and location of the schools in which the teacher worked, the length of teaching experience and the teacher's educational background. An important factor in the selection of participants was whether or not they were in a position to and would indeed impart the information required. Burgess (1984) classes this method as 'judgement and opportunistic sampling' and writes of it:

> These forms of non-probability sampling involve the selection of actions, events and people. In judgement sampling informants may be selected for study according to a number of criteria established by the researcher [...] Meanwhile, opportunistic sampling is used to refer to the process whereby the field researchers find informants who provide them with data. Here the researcher selects individuals with whom it is possible to co-operate. (Burgess, 1984: 55)

The sample was taken from teachers with responsibility for children in the infant and lower junior age range as, at the time of study, it was these teachers who had the greatest amount of experience of teaching science within the statutory requirements of the National Curriculum.

Each of the five schools were situated in a Metropolitan District in the North of England. The primary schools in the authority vary considerably in size and in the cultural and social mix of their pupil populations. Table 12.1 below provides information on the schools in which the research took place and provides background information on the participant teachers and their pupils.

My own role within the research was one of participant-as-observer, described by Burgess (1984) as one in which 'the researcher participates as well as observes by developing relationships with informants' (p. 81). He elaborates on his view of this role by quoting Donald Roy:

> The participant-as-observer not only makes no secret of his investigation; he makes it known that research is his overriding interest. He is there to observe. To mention a second distinction that I feel is important, the participant-as-observer is not tied down, he is free to run around as research interests beckon. (Burgess, 1984: 81)

It must be admitted that at the outset of research I had envisaged my role as being more than that of observer-as-participant in that I expected a relatively high level of formality, particularly with teachers and children with whom I had made little or no previous contact. An introductory pre-visit was made to all participating classes, but even without this, I should through experience have anticipated that the gregarious nature of young children and the people who teach them would have ensured that as soon as I walked into a classroom I would become an integral part of the society therein.

Table 12.1 Summary of details of participant schools, teachers and pupils

Teacher Code	Description of school	Year group of class	Years of teaching experience	Science background
A	150 pupil infant and nursery Situated in a 'middle-class' area on the outskirts of a large town	1	13	No formal qualifications Has not attended a recent science-focused coursef Joint holder of post of responsibility for science
B	350 pupil junior and infant Situated in a small semi rural town with a broad socioeconomic mix	2	23	No formal qualifications Has recently attended a science knowledge upgrade course Does not hold responsibility for science
C	280 pupil junior, infant and nursery Situated in one of the less affluent areas of a large town	3	14	No formal qualifications Has not attended a recent science-focused INSET course Does not hold post of responsibility for science
D	210 pupil first (5–9 years) Situated in prosperous mainly residential small town	3 & 4 mixed	7	O Level Chemistry O and A Level Biology Has recently attended a '20-Day' science course Regularly attends LEA science INSET Science co-ordinator for the school
E	280 pupil junior Situated in a small industrial town and serving a principally Muslim community	3 & 4 mixed	3	BSc (Chemistry and Physiology) Has recently attended a science knowledge upgrade course Does not hold a post of responsibility for science

Data Collection

For data collection a number of related methods were employed. A questionnaire was used to obtain factual information and to provide teachers with an opportunity to express their personal views on science and its teaching. Further perceptions and opinions from both teachers and pupils were obtained by interview before and after each session. In each classroom, the teacher divided the class into sub-groups of between four and ten pupils, with six being the most common number. In each of the observed sessions a particular group was focused on throughout the science activity. Each session was of a morning's or afternoon's duration depending upon when the class would normally be engaged on science-based activities. This 'normality' thus offered a structure for the timing of the research visits. Each class was observed during one pre-visit and three research sessions.

Teacher interviews were carried out outside the class contact time and pupil interviews during the session. For both teachers and children the interviews were located within a framework of open-ended questions which allowed for the development of any other, related issues that arose. During the pre-activity interview with the teacher the questions centred around the structure of the activity, reasons for its selection and the learning objectives. Such discussion facilitated the identification of the process based learning the teacher was hoping to promote through the practical application of the skills and scientific investigation of the concepts to be developed via the knowledge and understanding basis for the planned activities. The post-activity interview focused on the teacher's perceptions of how well the objectives had been met and how the teacher felt the children had responded.

The pre-activity interview with the children was carried out between the teacher's introduction and the commencement of the activity. Questions focused on what the children had made of the introduction, had they known what they had been asked to do and had they any comments to make on what they were expected to gain from doing the activity? The post-activity interview asked the children to reflect on what they had done and on what they had learnt. They were asked their views on why they had been asked to do the activity and whether this was a good way to learn about science and why.

Each activity was observed so that the teacher inputs and interventions and the resulting reactions of the pupils could be identified and monitored. During the observation a record was made of the children working using a video camera. The record comprised of 'windows' on the activity, that is, short pieces of film depicting the stages the activity went through as it progressed. This was shown to the children after the activity had been completed in the hope that it would stimulate discussion of what they did and why. Unfortunately, what had seemed a good idea at the planning stage proved very disappointing in practice. As Hopkins (1985) intimates, the novelty of seeing themselves 'on the telly' proved too distracting for the children, irrespective of how and when the film was shown to them. Some success was gained by showing the children the film once and then asking questions as it was run a second time, but even using this method the time and effort spent and cost incurred could not be justified in terms of the information gained.

Of the research methods employed, interviewing provided a substantial amount of in-depth information. One initial concern was how young children would respond to interviewing by a relative stranger. The concern was unfounded; at all times the children were open and forthright in their views. They thoroughly enjoyed being given the opportunity to express their feelings about what and how they were taught, and seemed to appreciate that someone was bothering to ask them such questions. The level of professionalism shown by the teachers was outstanding, their general attitude being that it was worth putting up with the inconvenience of having the researcher around, because in the long run there could be benefits for the children and for themselves.

Research Findings

Initial examination of the data revealed that analysis and reporting could be facilitated by categorising the information. This decision was also influenced by a previous study in which 35 teachers had been asked, via a questionnaire, for their perceptions of primary science, and by Engelhart's (1972) discussion of content analysis in his discussion of 'classroom climate studies'. The categories utilised in this study were finalised when data collection was complete and initial examination had commenced. Analysis was thus undertaken by grouping the findings under six headings, which, it was felt, represented the important aspects of the teaching programme, as a whole:

(1) Activity planning;
(2) Organisational issues;
(3) Activity management;
(4) Teachers' understanding of science;
(5) Teaching and learning issues;
(6) Pupils' perspectives.

They would also facilitate the identification and discussion of the principle features of science and the factors influencing delivery.

Activity Planning

In the primary phase of education, science is commonly taught from a thematic base. Each of the five teachers involved in this study identified the topic as the base upon which the majority of their activities were planned; but the premise upon which the topics were founded varied from teacher to teacher and from school to school. The topic planned by teacher A could be described as contextual in that the linking theme was a number of nursery rhymes, each one encompassing a different area of experience. This contrasted with the 'Ships' topic planned by teacher D, which could be regarded as conceptual, in that it looked to develop across and via a range of activities, a specific area of scientific knowledge concerned with the principles surrounding floating and sinking.

The context in which activities are set does not have to be unique or sophisticated, quite the opposite in fact. Discussion with pupils suggested that simple, yet linked themes were appreciated. The pupils at the school studying 'Ships' demonstrated an overall understanding of the logic in investigating floating and sinking in this context. The children working from nursery rhymes, however, were clearly struggling to link the sticking together of biscuits in order to evaluate edible adhesives with the story of Hansel and Gretal.

Although the current topic base featured strongly whenever planning was discussed it was not the only rationale identified. Opportunities were also taken from particular events such as festivals within the school calendar – Bonfire night, Diwali, and Christmas featured in supporting science work. A third rationale of activities relating to a discrete knowledge area were a feature of at least one teacher's planning. A 'light' activity planned by an infant teacher did not have a thematic base; it was an additional activity inserted between two topics. Discussion with these children revealed an acceptance that if their teacher had planned something for them it would be interesting and they would gain something from doing it. If pupils have confidence in their teacher's ability to identify what is worth learning, it seems they might enter a classroom with a level of expectancy that can be turned, by the skilful practitioner, into meaningful activity.

Teacher enthusiasm for the topics around which the activities were built seemed to link with the mode of identification. As might be anticipated, if the topic had been selected by the teacher herself there was generally greater commitment and sense of ownership than if it had been identified for that teacher by, for example, the subject co-ordinator. Teacher B illustrated why she felt it was important for the class teacher to have 'control' over the topic with the following example:

'Rather than do changes in food as a topic I find it better to pick it out where it fits in and take the opportunity to put some purpose to it.'

In all cases, irrespective of how the topic had been identified, the planning of activities was seen as the responsibility of the class teacher.

When teachers were asked where their 'inspiration' for the activities came from they gave a variety of responses such as a combination of previous experience, information acquired from other teachers and material obtained from commercial sources. As one of the teachers explained:

'I think it's just experience, either something you've done before or you've seen someone else doing it and others from books. It's a mixture basically or copying things from schools. You see something on a wall and think that looks nice, we could do it like this.' (Teacher E)

Commercially produced science schemes were available in two of the five schools but these were used in the same manner as other commercially produced materials; teachers 'dipped into them' at the planning stage in search of an activity or discussion relevant to their current work. Schemes were never used in their entirety, but rather as an aid to the teachers' planning. At no time during interview or other informal discussion did any teacher make reference to a school scheme of work for science. Perhaps this has since begun to change with the current requirement for curriculum policy documents.

Although all the teachers gave the children the opportunity to express their own ideas during the ongoing activity, the children's influence upon the activity, at the planning stage, was negligible. Instances occurred of children putting forward legitimate, alternative investigative procedures. In some instances it was observed that the children's ideas were manipulated, being made to 'fit in' with the teacher's own agenda. In other instances, the ideas were acknowledged but not pursued. In every case the activity structure had been determined by the teacher before consulting the children.

Organisational Issues

During the observed sessions all but one of the classes were organised on an 'integrated' basis; that is, each class was divided into workgroups, with each group working on a different area of the curriculum. The exception was the Year 3 class of teacher C. In this case science was taught to the whole class at the same time, although here, too, the class was divided into workgroups for the practical elements of the lessons.

In only three of the 15 observed sessions did the group of children work together as a cohesive unit. In two of these three sessions the teacher worked with the group throughout, in effect directing the activity and being the catalyst for cohesion. In the third session the group had only one piece of apparatus between them and therefore had no alternative but to co-operate with each other in order to access the apparatus and complete the activity. On occasion, these workgroups were sub-divided by the teacher into smaller groups of two or three pupils. At other times the children took it upon themselves to sub-divide the group. On two occasions the group structure ceased to exist and the children worked individually. There appeared to be no optimum size of group and the principle that most of the teachers seemed to apply was to allow a degree of flexibility so that group size could be matched to activity.

With the exception of one session in which the class was allowed to form 'friendship groups', group composition was determined by the teacher. Of the five teachers, one had a system of mixed ability groups, one had large mixed ability workgroups that were divided into smaller ability sub-groups and the other three teachers grouped by ability. The criteria upon which ability was judged varied considerably between the individual teachers. Teachers D and E grouped children according to their 'scientific' ability. Teachers A and B used what can only be described as a general ability level, and teacher C based her groups on language ability.

The impact of using language ability as the criteria to structure science groups became evident during one particular research visit. On this occasion, the teacher had planned an activity that involved the children in the careful observation of a burning candle and an investigation of what happens when a burning candle is enclosed in a container. The research focused on a group of six pupils described by the teachers as the 'brighter girls'. She added:

'They are the better group language wise ... they would tend to be the ones you could leave to get on and not come back to as much.' (Teacher C)

Observation of this group proved revealing and worrying. After watching what happened when a small glass tumbler was placed over a lighted

candle, each group member expressed surprise at the result. Explaining to
the rest of the group, one pupil said that this had happened because,
when the tumbler had been turned upside down, the air in it had dropped
on to the flame and blown it out. She supported her argument by asking
the group to think about what would have happened if there had been a
small amount of water in the tumbler instead of air. After observing a
candle stay alight for a longer period of time in a large tumbler, the same
pupil said that this was because the air had further to drop before it
reached the flame. Other members of the group appeared to accept this
explanation and only one other tentative suggestion was made, that the
thickness of the glass had something to do with it. When the teacher
joined the group she assumed that, because they had observed accurately,
the children had reached a point where they could take on board the
concept being explored, namely that the length of time the candle burned
was related to the amount of oxygen in the air. In effect, because the
children's ideas about 'the air around us' were insufficiently developed,
they were clearly unready to accommodate this new concept. When
asked, at the end of the lesson, what they felt they had learned, the
children were still talking about air 'getting straight to the candle and
blowing it out'. Although they were deemed 'bright' from a language
point of view, the scientific concepts of this group of children, in this area
at least, were clearly not well developed. Judging from this teacher's
comments about one of the 'less able' groups: – 'Once Luke had
mentioned the fact that it was the oxygen they quite quickly got the idea
that there was less oxygen in the smaller container.' – opinions regarding
children's scientific capabilities formed on the basis of their language
ability may be extremely misleading.

Activity management

One notable difference between the five teachers was the time taken
both to introduce the activity to the class at the beginning of the lesson
and to bring it to a well-rounded conclusion at the end. Teacher B always
spent in excess of 45 minutes interacting with her infant class before they
commenced the practical element and no less than 20 minutes concluding
it. It was noticeable that when these children were interviewed they all
wanted to contribute to the discussion and, in doing so, demonstrated
that they knew not only what they were doing but also how the activity
related to previous activities and experiences and, in some cases, how it
could be developed further. The remaining teachers tended to spend a
shorter time, giving a general introduction to the whole class and
reinforcing this with more detailed group input, once the activity had

commenced. This often resulted in the children starting the activity without a clear picture of its purpose. While watching a video of the activity they had just completed one group of Year 3 pupils were asked when it had become clear to them what they had to do. They replied that it was not until about half-way through that they fully understood what the teacher was after. In a different school teacher A expressed her disappointment at the outcome of the activity and remarked:

'They seemed very subdued. They didn't seem to understand what we were getting at at all. Even when we were discussing differences they weren't really with it, were they?'

One common feature was the degree of structure that all the teachers built into the activities. Teacher B who had planned an activity that had a structured element followed by a much more open investigation explained her thinking:

'If you structure them first they have something tangible to do and they drift into the other. If you just put it out and tell them to get on with it I don't think you get anything. I like to get my sessions set. It's the whole classroom management as much as anything because I like them all to know what they are doing. Those first few minutes are so important as to whether you manage the rest of the period or you don't.'

The strategies the children were asked to employ were many and varied; observation to find out about facial features; problem solving to find the best sewing thread; open investigation to find out about shadows; closed investigation to find out what happens to a burning candle when a tumbler is placed over it. The most common strategy used was the 'semi-open investigation', that is, an open investigation with parameters established by the teacher. For example, one teacher had identified an activity in which the children were to investigate the insulating properties of fabrics. The potential of the activity as an investigation is limitless but, by pre-determining the fabrics the children were allowed to use and the methodology they were to employ, the teacher kept within pre-determined boundaries.

No one investigative approach, be it observation, problem solving, open investigation, closed investigation, or any other, appeared to have inherent, comparative advantages. The teachers employed between them the full range of approaches; some teachers were, however, more flexible than others. Teacher B for instance was seen to use observation, semi-open and open investigations in one session alone, while teacher C planned closed investigations throughout the period of the research.

Teachers' understanding of the science

Two factors emerged relevant to the level of the teachers' understanding of both the scientific process and the knowledge base of scientific concepts. First, the part that science had played in their own education, and secondly, the science-focused courses they had attended since the advent of the National Curriculum. Of the two factors, the latter seemed from their comments to have been the most significant. Three of the teachers had attended recent courses, one of them as a participant on a DES funded 20-day course and two as members of a 'Core Knowledge Upgrade' course organised by the LEA's Science Advisory Team (see Table 12.1.) One of these two was a science graduate, so it was perhaps not surprising to find that her understanding was sound. The other teacher had no formal science education and, therefore, when teaching science, relied on her teaching experience backed by the quality of the information, knowledge and skills acquired from the courses she had attended. Throughout the research period all three of these teachers demonstrated an ability to identify clearly the concepts and/or skills they were looking to develop. Discussing an investigation of light the teacher with no formal science training, described the scientific focus as:

> 'To know that light passes through some materials and not through others and causes a shadow where it doesn't. That's what I hope the children will get out of it.' (Teacher B)

She had targeted precisely the knowledge she was striving to promote. Teacher D, who had recently had the benefit of a DES (DfEE) designated science course explained how she was building conceptual progression into the floating and sinking activities she was providing:

> 'I am extending the activity you saw last time. Trying to take this group one step further. Seeing if there is some reason for it floating or sinking. They're still saying if it changes shape it changes weight so I've got the scales out. The last part of the activity leads into plasticine boats.'

The three teachers who had attended recent training courses also had the knowledge and understanding to evaluate continually the activities, make adjustments to improve their performance and to modify them in order to correct malfunctions. Teacher E presented one group of children with the task of investigating a selection of fabrics to find out which were waterproof, which were showerproof and which were neither. When asked at the end of the activity whether she would make any changes to the activity before presenting it to another group of children she explained:

'I would take out the showerproof category and introduce it later, at the end of a simpler investigation. Then we could do the test again adding in this new factor. As we were going along I realised that showerproof is really hard to record and to find out. I didn't want to stop them because they had set the criteria for themselves and that I didn't want to change it as this was a step forward for the group.'

The remaining teachers had no science qualification nor had they recently attended a science course. Their level of confidence and scientific understanding was noticeably weaker. An activity planned by one of these teachers asked the children to look in a mirror and carefully draw their own reflection. When asked what the science focus of the activity was the teacher had difficulty identifying it:

'Well, it's careful observation, comparison with others, looking at the differences, how people aren't the same, just talking about the features you have got and drawing it. Thinking about where your eyes are in relation to your ears etc. Instead of just giving them a piece of paper and saying draw yourself because they just draw something that vaguely resembles some ... I don't know what really.' (Teacher A)

At the end of the session she expressed dissatisfaction with the children's response, they were apparently as confused as she was as to what the activity was all about:

'It seemed to miss the point completely with them. I think eventually the two girls were looking and thinking with a lot of, well is it here or is it there and what colour ... but I don't know if they noticed differences between each other, which I thought would have been pretty obvious.' (Teacher A)

Teaching and learning issues

Invariably, when asked for the scientific focus of an activity, the teachers would identify either skills or concepts, but on only two occasions did respondents offer both. Teachers who identified a knowledge area as the target might, with prompting, add a skill or number of skills, but these were often vague and expressed without much conviction:

'It's sort of an exploratory activity. It's a hands on, first-hand experience activity.' (Teacher A)

Teacher B, who had a clear vision of the concept areas she was hoping to develop, explained her approach to Attainment Target 1:

'That's the one that goes on all the time isn't it. You hope they are doing that to get to the attainment target all the time, don't you. They will have done some finding out and some recording, so that's two attainment targets.'

Similarly, teachers who could outline the skills they were hoping to promote through the activity were less than specific when it came to knowledge areas, often giving blanket responses such as 'materials' or 'forces' when asked to outline the knowledge content of an activity.

This bias towards either skills or concepts also affected teachers' approaches to continuity and progression. One teacher, for example, had structured a series of investigations that progressively developed the children's investigative skills. All the activities, however, concentrated on the same concept area and therefore there was little progression of knowledge. In contrast, the nursery rhyme topic moved, in consecutive weeks, from an activity about the differences between individuals to one about how materials change and then on to one concerned with magnetism. After the magnetism activity the teacher explained that it had been a precursor to the children investigating reflection of light. By constantly being moved from one knowledge area to another the children were being given little opportunity to concept-build.

Only one of the teachers actually stated that she planned activities with a particular group of children in mind. Another intimated that, in the light of experience, she would modify her planned programme for certain children, but these were the only two examples observed during the research of differentiation at the point of input. Far more common was the situation whereby the teacher planned an activity and delivered it to all the class irrespective of individual pupil activity. These teachers seemed to be relying on differentiation by outcome. This worked satisfactorily when the activity was sufficiently 'open' but was less successful where the activity had a defined structure. After one such activity, Teacher E indicated that she had recognised the problem and remarked:

'I don't think Khatisar got anything out of it. She was very confused so I don't think she got what I was aiming for. She enjoyed taking part and doing the activity but she didn't understand why she was doing it.'

Pupils' perspectives

On one thing the children were in agreement, finding out for themselves was fun. It says much for the efforts of the teachers that only one child out of the 85 interviewed said that he had not enjoyed the activity. His reason? He didn't like the shadows, they frightened him! At three of the five schools the children knew exactly what the subject area was that they were involved in – it was science. Their teachers used the term frequently and the children had come to associate the word with a practical lesson in which they would be given the opportunity to investigate for themselves. All three teachers had received recent science input, via courses. The identification of science in this way ensured that the pupils always knew what was required of them, they had come to have expectations of the lesson and also to accept that the teacher would have expectations of them in terms of how they set about the task in hand. Many of these children used the term 'science' to form links between different experiences. When asked, after investigating the strengths of threads if they could think of anything else they had done that was science, a trio of Year 4 children replied:

'We went into the boiler house and used our hands to find out where it was hot and where it was cold.'

'We buried some paper and other things in the ground and made a chart of disappearing and not disappearing.'

'We put some water in a place and we left it and we finded out does the water go away?'

Children who were not familiar with the term 'science' used their own heading under which to catergorise the activities. Titles such as a 'finding out activity' or a 'sticking activity' were used and investigations that involved food were inevitably 'cooking' or 'baking' activities.

On the subject of how they learn best the children were unequivocal. They had to do the activity and find out for themselves. However the question was put to them the answers were always the same:

'It wouldn't have been interesting at all because you have to find out for yourself.'

'You've got to do it on your own and it's only when you figure it out for yourself that you learn.'

Summary and Discussion of the Findings

A thematic approach to the planning of science was observed frequently during this study. This can be an effective way of providing context for scientific activities when the area of experience that the teacher wishes to develop has been clearly identified and the theme is built around these objectives. It is far less effective when the science is simply accommodated by the theme or topic. In the planning and provision of scientific activities, the most important question appears not be which mode of delivery to employ, topic, thematic or discrete, but rather how to ensure that the experiences provided for children are stimulating and scientifically rewarding and meaningful. The need for in-service training in the skills of activity planning for science continues across both primary key stages.

The degree of structure that all the teachers built into the activities was very marked. Could it be that teachers feel that there is an in-built structure to science that they have to respect? It is possible that the teachers do not yet feel confident enough with the subject area to allow the children too much freedom. Is this level of formality present in other subject areas and is more 'open' learning far less common than we think it is? These questions cannot be answered by this study but what is apparent is that these five teachers, none of whom regarded themselves as formal practitioners, delivered science within a framework that afforded them a high level of control over the activities and their outcomes.

Whole-class discussion took place frequently and the majority of the teachers elicited the children's ideas as to how the information they were seeking could be obtained. Little evidence was found, however, of the teachers incorporating the children's ideas into the activity planning. This brings into question the value of consulting the children at this stage when the outcomes from the consultation are not then to be used constructively. It must be off-putting for a child to submit a good idea and not have the opportunity to pursue it. Why this occurred was difficult to assess. Could it be that teachers feel obliged to consult the children but do not know what to do with the information when they have got it, or is it simply that working to a structure that they themselves have identified provides them with more security? As Bennett, Wragg & Carre (1991) have shown, many primary teachers do doubt their own ability to deliver National Curriculum science.

All the teachers employed some form of group structure when organising the children for practical work. The size of the groups varied and was at times governed by the available resources. The ultimate influence on the group size, however, appeared to be the pupils themselves. Teacher-structured groups greater than three always broke into sub-groups and at times even pairs separated. There did not seem to be any disadvantage in this 'free-market' and the children appeared very adept at selecting someone with whom they could work productively. It is an almost impossible task for the teacher continually to group and regroup children so that they are socially and academically well matched, and there is a lot to be said for employing a system that allows the children to make at least some of the decisions themselves.

If children are to be ability grouped for scientific activities the grouping should be based on their scientific ability or experience. This may seem a very obvious statement to make; however, this research suggests that for these teachers this was not as easy to achieve as it may at first seem. Grouping by subject ability has far-reaching implications for the 'integrated subject' approach to classroom management commonly found during this study. If this organisational strategy is to be employed, is it reasonable to expect teachers to restructure the groups every time the children move from one subject area another? The logistics of such a system do not bear thinking about, hence perhaps the 'catch-all' ability grouping observed. As children move through school their differentials of ability and experience may widen. At what age the strategies of the 'integrated day' and 'ability grouping' may become totally incompatible is difficult to assess at the present time, but this could prove an enlightening area for future study.

Planning scientific tasks for children that are not based on their known scientific skills, knowledge and experience can result in the children 'groping about in the dark' and forming or consolidating misconceptions, as the children with the candle under the tumbler were doing. This would appear to be the direction of Osborne & Freyberg's (1985: 89) thinking when they concluded that: 'If a scientific proposition is too sophisticated for children, in relation to their prior experience and level of cognitive maturity, then it will not be appreciated.' It could also, of course, result in work that is below the capabilities of the children and which fails to be stimulating or developmental. While it may be unrealistic to expect teachers to differentiate all the activities they plan, allowance must surely be made for the spread of abilities that exists in all classrooms. Activities perhaps need to be evaluated at the planning stage, to ensure their suitability for all the children to whom they are to be delivered. Little evidence was found to indicate that this evaluation does take place at the present time, although some teachers may now be moving towards it.

In its initial non-statutory guidance for science the National Curriculum Council (NCC, 1989b) intimated that when providing activities for children, teachers should strive to simultaneously develop the skills and concepts of science. They suggested that: 'Teachers will need to review their teaching styles to ensure that investigative work uses, reinforces and develops the concepts of science.' (NCC, 1989b: D1).

This idea of 'balance' between skills and concepts is reinforced in the latest statutory orders for science issued by the DfE (1995). At both Key Stages 1 and 2 the Programmes of Study relating to Experimental and Investigative Science states that activities that encourage the development of experimental and investigative methods should also encourage pupils to use and develop their scientific knowledge and understanding. It would appear, from the comments they made, that these teachers are currently experiencing some difficulty in striking this kind of balance.

There is, not surprisingly, a link between the level of teachers' understanding of science and their confidence in their abilities to teach it effectively. Teachers who had a science element in their education or initial training have an advantage over those who have not; but perhaps a more significant factor was whether or not they had recently attended a science upgrading course that would combine subject knowledge with pedagogy. Such courses not only impart knowledge but also allow teachers to participate, at their own level, in the learning process. It is this first-hand experience of how scientific knowledge and skills are developed that appears to be as important for adults as it is for children. The teachers, having been put into the situation themselves, begin to appreciate the implication of the activities planned for their pupils. Teachers who have been on such courses may still make conceptual errors, but appear to have a deeper understanding of the processes that the children are experiencing.

There can perhaps be no greater justification for involving children in the investigative process than that the learners themselves proclaim it to be an effective and enjoyable way to learn. Through active involvement they can come to an understanding of how and why events unfold as they do. Children are naturally curious. While they may not need to be told to investigate, they do need to be skilfully presented with a wide range of appropriate opportunities. The teacher's role is to structure these investigative experiences so that the learner can develop his/her own understanding of the underlying concepts and the processes of scientific learning. This study hopes to have gone a little way towards illuminating influential factors relating to this. It also suggests that post-Dearing, the factors continue to require consideration.

13 Postscript: Moving Forward with a Research Agenda

PAT BROADHEAD

The introductory chapter raised a question concerned with the possibilities of now beginning to develop a conceptually founded framework concerned with and subsequently underpinning provision across the span of the early years and embracing all its domains. Chapter 1 also located the continuum of development and learning, with which this publication is most substantially concerned, within the framework, to be considered as integral to it and to the illumination of practice. The opening chapter also pointed to the roles of educators and caregivers in the support of children's learning and development. What, then, can the research reported here offer by way of support for an all-embracing conceptualisation of the early years and for continuity, consistency and appropriateness within an early years continuum?

Let us examine what is offered that might pertain to the importance of the educare principle discussed in Chapter 1. Chapters by Judy Arrowsmith (Chapter 6), Sally Beveridge (Chapter 2), Dianne Lamont (Chapter 4) and Sheila Rye (Chapter 5) have much to offer here, each of them focusing as they do on aspects of parental involvement and the key role of the family in the learning and development of young children. This ranges from the need to take account of parental and professional perspectives on integrating special needs children, to parents working and learning alongside practitioners, to fruitful liaison with parents for whom English is a second language as it is for their children. In addition, Val Monaghan's (Chapter 3) research into language development through story revealed some potential in a continuation of learning contexts across home and school settings. Judy Arrowsmith's research helps illuminate the issue of parental involvement into the later years of the early years continuum with professionals here particularly uncertain as to how to promote it, but through participation in a research project, coming to see the potential of such partnerships in relation to school development planning. Thus it seems that, in the later years, parental partnerships might shift somewhat, remaining none the less valuable but with a broadening out from parental concern for their own child (still evident) to a greater involvement in wider aspects of their child's learning community. These chapters show the benefits of such partnerships for staff, parents and children in enhancing the quality of provisions at school and potentially, at home also. They reveal the extent to which parents and staff are willing and able to become involved in such partnerships when informed leadership and facilitative conditions can generate mutual respect for each other's contribution and including the children's contributions. If there is general acceptance for a premise that early years experience does lay the foundation for future learning, then part of the child's entitlement is surely to be with supportive, informed adults who understand the nature of the child's experiences both at home and in provision. However, we have seen from research reported here, a real need for these adult partners to overcome a broad range of personal anxieties and uncertainties before the child begins to fully benefit both in educational and in nurturing contexts.

What kind of teaching–learning environment do young children benefit from as they move from the very early years to a junior setting? How does the construct of 'curriculum' equate with that of 'appropriate structure' as the years go by? Some answers to these questions seem to lie in part in exploring the relative weighting accorded to the educational provision and the nurturance aspects, with the individual child's quest for knowledge and the adult's capacity for supporting this acting as pivotal points. In relation to both these proposed pivotal points, several chapters have clearly shown the young child's passion for knowledge, in a variety of guises and the clear implications for adults in supporting their quest for knowledge and understanding. Val Monaghan's (Chapter 3) study of nursery children depicted both parents' and children's pleasure at the evident growth in language and literacy skills. This partnership in learning resulted in increased sophistication of the skills and an enhanced understanding by adults – both professionals and parents – of how to facilitate this growing sophistication. Val Monaghan drew on some of the wide body of literature which locates the emergence of language and literacy skills as the foundation for all future learning and development. The parental involvement dimension once again reiterated the singular significance of parents as partners in the emergence and growth of essential, foundation skills. The structure she offered to the experimental group was explicit and yet flexible, with individual children and their parents clearly able to set particular and enjoyable agendas within that structure.

Similarly, with Dianne Lamont's (Chapter 4) study; through involvement in a research cycle, staff became better placed in making decisions about provision from a developmental standpoint with knowledge of individuals and their previous achievements coming to influence this decision making. Ann MacNamara's (Chapter 8) study of nursery and reception children revealed the kinds of evident, prior knowledge that teachers might helpfully exploit or unhelpfully hinder in its subsequent development. This pertained to one particular and, as with Val Monaghan's study, foundational aspect of learning, the skill of subitising. Ann MacNamara also considered the impact of staffing, organisation and resourcing in relation to inclinations or opportunities children might have for demonstrating prior learning to the adults around them. The implications for the subsequent structuring of opportunities for learning and development become apparent. For example, in relation to mathematics both Carol Aubrey (Chapter 9) and Ann MacNamara have drawn attention to the dangers of over-reliance on scheme maths for reception children. Carol Aubrey's research also revealed both the novice and the experienced teacher identifying inherent limitations in complete reliance on discovery learning in relation to the conceptual growth of mathematical understanding (as Val Monaghan did also with the growth of abstract thinking). The novice and experienced teacher had each come to believe that a teacher-determined structure was necessary within a wider context of acknowledging the individual need. The possibilities of overcoming any limitations were illuminated by the focus of her research into the development of pedagogical subject knowledge – a crucial area for further study in the early years field. The research reveals the importance of an awareness by the teacher of the relationship between assessment of prior knowledge and instruction (alongside Ann MacNamara's revealed need of a capacity for accessing that prior knowledge) and the need for the teacher to model cognitive strategies and, crucially, provide support for the children's early efforts. Once again we see implications for staffing levels and for pupil organisation as well as for levels of professional knowledge and understanding.

Sheridan Earnshaw's (Chapter 11) and Keith Bardon's (Chapter 12) research revealed older, early years children as confident investigators when their environment provides both appropriately structured scientific opportunities and informed, interactive adults who understand the scientific concepts and principles under investigation. They each offer teacher perspectives on the need for appropriate personal knowledge of the subject and of how to teach it. Without that subject knowledge and related pedagogical knowledge, the early years learner clearly cannot be properly supported in a quest for understanding. Given the demise of LEA provision in supporting educators' ongoing professional growth, from where will the necessary input now come?

At each point, from the very young child with the need for experience and for language to describe it, to the growing child who lays claim to skills that will develop their emerging conceptual frameworks by continually supplementing their existing knowledge bases, we have seen that the informed adult is one who understands how to see the early years child in an appropriate context of nurturing and education. Angela Anning & Sue Billet (Chapter 7), making reference to the substantial body of relevant research literature as well as drawing on their own findings in small and large schools, add to a prevailing picture of four and five year olds in an almost cusp-like position at the intersecting arcs of provision for the very young learner and provision for the more mature early years learner. Their research also highlights, yet again, the parallel implications of relevant adult knowledge alongside children's needs for intellectual stimulation in appropriate contexts.

Within the span of early years, 'appropriate contexts' need not preclude subject-related issues. We have read of confident mathematicians, scientists and language users. Keith Bardon has raised an interesting, associated question concerning the period within which the integrated day may become a less appropriate format in a consideration of what constitutes appropriate provision. A belief that the young child does not conceptualise her/his world in subject terms is well established in the early years, hence an emphasis on integration. However, the adults making the provision have learned to see the world in subject terms, with varying levels of personal knowledge across the respective subjects. In providing for the early years child, educators must strive to facilitate connections across these subjects. In the absence of related knowledge, how can these connections be made? A capacity to 'connect subjects', to cross-reference and integrate learning in a rigorous and accessible way may need to be rooted in knowledge of child development; is it a discipline in its own right? Might further investigation be timely?

The contribution of assessment and evaluation across the early years continuum surely has something to offer at this point. Diane Shorrock's chapter offers considerable substance here, outlining and acknowledging both the strengths and limitations of current legislative requirements on Key Stage 1 teachers. In support, the research from Val Monaghan, Ann MacNamara, Carol Aubrey, Sheridan Earnshaw and Keith Bardon broadens out a consideration of how teacher knowledge about content and about children's potential at particular ages and phases can combine with diagnostic assessments to inform planning and provision from the nursery to the early junior setting. The work of Dianne Lamont and Sheila Rye also point to a need to progress sensitively and thoughtfully when taking colleagues along such a path while also setting targets and maintaining momentum.

In conclusion, this final section proposes two main thrusts in relation to future research. The first of these thrusts relates to the nature of young children's learning and links with development across different forms of early years provision. Margaret Clark (1988), drawing on the work of others reiterated the need to study the continuity of children's experience and curriculum between the ages of three and eight. Account needs also to be taken of the important research agenda which Sally Beveridge offers in relation to the integration of children with special needs within such a continuum. It would seem timely to broaden out and take account of the years from birth to eight. This will assist in more fully illuminating the key issues of family and of parental partnerships and professionals. It would seem increasingly imperative that such research take account of the educare principle.

The more recent ramifications of a National Curriculum, interposed, mid way, brings renewed urgency. Added to this, moves towards integrating provision for the pre-statutory school-age child are gaining momentum across local councils, wherever funding allows. There is well-substantiated research evidence to show that provision for the four year old and for many five year olds in school is consistently inappropriate. There are moves towards a more subject-oriented curriculum for the junior child from seven onwards. More now needs to be known and understood about how children at different ages and phases, within the early years continuum, learn within their respective settings; such research would inform perspectives on appropriate provision across the continuum.

The second of the two research thrusts proposed pertains to how practitioners develop their understandings of children's learning processes in early years settings. It is now well recognised that initial training, for any practitioner, can only go so far in providing a base-line of knowledge and understanding. The research reported here adds weight to the call for ongoing training and development if practice is to be enhanced; this is evident in relation to a range of contexts and a range of needs. Alongside this and clearly impacting, several chapters have considered the implications of the rapidly diminishing authority-led role in relation to local training needs. More needs to be known about how practitioners across the phases and within the range of types of provision in early years extend their understanding of care, development and education and how they perceive relationships between the three interfacing areas. Several chapters have revealed the extent to which practitioners have been prepared to go in search of enhanced practice and how this has led to benefits for children's learning and development. Access to research is undoubtedly an important part of the route to practice enhancement and improved opportunities for children's learning to occur. There are clearly also other factors in the equation; this publication has revealed something of the links between effective assessment and enhanced provision and of how teacher knowledge is linked to effective pedagogical practices. If further insights could be gained into these processes of teacher development and if these insights were to be placed alongside a better understanding of children's learning in a range of settings, important perspectives might emerge upon which a conceptual framework could perhaps be founded.

It is hoped that the near future might witness a renewed commitment to substantially funded research in the early years of education; that this might lead to enhanced understanding of learning and development in a range of settings and of how learning and development might be supported through ongoing practitioner education and quality provision. Earlier research from higher status times should clearly not be discounted, although equally clearly it now needs re-considering within a broader conceptualising of the early years domain. The priorities and topics identified in Chapter 1 remain underfunded and under-researched. More recent events and research have added impetus. Interest in early years research has been maintained despite lack of funding. Adding to and locating these informed perspectives within an overarching conceptual framework has real potential for informing and for being informed by a continuum of development and learning.

References

Alexander, R., Rose, J. and Woodhead, C. (1992) *Curriculum Organisation and Classroom Practice in Primary Schools*. London: HMSO.

Anning, A. (1991) *The First Years at School*. Milton Keynes: Open University Press.

Antell, S.E. and Keating, D.B. (1983) Perception of numerical invariance in neonates. *Child Development* 54, 695–701.

Applebee, A.N. (1983) *The Child's Concept of Story: The Pre-school Years*. Chicago: University of Chicago Press.

Athey, C. (1990) *Extending Thought in Young Children*. London: Paul Chapman.

Aubrey, C. (1993) An investigation of the mathematical competences that young children bring into school. *British Educational Research Journal* 19 (1), 19–37.

— (1994a) An investigation of children's knowledge of mathematics at school entry and the knowledge their teachers hold about teaching and learning mathematics, about young learners and mathematics subject knowledge. *British Educational Research Journal* 20 (1), 105–20.

— (1994b) The construction of early years mathematics. In C. Aubrey (ed.) *The Role of Subject Knowledge in the Early Years of Schooling*. London: Falmer Press.

— (1995) Teacher and pupil interactions and the processes of mathematical instruction in four reception classrooms over children's first year in school. *British Educational Research Journal* 21 (1), 31–48.

Bailey, D.B. and Wolery, M. (1992) *Teaching Infants and Pre-schoolers with Disabilities*, 2nd ed. New York: Macmillan.

Barrett, G. (1986) *Starting School: An Evaluation of the Experience*. London: AMMA.

Beckwith, M. and Restle, F. (1966) Process of Enumeration. *Psychological Review* 73, 437–44.

Bennett, D. (1987) The aims of teachers and parents for children in their first year at school. In *Four Year Olds in School: Policy and Practice NFER/SCDC Report*. Windsor: NFER.

Bennett, N. and Kell, J.C. (1989) *A Good Start: Four Year Olds in Infant Schools*. Oxford: Basil Blackwell.

Bennett, N., Desforges, C., Cockburn, A. and Wilkinson, B. (1984) *The Quality of Pupil Learning Experience*. London: Lawrence Erlbaum.

Bennett, N., Wragg, E. and Carre, C. (1991) Primary teachers and the National Curriculum. *Junior Education*, November 1991, 10–13.

Blank, M.S., Rose, S.A. and Berlin, L.J. (1978) *The Language of Learning*. London: Grune & Stratton.

Board of Education (1931) *Report of the Consultative Committee on the Primary School* (Hadow Report). London: HMSO.

Brophy, J. (ed.) (1991) *Advances in Research on Teaching*, Vol. 2. Greenwich, CT: JAI Press.

Bruner, J. (1986) *Actual Minds, Possible Worlds*. London: Harvard University Press.

Burgess, R.G. (1984) *In the Field – An Introduction to Field Research*. London: Unwin Hyman.

Burningham, J. (1983) *The Shopping Basket*. Jonathan Cape.

CACE (Central Advisory Council for Education, England) (1967) *Children and their Primary Schools* (The Plowden Report). London: HMSO.

Carpenter, T. and Moser, J. (1983) The acquisition of addition and subtraction concepts. In A. Lesh and C. Landau (eds) *Acquisition of Mathematical Concepts and Processes*. New York: Academic Press.

Chinlund, C. (1988) What affects 3, 4 and 5 year old children's ability to subitize small numbers? Unpublished doctoral dissertation. State University of New York at Albany.

Cicourel, A.V. (1981) Notes on the integration of micro- and macro-levels of analysis. In K. Knorr-Cetina and A.V. Cicourel (eds) *Advances in Social Theory and Methodology: Toward an Integration of Micro- and Macro-Sociologies*. London: Routledge & Kegan Paul.

Clark, M.M. (1988) *Children Under Five: Educational Research and Evidence*. London: Gordon & Breach.

Cleave, S. and Brown, S. (1989) *Meeting their Needs*. Windsor: NFER/Nelson.

— (1991a) *Quality Matters*. Windsor: NFER/Nelson.

— (1991b) *Early to School: Four Year Olds in Infant Classes*. Berkshire: NFER-Nelson.

David, T. (1990) *Under Five - Under Educated?* Buckingham: Open University Press.

DES (Department of Education and Science) (1978) *Special Educational Needs* (The Warnock Report). Cmnd. 212. London: HMSO.

DES (1985) *Science 5–16: A Statement of Policy*. London: Department of Education and Science and the Welsh Office, HMSO.

DES (1986) *Achievement in Primary Schools*. London: HMSO.

— (1988) *National Curriculum Task Group on Assessment and Testing: A Report* (The TGAT Report). London: HMSO.

— (1989a) *The Education of Children Under Five*. London: HMSO.

— (1989b) *Report by HMI Inspectors on a Survey of the Quality of Education for Four Year Olds in Primary Classes*, Ref. 339/89/NS. London: DES.

— (1990) *Starting with Quality* (The Rumbold Report). London: DES.

— (1991a) *Science in the National Curriculum*. London: Department of Education and Science and the Welsh Office, HMSO.

— (1991b) *Statistical Bulletin 7/91*. London: DES.

Desforges, C. and Cockburn, A. (1987) *Understanding the Mathematics Teacher*. Lewes: Falmer Press

DfEE (1995) *Science in the National Curriculum*. London: Department for Education and Employment and the Welsh Office: HMSO.

Dodd, L. (1988) *Wake up Bear*. Picture Puffin.

Donaldson, M. (1978) *Children's Minds*. Glasgow: Fontana Press.

Doyle, W. (1983) Academic work. *Review of Educational Research* 53 (2), 159–99.

— (1986) Content representation in teachers' definitions of academic work. *Journal of Curriculum Studies* 18 (4), 365–79.

Edwards, D. and Mercer, N. (1987) *Common Knowledge: The Development of Understanding in the Classroom*. London: Methuen.

Edwards, V. and Redfern, A. (1988) *At Home in School*. London: Routledge.

Egan, K. (1988) *Primary Understanding*. London: Routledge.

Elliot, J. (1985) Education action research. In J. Nisbett and S. Nisbett (eds) *Research Policy & Practice, World Yearbook of Education*. London: Kogan Page.

— (1991) *Action Research for Educational Change*. Milton Keynes: Open University Press.

Engelhart, M.D. (1972) *Methods of Educational Research*. Chicago: Rand McNally.

Garland, S. (1985) *Going Shopping*. Picture Puffin.

Gelman, R. (1977) How young children reason about small numbers. In N.J. Castellan (ed.) *Cognitive Theory*. New Jersey: Erlbaum.

Gelman, R. and Gallistel, C.R. (1978) *The Child's Understanding of Number*. Cambridge: Harvard University Press.

Gilkes, J. (1987) *Developing Nursery Education*. Milton Keynes: Open University Press.

Gipps, C., Steadman, S. and Blackstone, T. (1983) *Testing children: Standardised Testing in Schools and LEAs*. London: Heinemann.

Good, T.L., Grouws, D.A. and Ebmeier, H. (1983) *Active Mathematics Teaching*. New York: Longman.

Harlen, W. (1985) *Teaching and Learning Primary Science*. London: Harper & Row.

Hegarty, S., Pocklington, K. and Lucas, D. (1981) *Educating Pupils with Special Needs in the Ordinary School*. Windsor: NFER-Nelson.

Hevey, D. (1986) *The Continuing Under Fives Muddle!* Survey for the Voluntary Organisation Liaison Council for Under Fives.

HMI (1990) *The Implementation of the National Curriculum in Primary Schools*. London: HMSO.

HMI/Scottish Office Education Department (SOED) (1991) *The Role of School Development Plans in Managing School Effectiveness*. Edinburgh: SED.

HMSO (1989) *Science in the National Curriculum*. London: DES.

— (1990) *Starting with Quality* (The Rumbold Report). London: HMSO.

— (1991) *Assessment, Recording and Reporting:A Report by HM Inspectorate on the First Year 1989–1990*. London: DES.

Hopkins, D. (1985) *A Teacher's Guide to Classroom Research*. Milton Keynes: Open University Press.

Hughes, M., Wikeley, F. and Nash, T. (1990) *Parents and the National Curriculum: An Interim Report*. Exeter: University of Exeter, School of Education.

Hutt, S.J., Tyler, S., Hutt, C. and Christopherson, H. (1989) *Exploration and Learning: A Natural History of the Pre-school*. London: Routledge.

Kaufmann, E.L., Lord, M.W., Reese, T.W. and Volkmann, J. (1949) The discrimination of visual number. *American Journal of Psychology* 62, 498–525.

Kemmis, A. (1985) Action research and the politics of reflection. In D. Boud, R. Keogh and R. Walker (eds) *Reflection: Turning Experience into Learning*. London: Kogan Page.

Klahr, D. (1973) Quantification Process. In W. Chase (ed.) *Visual Information Processing*. New York: Academic Press.

Klahr, D. and Wallace, J.G. (1976) *Cognitive Development, An Information Processing View*. New Jersey: Laurence Erlbaum Associates.

Leinhardt, G. (1987) Development of an expert explanation: An analysis of a sequence of subtraction lessons. *Cognition and Instruction* 4 (4), 225–82.

— (1989) Math lessons: A contrast of novice and expert competence. *Journal for Research in Mathematics Education* 20 (1), 52–75.

Leinhardt, G. and Smith, D.A. (1985) Expertise in mathematics instruction: Subject matter knowledge. *Journal of Educational Psychology* 77 (3), 247–71.

Leinhardt, G., Putnam, R.T., Stein, M.K. and Baxter, J. (1991) Where subject knowledge matters. In J.Brophy (ed.) *Advances in Research on Teaching*, Vol. 2. Greenwich, CT: JAI Press.

MacNamara, E.A. (1990) Subitizing and addition of numbers in young children. Unpublished MEd dissertation, University of Leeds.

McCann, A. (1990) Culture and behaviour: A study of Miripani infant pupils. In R. Webb (ed.) *Practitioner Research in the Primary School*. London: Falmer Press.

McNiff, J. (1988) *Action and Research: Principles and Practice*. Basingstoke: Macmillan Education.

Measor, L. (1985) Interviewing: A strategy in qualitative research. In R. Burgess (ed.) *Strategies of Educational Research*. Lewes: Falmer Press.

Mitchell, D. and Brown, R.I. (eds) (1991) *Early Intervention Studies for Young Children with Special Needs*. London: Chapman & Hall.

Moon, B., Isaac, J. and Powney, J. (1990) *Judging Standards and Effectiveness in Education*. London: Hodder & Stoughton.

Mortimore, P., Sammons, P., Stoll, L., Lewis, D. and Ecob, R. (1988) *School Matters: The Junior Years*. Somerset: Open Books.

NCC (National Curriculum Council) (1989a) *A Framework for the Primary Curriculum*. York: NCC.

— (1989b) *Science Non-Statutory Guidance*. York: NCC.

NFER (1992) *An Enquiry into LEA Evidence on Standards of Reading of Seven Year Old Children*. Windsor: NFER.

Oakley, A. (1981) Interviewing women: A contradiction in terms. In H. Roberts (ed.) *Doing Feminist Research*. London: Routledge.

OFSTED (1993) *Curriculum Organisation and Classroom Practice in Primary Schools: A Follow-up Report*. London: HMSO.

Osborn, A.F. (1981) Under fives in schools in England and Wales, 1971–79. *Educational Research* 23 (2), 96–103.

Osborn, A.F. and Milbank, J.E. (1987) *The Effects of Early Education. Report from the Child Health and Education Study*. Oxford: Clarendon Press.

Osborne, R. and Freyberg, P. (1985) *Learning in Science – The Implications of Children's Science*. Birkenhead, Auckland: Heinemann.

Potter, M.C. and Levy, E. (1968) Spatial enumeration without counting. *Child Development* 39, 265–83.

Poulson, L. (1991) Narrative in the infant classroom. *English in Education* 25 (1), 18–23.

Romberg, T. and Carpenter, T. (1986) Research on teaching and learning mathematics. In M.C. Wittrock (ed.) *Handbook on Research on Teaching*, 3rd Ed. London: Collier MacMillan.

Rowland, S. (1988) My body of knowledge. In J. Nias and S. Groundwater-Smith (eds) *The Enquiring Teacher, Supporting and Sustaining Teacher Research*. London: Falmer Press.

Sandow, S., Stafford, D. and Stafford, P. (1987) *An Agreed Understanding? Parent–Professional Communication and the 1981 Education Act*. Windsor: NFER-Nelson.

Satterley, D. (1981) *Assessment in Schools*. Oxford: Basil Blackwell.

Scardamalia, M. and Bereiter, C. (1989) Conceptions of teaching and approaches to core problems. In M.C. Maynard (ed.) *Knowledge Base for the Beginning Teacher*. Oxford: Pergamon.

Schaeffer, B., Eggleston, V.H. and Scott, J.L. (1974) Number development in young children. *Cognitive Psychology* 6, 357–79.

Schoenfield, A.H. (1985) *Mathematical Problem-solving*. New York: Academic Press.

Sedgwick, H. (1982) Visual modes of spatial perception. In M. Potegal (ed.) *Spatial Perception*. London: Academic Press.

Shorrocks, D. (1993) *Implementing National Curriculum Assessment in the Primary School*. London: Hodder & Stoughton.

Shorrocks, D., Daniels, S., Frobisher, L., Nelson, N., Waterson, A. and Bell, J. (1992) *The Evaluation of National Curriculum Assessment at Key Stage 1. Final Report of the ENCA 1 Project* (School of Education, University of Leeds). London: SEAC.

Shorrocks, D., Daniels, S., Stainton, R. and Ring, K. (1993) *Testing and Assessing Six and Seven Year Olds: The Evaluation of the 1992 Key Stage 1 National Curriculum Assessments*. London: The National Union of Teachers.

Shulman, L. (1986) Those who understand: Knowledge growth in teaching. *Educational Researcher* 15 (2), 4–14.

SOED (1992) *Using Ethos Indicators in Primary School Self Evaluation: Taking Account of the Views of Parents, Pupils and Teachers*. Edinburgh: SOED.

Somekh, B. (1993) Flies on the walls of their classroom. *TES*, 23 July, 11.

Starkey, P. and Cooper, R.G. (1980) Perception of numbers by human infants. *Science* 210, 1033–5.

Stein, M.K., Baxter, J.A. and Leinhardt, G. (1990) Subject-matter knowledge and elementary instruction: A case from functions and graphing. *American Educational Research Journal* 27, 639–63.

Stierer, B. (1991) Assessing children at the start of school: Issues, dilemmas and current developments. *Curriculum Journal* 1 (2), 155–69.

Sutton, R. (1991) *Assessment: A Framework for Teachers*. Berkshire: NFER-Nelson.

Sylva, K. (1991) Educational aspects of day care in England and Wales. In P. Moss and E. Melhuish (eds) *Current Issues in Day Care for Young Children*. London: HMSO.

Sylva, K., Roy, C. and Painter, M. (1980) *Childwatching at Playgroup and Nursery School*. London: Grant McIntyre.

Taves, E.H. (1941) Two mechanisms for the perception of visual numerousness. *Archives of Psychology* 37, 1–47.

Taylor, S. (1993) *Nursery World* 9 (9), 4.

Thorndike, R.L. and Hagen, P. (1977) *Measurement and Evaluation in Psychology and Education*. New York: Wiley.

Tizard, B. and Hughes, M. (1984) *Young Children Learning. Talking and Thinking at Home & School*. London: Fontana Press.

Tizard, B., Mortimore, J. and Burchell, B. (1981) *Involving Parents in Nursery and Infant Schools*. London: Grant McIntyre.

Tough, J. (1976) *Listening to Children Talking*. London: Ward Lock.

Wade, B. (1984) *Story at Home and School*. Birmingham: University of Birmingham.

Wang, M.C. and Palincsar, A.S. (1989) Teaching students to assume an active role in their learning. In M.C. Reynolds (ed.) *Knowledge Base of the Beginning Teacher*. Oxford: Pergamon.

Watt, L.M. and Watt, D.L. (1993) Teacher research, action research: The logo action research collaborative. *Educational Action Research* 1 (1), 35–63.

Webb, R. (1990a) The origins and aspirations of practitioner research. In R. Webb (ed.) *Practitioner Research in the Primary School*. London: Falmer Press.

— (1990b) The process and purpose of practitioner research. In R. Webb (ed.) *Practitioner Research in the Primary School*. London: Falmer Press.

Wells, G. (1985) *Language, Learning and Education*. Windsor: NFER-Nelson.

— (1986) *The Meaning Makers. Children Learning Language and Using Language to Learn*. London: Hodder & Stoughton.

Westgate, D. and Hughes, M. (1989) Nursery nurses as talk partners. *Education 3–13*, 17, 2 June 54–9.

White, M. and Cameron, S. (1987) *The Portage Early Education Programme*. Windsor: NFER-Nelson.

Wolfendale, S. (1983) *Parental Participation in Children's Development and Education*. London: Gordon & Breach.

Wood, D.J., Bruner, J.S. and Ross, G. (1976) The role of tutoring in problem-solving. *Journal of Child Psychology and Psychiatry* 17 (2), 89–100.

Woods, P. (1988) Educational ethnography in Britain. In R.R. Sharman and R.B. Webb (eds) *Qualitative Research in Education: Focus Methods*. London: Falmer Press.